ALOUD

ALOUD

VOICES FROM THE NUYORICAN POETS CAFE

EDITED BY

MIGUEL ALGARÍN

AND

BOB HOLMAN

a john macrae book
henry holt and company   new york

Henry Holt and Company, Inc.
Publishers since 1866
115 West 18th Street
New York, New York 10011

Henry Holt® is a registered
trademark of Henry Holt and Company, Inc.

Published in Canada by Fitzhenry & Whiteside Ltd.,
195 Allstate Parkway, Markham, Ontario L3R 4T8.
Published simultaneously in cloth and paper in 1994.

Library of Congress Cataloging-in-Publication Data
Aloud: Voices from the Nuyorican Poets Cafe/edited by Miguel
Algarín and Bob Holman.
p.   cm.
"A John Macrae book."
1. Puerto Ricans—New York (N.Y.)—Poetry.   2. American poet-
ry—Puerto Rican authors.   3. American poetry—New York (N.Y.)
4. American poetry—20th century.   5. Nuyorican Poets Cafe.
I. Algarín, Miguel.   II. Holman, Bob.
PS591.P8A46   1994   94-1240
811'.540808687295—dc20   CIP

ISBN 0-8050-3275-4
ISBN 0-8050-3257-6 (An Owl Book: pbk.)

First Edition—1994

BOOK DESIGN BY CLAIRE NAYLON VACCARO

Printed in the United States of America
All first editions are printed on acid-free paper. ∞

10   9   8   7   6   5   4   3   2   1
10   9   8   7   6   5   4
(pbk.)

TO THE
POETS OF THE FUTURE,
ALOUD AT THE
NUYORICAN POETS CAFE

CONTENTS

II. POETRY OF THE 1990S

III. FOUNDING POEMS

IV. THE OPEN ROOM

If you're not suitable for the future,
you probably won't make it in the present either.

—Sun Ra

ALOUD

CONGRATULATIONS. YOU HAVE FOUND THE HIDDEN BOOK.

Invocation by Bob Holman

DO NOT READ THIS BOOK!

You don't have to. *This book reads to you.*

This book is a SHOUT for all those who have heard the poem's direct flight from mouth to ear.

Hear this book with your eyes! When the Mouth marries the Eye, the Ear officiates (see Tristan Tzara's "The Gas Heart." Better yet, perform that tiny masterpiece!).

These poems know poetry is a contact sport! The poem is not written until you read it!

In Chinese, there is no verb without a noun; it is contained in the character. There is no running without a deer to run, and three deer is "Beautiful." *It* is not raining. What (who) is *It*?! "No Tag Backs" (Paul Beatty). (Rain is.) (Try Pound/Fenalossa's *The Chinese Written Character as a Medium for Poetry.*)

Where were we? We *are* at the Cafe, the Poets Cafe, the Nuyorican Poets Cafe, home for the tradition that has no home but your ear. The home of the art that has been homeless ever since Plato kicked the poets out of the *Republic.*

Until now . . .

Welcome to the inside of the explosion! This is where you actually see the Thing Itself (*Where all the ideas are?*—Dr. Williams) explode and then watch the exploded bits themselves explode. That is how fast poetry is becoming a spinning force in our nation's dailiness, late in the second millennium.

"Help Me/I Can See," as Rev. Pedro Pietri's donations can says. This book dares state the obvious—RAP IS POETRY—and its spoken essence is central to the popularization of poetry. Rap is taking its place, aloud, as a

1

new poetic form, with ancient griot roots. Hip hop is a cultural throughline for the Oral Tradition. Word goes public! Poetry has found a way to drill through the wax that had been collecting for decades! Poetry is no longer an exhibit in a Dust Museum. Poetry is alive; poetry is allowed.

The speed of the modem gets you my poem simultaneously! Faster than Mayakovsky's plane with propeller whirring that he requested be ever at the ready outside his studio window, ready to ferry the finished poem to publisher, lickety-split. Faster than Frank O'Hara's telephoned "Personism Manifesto." Now all technology bows to the poem itself, the singular voice rising above the pablum noise of a society filled with blandspeak, political blahblah, commercial absurdwords.... "Content," as they told me at MTV, "is making a comeback. Meaning is going to be big in the nineties." And lo: there are poets, poets from this book, on MTV! It's the nineties! Poems are being *written* with television cameras, composed in recording studios, downloaded via computer networks....

And at the Cafe at two or three in the morning, Gwendolyn Brooks can still be found in residence, or Andrei Voznesensky, or Guillermo Gomez-Peña, or Allen Ginsberg, Adrienne Rich, Amiri Baraka, Quincy Troupe, Jayne Cortez, Robert Creeley, Michael Franti—listening to the Open Room poet mumble that this poem has no title. Because finally *Voices from the Nuyorican Poets Cafe* is a place, 236 East Third Street to be exact, between Avenues B and C in the heart of Midtown. (Midtown Loisaida, that is.)

That is not the cover of a book you opened, that is Julio Dalmau at the door, hassling you for five bucks cover to see the Slam. And there is Lois Griffith just inside, the spirit of the place. Willie Correa is in the booth, tweaking the sound system, Roland Legiardi-Laura is setting up the projector, and Sonia Lopez is straightening a painting on the porous brick walls. Miguel is there at the corner of the bar with his marble notebook. You want to read at the Cafe, you sign up in the book. The mike is ready, you are on stage now. This space is reserved for the poem you are about to read, the Next Poem:

THE SIDEWALK OF HIGH ART

Introduction by Miguel Algarín

I. THE SCATTERING OF THE ASHES: THE BURIAL OF A POET

Many years ago, two poets made a promise to each other, and the promise was deceptively simple. One poet promised the other that by the next evening he would come back with a poem that would lay out in detail what was to be done upon his death.

> *Just once before I die*
> *I want to climb up on a*
> *tenement sky*
> *to dream my lungs out till*
> *I cry*
> *then scatter my ashes thru*
> *the Lower East Side.*

So it came to pass that Miguel Piñero would die, on June 17, 1988. We had been scheduled to do a reading tour of the Southwest, preparations had been made, all our Chicano friends were prepared to feed us menudo for the cruda and taquitos to go along with the tequila.

But that night, Miky did not come home. Miky belonged to the streets, on the concrete and the asphalt of New York, and his disappearances were not rare. It was his operational mode. The streets were where he felt best. It was in the early morning that a phone call came through: Miky had not been reveling and indulging in his excesses but had fallen ill and been admitted to St. Vincent's. My move toward the hospital was automatic, frenetic, and impulsive. I had to look out for my main mellow man, who was both my shadow and my angel.

There's always an eerie silence around the beds of people in intensive care. The only sounds are the electronic machinery insisting on their digital countdowns, insisting with their automatic accuracy how much or how little life is left. Miky's eyes were closed, he seemed deeply asleep, and as I approached him I remember saying to my sister that maybe we ought to wait outside, wait till he wakes, and then we can speak, and then we can visit, and then we can show him our love. But Miky, with that third eye always open to the universe, had in a flash felt my sister's and my presence, and although he could not immediately open his eyes, his fingers moved and his arms twitched, and I knew to enter, that he was conscious and I could speak and be heard, though responses were not to be easily had. I said, "Miky, my love, rest."

I moved toward the bed and put my hand in his, though it was difficult getting to his fingers through the tangle of intravenous lines. He surprised me with the strength of his grasp, and I said, "Tomorrow, we'll leave tomorrow, and if we can't leave tomorrow, we'll reschedule and leave when all is well again." His fingernails had grown long, and his grasp grew tighter and his nails dug into my palm. He wanted to say something, so I tried again: "I'm going to call Jimmy in Albuquerque and tell him that we'll come out next month." He pulled me toward the bed, I saw his eyes slowly open, and his lips barely moved as I bent down and put my ear up to his lips, and he kissed my ear, his hand grasped harder, and he said, "This is our last tour, we must keep all our dates, I will be here when you come back, and anyway, you know what you need to do if I die." I knew exactly what I had to do, and yet I couldn't imagine I would actually have to do it. He seemed impatient with me for staying as long as I did, and he gave me a glance that said everything it had to about my lingering: "Don't you have to catch a plane, Miguel? Why aren't you on your way?" I was shaken, and I knew that I didn't want to leave him. Yet his instructions were very clear.

That afternoon I left for Albuquerque to meet Jimmy Santiago Baca, to enter the holy land of the Chicanos' semiarid, drier-than-dry air and the spiritual world of Quetzalcoatl. The readings went as scheduled. Everywhere I read, everyone was moved and saddened by Miky's absence. His death was announced at 2:30 A.M., June 17, by his brother in a long-distance call from New York. My impulse was to climb on a plane to New York immediately. Miky had, however, instructed me to finish the tour, so I left Albuquerque for Taos. A poet's dying will is something that must be enacted and not foiled. So I performed in Taos, got off the stage and into a car, and on my way back to Albuquerque I thought, "I better study my instructions before I arrive in New York." The muscular, now familiar refrain of the poem kept coming at me; it both refreshed and frightened me. Miky's living will now resided in his verbs:

> *So let me sing my song tonight*
> *let me feel out of sight*
> *and let all eyes be dry*
> *when they scatter my ashes thru*
> *the Lower East Side.*

That was my task.

When I arrived in New York, I went immediately to the Wollensky Funeral Parlor, where a great poet lay in state. I knew I was to conduct the ceremonies attendant upon a Nuyorican* poet, which meant that there would be a call let out: "I want musicians, I want drummers, and may all the poets come prepared to read, to testify in heightened language to a life lived as a lifelong sonnet." I knew I had to put the poem into action, and I knew that the whole of the community would have to help me lift the poem off the page.

That night Amiri Baraka, Pedro Pietri, Jose-Angel Figueroa, Nancy Mercado, Eddie Figueroa, Julio Dalmau, Amina Baraka, Louis Reyes Rivera, Luis Guzman, and many, many other writers, musicians, and friends showed to celebrate the passing of a man who had left a legacy of poetry and theater behind.

When a poet dies, a whole community is affected, and the Lower East Side was abuzz with despair, sadness, and the keen awareness of the solitude that was coming. We all knew we would no longer see Miky on the streets of the Lower East Side, giving and taking at will whatever and whenever he wanted.

The preparations for the ceremony of the scattering of the ashes forged an unbreakable bond between the artists and the working people of the Lower East Side. Miky had asked that his ashes be scattered

> *From Houston to 14th Street*
> *from Second Avenue to the mighty D*

---

*Nuyorican (nü yòr 'ē kən) (New York + Puerto Rican) 1. Originally Puerto Rican epithet for those of Puerto Rican heritage born in New York: their Spanish was different (Spanglish), their way of dress and look were different. They were a stateless people (like most U.S. poets) until the Cafe became their homeland. 2. After Algarín and Piñero, a proud poet speaking New York Puerto Rican. 3. A denizen of the Nuyorican Poets Cafe. 4. New York's riches.

He wanted his ashes scattered where

the hustlers & suckers meet
the faggots & freaks will all get
high
on the ashes that have been scattered
thru the Lower East Side.

Miky wanted singing. He didn't want tears. As we prepared the empty lot next to the Cafe, people came from everywhere to join our procession. A wonderful installation had been created in that garbage-strewn lot by Arturo Lindsay. He had prepared an effigy to be burnt at the site. Drummers surrounded the installation, poets were ready to offer spontaneous testimonials at the installation, and our teacher Jorge Brandon spoke the first words. Brandon, the great master of the oral tradition at the ripe young age of 85, spoke with accuracy and pitch that belied his age and appearance. It was high oratory at its finest. The effigy was lit, and as it burned, a poet stepped up, read a poem, then dropped it into the fire; as that poem burned, another poet would step forward, recite, then drop a poem into the flames. It was clear that Miky's instructions had been letter-perfect. There was simply no other place to start the procession of the scattering of the ashes than the Nuyorican Poets Cafe, which he had founded with me. The lot was perfect—not manicured, but littered and disheveled and unpretentiously alive. We had cleared only a small circle for the installation, leaving the rest in its natural state: broken glass, strewn brick, unearthed boilers, and local garbage. The poem continued:

There's no other place for me to be
there's no other place that I can see
there's no other town around that
brings you up or keeps you down
no food little heat sweeps by
fancy cars & pimps' bars & juke saloons
& greasy spoons make my spirits fly
with my ashes scattered thru the
Lower East Side...

The poem began to leap off the page and become the thing itself—words were becoming action.

I was handed the quart-sized can that contained Miky's ashes. My hands trembled as Joey Castro took the can from me. I asked him to please open it. He pulled out his pocketknife and began to pry the lid gently, respectfully, and yet fearfully. I'll never forget the look on his face when the lid popped lightly and we saw the ashes for the very first time. How very odd—the frame of a man weighs less than two and a half pounds of dust. And what did I have in the quart can? I had the ashes of a man who proclaimed himself to be

> *A thief, a junkie I've been*
> *committed every known sin*
> *Jews and Gentiles . . . Bums and Men*
> *of style . . . run away child*
> *police shooting wild . . .*
> *mother's futile wails . . . pushers*
> *making sales . . . dope wheelers*
> *& cocaine dealers . . . smoking pot*
> *streets are hot & feed off those who bleed to death . . .*
>
> *all that's true*
> *all that's true*
> *all that is true*
> *but this ain't no lie*
> *when I ask that my ashes be scattered thru*
> *the Lower East Side.*

So the procession left the yard on the west side of the Cafe and began its voyage through the Lower East Side in concurrence with the configuration that the poem had laid out: *From Houston to 14th Street / from Second Avenue to the mighty D.* As we walked, I would scatter the ashes and people would say, "Who's that, who goes there?" The answer would initially come from me, "It's Miky Piñero." The response would be astounding, "It's Miky Piñero!" One person would cry out, and then another, "It's Miky Piñero," and then another, "It's Miky Piñero." It was a litany, the repetition of the rosary. People passed the word out in waves of sorrow, communicating to each other that the dispersal had begun, that Miky's ashes were being spread. Piñero was having the burial of his dreams, his poem breathing, moving and bonding people. By the time we reached Avenue D the procession was huge. People walking their dogs, going into stores, and standing at bus stops would forget the object of their mission and join us. It was as if they were impelled by a force bigger than themselves. If they were on the way to work, they didn't go. If they were on their way to the store, they wouldn't go. If they were going to the park, they didn't go. If they were walking their dog, they joined us. The murmuring grew into an audible incantation: "It's Miky Piñero, it's the poet, it's the guy who wrote *Short Eyes,* it's the guy on TV, on 'Miami Vice,' it's the guy that gave me twenty dollars when I needed it." It was the man that we all knew by many names and in many places.

Great ceremonies are followed by cataclysmic changes. After the procession ended, a great food-and-drink reception had been planned at Roland Legiardi-Laura's loft. The planning for the reception had been spontaneous and exciting. Roland had permitted the use of his place for the send-off of a great poet, and I had found what I was searching for: a big, well-lit space where we could all come to make an offering after the scattering of the ashes. The wake would be accompanied by great food, drink, and recitals. In the midst of this rejoicing, Bob Holman approached me and said, "Miguel, it's time to reopen the Cafe. This is the moment, you know, and Miky is insisting on it, and we are ready. Let's move on it, let's open the Nuyorican Poets Cafe again."

Bob Holman's words later began to unravel a need that had been lying dormant in me ever since I had closed the doors of the Cafe for what had become a prolonged period. Yes, Miky's death was to be a new beginning. From the ashes, life. From the whispered promise made by one poet to another, the oral tradition was to find a permanent home at the Nuyorican Poets Cafe.

II. THE POETRY OF THE 1990S: FIN DE SIECLE

The philosophy and purpose of the Nuyorican Poets Cafe has always been to reveal poetry as a living art. Even as the eye scans the lines of a poem, poetry is in flux in the United States. From Baja California to Seattle to Detroit, from the dance clubs with rap lyrics booming to the schools where Gil Scott-Heron plays to the churches where poetry series thrive to community centers with poets-in-residence and coffeehouses throughout the whole of the nation, the spoken word is on fire.

Presidents invite poets to their inaugural platform, and we are now finally paying attention to the need most nations in the world have for a poet laureate: a person who puts into verse the national feelings. Poetry is not *finding* its way, it *has found* its way, back into everyday life. It is not only meaningful, it is also fun. In *New York Newsday,* Patricia Volk has said of the Nuyorican Poets Cafe, "If you've wondered what effect MTV, the quickness of the city, and life being a vital particle away from death have had on poetry, you'll find out here. The Nuyorican is New York's arena for the spoken word, the poetic counterpart to the second floor of the Whitney Biennial. It's not a floating head above a lectern. It's about getting people excited, about what you say and how you say it. The word is so good, it reminds you that no matter how bizarre life gets, you need poetry."

Poetry at this moment, the last decade of the century, is a growing, developing, challenging force. We have, at the end of the millennium, brought it to life and televised it to the masses. The driving force has been to rekindle the word and the meaning of words. The effort has been to diversify, to turn over mass advertising's dissipation and abuse of language, and to rescue language from the deadening political "isms" that have enveloped it.

The new poetry, or rather the poetry of the nineties, seeks to promote a tolerance and understanding between people. The aim is to dissolve the social, cultural, and political boundaries that generalize the human experience and make it meaningless. The poets at the Cafe have gone a long way toward changing the so-called black/white dialogue that has been the breeding ground for social, cultural, and political conflict in the United States. It is clear that we now are entering a new era, where the dialogue is multi-ethnic and necessitates a larger field of verbal action to explain the cultural and political reality of North America. Poets have opened the dialogue and entered into new conversations. Their poems now create new metaphors that yield new patterns of trust, creating intercultural links among the many ethnic groups that are not characterized by the simplistic term *black/white dialogue.*

The poets of the Nuyorican Poets Cafe take responsibility for breaking all boundaries that limit and diminish the impact of their work. It is at the heart of the matter to move their work from the Cafe into other communities of the city in order to break racial patterns that tend to isolate these communities into ethnic pockets that are enclosed and without intercommunication. After Pete Spiro's play *Howya Doin' Franky Banana* is produced at the Cafe, it will move to the Frank Silvera Writers' Workshop in Harlem and the Belmont Italian-American Workshop in the Bronx. Thus the artist becomes a catalyst through which social change is made. It is rewarding when Garland Thompson, the director of the famed Frank Silvera Writers' Workshop, can write to us that "it was a truly exciting new multicultural concept and experiment of yours . . . to present a provocative new work by a talented white playwright, Pete Spiro, directed by an African-American director, Rome Neal, at the Frank Silvera Workshop, one of Harlem's oldest new playwrights' developmental theatres."

It is clear that there's an urgency among us. We must listen to one another. We must respect one another's habits. And we must start to share the truth and integrity that the voice of the poet so generously provides.

The poet of the nineties is involved in the politics of the movement. There need be no separation between politics and poetry. The aesthetic that informs the poet is of necessity involved in the social conditions that the people of the world are in. Martín Espada cannot write about the Puerto Rican without identifying the aggression that Puerto Rican people face both on the mainland and in the island. In his poem "Rebellion Is the Circle of a Lover's Hands," he celebrates the fiftieth anniversary of the Ponce Massacre, grounding the memory of people:

> The marchers gathered, Nationalists
> massed beneath the delicate white balconies
> of Marina Street,
> and the colonial governor
> pronounced the order with patrician calm . . .

The order was to repress the peaceful demonstration. The result was a painful bloodletting that remains etched in the consciousness of the Puerto Rican people. Jorge Brandon has been, for the last thirty years, reciting his poem "La Masacre de Ponce" on the streets of the Lower East Side to anybody who's willing to listen. Brandon's mission has been to say it aloud, to say it on street corners, to say it in the parks of this city, and now, once again, we find Espada, as Brandon, responding to what has been a primary mission of poetry, to inform the living of what has taken place in the past:

> But rebellion
> is the circle of a lover's hands,
> that must keep moving,
> always weaving.

However, the retelling of the stories of the past is not enough. The poet of the nineties has to be responsible for giving a direction, for illuminating a path. It is part of the political and aesthetic responsibility of the oral poet to tell people how to relieve themselves of the anxiety of the day, and it is precisely that task that Bimbo Rivas assigned himself, when he, one of Jorge Brandon's disciples, would exclaim aloud:

> *A Job*
> *I NEED A JOB TODAY*
> *Folks that got a job*
> *a job that does its job*
> *can see some sense in this relate*
> *folks that lost their faith*
> *that rot away with pain*
> *DAY AFTER DAY*
> *Strike at each other*
> *hoping to find*
> *in greater pain*
> *a sedative*
> *it's all too relative*
> *my friends*
> *a man without a JOB*
> *is lost in the labyrinth of*
> *HELL.*

Bimbo's play on the word *JOB*—its biblical reference to Job—is clear. If people do not strive to make a change, they will, like Job, remain in eternal pain. The intent is clear. Speak about how people hurt, yet at the same time give them a directive, a sense of future release. The poetry of politics and war, urban war in Bimbo's case, necessitates that the poet tell the tales of the past and that there also be a generous admission: the possibility of hope.

From the battlefields of the inner-city ghettos to the exquisite semiarid landscape of the Black Mesa, the thread of wanting to relate the self to the land upon which one stands runs powerfully and richly. For Jimmy Santiago Baca, talking about the land is not talking about squatting a building on the Lower East Side, but instead moving out into the desert and communing with the earth. So that when Baca says, in his poem "Black Mesa,"

> *The northern most U-tip*
> *of Chihuahua desert*
> *infuses*

my house
with its dark shadow,
and leans my thoughts
in its direction
as wind bends a row of trees
toward it.

I want to visit
it
before winter comes . . .

we have a poet seeking the self in the land. Lifting the details of the terrain into the poem reveals the self and shows how the land explains the self to the poet. It is exciting to encounter a Southwestern poet who shows us how rooted in the land he is, much like a mesquite tree is rooted in the earth. Here the politics of land and people are one, as the poet reinvents the self through the history of the terrain:

I re-imagine myself here,
and pant the same breath
squeezed from these rocks 1000 years ago.

Baca educates himself through his empirical observation of the land. He finds his security in the rocks that lie about. The land is concrete information that feeds the body and the soul and reveals the future. It is an American saga: the land plus people becoming the backbone of America.

In the Northeast, however, the clutter, the vertical living that contrasts so deeply with the horizontal existence of the Southwest, affects the ways in which we bare language, peel away its civilities and its decorum, and employ its raw, ribald, coarse, crude, and uncouth imaging. Love and sex are passionately dealt with in the poems of the nineties. The language of poetry is now associated with the great mass of people who are suffering the scathing effects of living so densely together. We cannot ignore how we rape each other, kill each other. Ill-bred and boorish, late-twentieth-century poetic language penetrates the thick urban blight so that Hattie Gossett can talk about "pussy and cash":

of course theres an endless pool of pussys on reserve waiting for you to
    bring them in

to run yo household take care of yo kids or grandmama or run yo business
if you know the secret password—whar da hoz is?—you can get some clean
   freelance pussy to help you through the night when you got to be farfar-
      far away
from yo regular pussy

The economy of sex goes hand in hand with the painful and often mutilating despair that sets in with love gone sour. When love is extended but not returned, the consequences are both scary and despairing. So that when the young girl in Sapphire's poem "in my father's house" serves the meal she's cooked and finds she's not invited to the dining table, she has learned a deep and wounding truth:

I went to sit down at the table
& stopped shocked.
my father had only set a place
for himself & my little brother.
"I thought you had already eaten," he offered.
I made no move to get another plate,
neither did he.
he served his son
the food I had prepared.
they ate,
I disappeared,
like the truth . . .

Love has been offered, and it has neither been received nor returned. The girl has been a tool that provides a meal that bonds father and son but leaves her out and ignored. The nineties are not only a politically unstable decade, but also a period of emotional and spiritual dryness. Still, Pedro Pietri's satirical wit makes us laugh at the total absurdity the last years of this millennium. He time and again manages to usurp our jaded despair and makes us laugh at ourselves:

woke up this morning
feeling excellent
picked up the telephone
dialed the number of
my equal opportunity employer

to inform him that I will not
be into work today
"Are you feeling sick?"
the boss asked me
"No Sir" I replied:
I am feeling too good
to report to work today,
if I feel sick tomorrow
I will come in early

The poets at the Cafe are saying, "Listen, and be aware of the energy and power of words. Do not abandon the self, retain the culture, return to thinking, stop the passive role of the observer, and take up the sport of life."

III. POETRY INTO THE TWENTY-FIRST CENTURY: THE DEMOCRATIZATION OF VERSE

Say it! No ideas but in things. Mr.
Paterson has gone away
to rest and write. Inside the bus one sees
his thoughts sitting and standing. His
thoughts alight and scatter—

Who are these people (how complex
the mathematic) among whom I see myself
in the regularly ordered plateglass of
his thoughts, glimmering before shoes and bicycles?
They walk incommunicado, the
equation is beyond solution, yet
its sense is clear—that they may live
his thought is listed in the Telephone
Directory—...

A wonder! A wonder!

From the ten houses (Alexander) Hamilton saw when he looked
(at the falls!) and kept his counsel, by the middle of the century—the
mills had drawn a heterogeneous population. There were in 1870,

*native born 20,711, which would of course include children of foreign
parents; foreign 12,868 of whom 237 were French, 1,420 German,
3,343 English—(Mr. Lambert who later built the Castle among
them), 5,124 Irish, 879 Scotch, 1,360 Hollanders and 170 Swiss—*
                                        —William Carlos Williams,
                                        Paterson

If Janet Jackson had been allowed to follow William Carlos Wil-
liams's insight, been able to "Say it! No ideas but in things," her voice
would have been the voice of the 1990s and her poetry closer to that of Tra-
cie Morris than to that of Maya Angelou. Jackson's insight into America
would have been on target had she been able to say, "So when you wear that
gear on your head backwards / it won't make the spot easy / for someone's
target practice." But she didn't. She spoke the elegant, often romantic,
never less than sonorous language of Maya Angelou. Ms. Angelou's work
has been a cornerstone for the development of African-American poetry;
however, for *Poetic Justice* to have been the film that it could have been, it
would have to have had as its protagonist a woman who talks more like
Wanda Coleman, Maggie Estep, or Dael Orlandersmith than the softer
verse that speaks of poetry as the "oneness of the human spirit." We are all
in a time capsule heading straight into the twenty-first century filled with
excitement, writing poems that land on their feet, poems about life's raw
edges, correctional institutions, emotional confinement, sexual choices, and
regrets. Jackson could have been talking the rough, molten steel of late-
nineties verse.

When Alexander Hamilton visited the Falls in Paterson, the popula-
tion that he found reflected the European immigration to the New World.
It is part of Dr. Williams's genius that his epic American poem can exqui-
sitely label with such exactitude the number of French, German, English,
Scotch, Dutch, and others who made up the general population around the
falls. These precisely enumerated people were the beginning of what was to
become the heart of the American industrial evolution, just as we at the
Nuyorican Poets Cafe, in keeping with the traditions of *Paterson*, open our
doors to the multi-ethnic, formally poetic world that comes to us to read, to
hear, to be heard. On any night that the doors open for our mock-Olympic
poetry Slams, the magic is in the playfulness of the occasion and the abso-
lute seriousness with which the poets and the audience interact. This is
interactive art. If we wanted to make a parallel to the video world, we could
call the Slam "Prime Time Interactive Literature."

The Grand Slam starts with our host, Bob Holman, reading his Dis-Claimer: "We disdain/competition and its ally war/and are fighting for our lives/and the spinning/of poetry's cocoon of action/in your dailiness. We refuse/to meld the contradictions but/will always walk the razor/for your love. 'The best poet/always loses.' " Judges, who have been selected whimsically from the audience, are introduced with such "qualifications" as being born in Brooklyn or having never been to a Slam before. These judges will rate the poem from zero ("a poem that should never have been written") to ten ("mutual simultaneous orgasm") using the "Dewey decimal rating system" to avoid ties and "the dreaded Sudden-Death Haiku Improv overtime round." Here we are in the realm of literate humor, with no discerning of "high" and "low," all in the service of bringing a new audience to poetry via a form of entertainment meant to tune up fresh ears to a use of language as art that has been considered dead by many. And after an hour or so of non-stop poetry, our host nods to the deejay in the booth and the room goes into a frenzy of dance, beer, wine, tea, and coffee, and that's called the Break. Winners go from the Grand Slam to the Nationals, which in 1993 featured poets from twenty-four cities.

The modern Slam is the creation of Marc Smith, who continues his weekly bare-knuckles events at the Green Mill in Chicago. The idea for the Slam grows out of ancient traditions of competitive and/or linked rhymes between orators—from the Greek mythological tale of Apollo and Marsyas to the African griots, from the *Sanjūrokunin sen,* or imaginary poetry team competitions, of tenth-century Japanese court poet Fujiwara no Kinto to the African-American "dozens." It is a tradition that still exists very actively on the island of Puerto Rico, where El Trovador improvises in the plaza, spontaneously pulling into the verse the life of the folks in the small town, the tragedies that have occurred in their families, the gossip that surrounds their private lives, and the celebratory passages that talk about births, deaths, weddings, and baptisms. All of this is compacted into ten-syllable lines with end rhymes. El Trovador moves from town to town in the outskirts of the big cities of the island and is received grandly by the townsfolk, who look forward to regaling him with laughter and drinks when he is entertaining, and/or criticizing and insulting him when he is either too rigid or too drunk to deliver the goods. This tradition of El Trovador coming to perform to the audience for their approval or being punished by their disapproval is totally alive at the Nuyorican Poets Cafe.

So, it is Grand Slam night, and the slammers are Regie Cabico, Shirley LeFlore, Julie Patton, and Anne Elliott. Our master of ceremonies excites the audience with a short, tight monologue that releases anxiety as it makes people laugh, both at themselves and at the competition that we are about to engage in. Shirley LeFlore, a poet in her fifties, opens the Slam, and with her we enter an almost magical world of Coltrane strains, where LeFlore riffs and talks of Miles, of Armstrong, of Chango, and in her flow she evokes the great poetic jazz tradition of Baraka at his most musical. She comes close to the smooth and angry jazzoetry that has been the characteristic music of African-American poetry of the fifties and early sixties. The crowd is pleased, she is given a warm, enthusiastic response, yet we're all aware of the great tradition from which this comes, and we are clear that her first poem is a riff away from the pantheon of the likes of Baraka, Jayne Cortez, and Gaylen Kane. The judges weigh in: she is given a 26 out of 30. I am moved by the willingness of the mostly young audience to involve themselves in a poem that is more characteristic of the Greenwich Village jazz-poetic scene than what they have probably come to hear. But who's to say? Chaos at the Cafe is a blessed state, not a problem.

The second poet, Julie Patton, moves in with long, winding lines that seem to flow along a passive downstream trip into a very private universe where references to Shakespeare and Faulkner and everyday life intermingle in a rhapsodic, seemingly haphazard manner that earns her a 27 for her effort. The poem she has read has been meandering, at times self-indulgent, but the audience hangs in there, following her bravura vocalizations where melody meets meaning. Julie has traveled from a stay at a writers' colony in the state of Washington to be with us tonight. It is exciting that a poet would travel across the country to come to the Nuyorican Poets Cafe in order to be heard, to be able to stretch out before our legendary young, rowdy, and critical audience.

Regie Cabico, the third slammer, enters the room like a bullet, a young gay Filipino talking rhapsodically about the "fresh golden fleeces" and the "nine inches" of fun that he desires. Cabico is a dynamo of metaphors spun out of an extraordinarily sensitive blend of gay audacity and Filipino sensibility. By the time that Regie explains "orgasms are onomatopoeia," the crowd is wild, screaming, shouting, talking back to him, involved in his poetic process. Poet and listeners have become one. The room is now the Temple of Poetry. Here we do not exalt it, we bring it down home. We do not lavish praises on the sensibility of the poet, we imbibe him. And then after we've embraced the poet's daring, we proceed to give him a numerological value. If it seems illogical, it is. If it seems irreverent, it is. If it seems funny, raucous, and vaudevillian, that too it is.

And the grade that Regie is given is a 29. Regie's delivery has been masterful, controlled, and intense. The excitement builds.

Anne Elliott is our fourth slammer. She has a classic Northern European look, which is an extraordinary contrast to the first three poets' presences. Her projection is melodic, though her verse is a muscular line of thought woven delicately and interlaced with musical accents. She is "the all-new Gregorian chant," as Holman has just characterized her from the stage. The audience has felt at one with his characterization, and indeed it is in sync with what we now begin to hear. Someone from the audience exclaims, "We are in the intestines of a dark devil!" This judgment is anonymous, it is impossible to identify who among the 250 people present has said it, yet it goes directly to the heart of the matter. The silent attention that is being given to her contrasts intensely with the reactive, interactive world that Regie Cabico had created. At the Nuyorican Poets Cafe we work by contrasts, and here we are at the extreme of two poetic poles. Elliott is given a 27.4. The audience reacts with an enveloping round of applause, signaling to her a deep appreciation of the mastery with which she's spun the melodic verse and the excitement she created, as if we were in the midst of a sustained passion.

The importance of the Slam, in fact the importance of poetry at the Cafe, is rooted in its capacity to draw in audiences ranging from our immediate working-class neighbors out for a beer and some fun to serious poetry lovers willing to engage the new poets the Cafe features to the artists themselves, who seek both exposure of their poems and exposure to other poets. The interrelationship between what has been heretofore thought of as a highbrow art and its appeal to a mass public has become a very important polemic, i.e., poetry seems to want to move into daily American life. The poem, the poet, and the audience grow in a deepening relationship that has become ever more public, ever more popular, and ever more engaging. No matter which way it is seen, it is remarkable to look out into the Nuyorican Poets Cafe Slam on a Wednesday night or on a Friday night and see young couples sitting, holding hands, embracing, and spending an evening out on the town in a poets' cafe for no other reason than that it is fun to be here, in this space, involved in this intensely interactive relationship between the poet expressing and the listener absorbing and actively responding. The time has finally arrived when poetry as an interlacing art is being heard from again. It informs, it motivates, it challenges, and it makes for pleasure. It is entertaining. It is a live form of recreation. It couldn't have been said twenty years ago; not even the Beats managed to take poetry out of the coffeehouses. Yet now it is on television, on radio, in the movie houses, and in numberless clubs around the country where live performances of the poem have taken root.

At the center of this movement is "the Largest Stage in the World." On any given night the master of ceremonies at the Nuyorican Poets Cafe can look out into the audience and spot the voices that have grown in the room and that have become recognized and beloved by the audience. So when Holman spots Sekou Sundiata in the room and calls him up to perform, the audience is enthusiastic and expectant that Sundiata will deliver a moment of intense pleasure and significant content. If poetry has become a pastime, it is a recreation that actively demands an involvement from the audience to grow, an audience that will seek inside themselves spaces which are unfamiliar to the ordinary ways in which we in the United States find pleasure. When Sekou steps up to the mike, we are suddenly inside a performance that is elevating the discourse in the room: Space, a character from Sundiata's play *The Circle Unbroken Is a Hard Bop,* begins to unravel his disjointed view of the world, and we in turn are made familiar with a personage we often run into in the subways and in the streets of the city. Space is a brilliant mind gone awry, having lost all connection to sequential thought. He splatters himself onto the sidewalk, into walls, onto the subway tracks in brilliant metaphoric effusions about how the CIA is taking over his mind, and about his masturbation in the name of Marilyn Monroe. Space's poem is a brilliant insight into what it means to be black, and a self-mocking assault on the audience and the fear that he, Space, can cause in his disjointed world.

Sekou's recital is a great lesson in self-discipline. Inside the play, Space spreads disruptively all over the stage, but before the audience on a Slam night, Space the character is contained inside the poet, and only the words are performed. If the listener has seen the dramatic rendition and contrasts that to this performance, an enormous lesson will have been learned about the theatricalization of poetry, the reason why poetry and theater are so intertwined, and why both are entering into the twenty-first century alive and well at the Nuyorican Poets Cafe.

Keenness, spontaneity, and trusting the moment are very important for the ceremonial master in the Nuyorican Poets Cafe. In keeping with the great commitment that the poets at the Cafe have made to writing the verse on the page and then lifting off the page into performing action, Holman's eyes survey the crowd, now spotting other poets who have grown in the room. Reg E. Gaines, who entered the room only ten minutes before, is caught and called up to center stage. When Gaines acquires control of the mike, we are in a very special place. Here is an African-American man who has discovered his poetic roots in the voice and sentiments of the Nuyorican poets. Reg E.'s command of Lucky CienFuegos's and Miguel Piñero's poems is astounding. He can, from memory, recite some of their most important poems from the mid-seventies. To recite in two languages is an exciting phenomenon, since it implies that the performer is capable of blending a Spanish verb with an object in English and delivering an impact that excites and arouses the listener.

The fearlessness with which young African-American poets are now confronting languages other than English and involving themselves in the exploration of self-expression in other forms of speech is new and probably the most welcome sign of a new internationalism alive in the young African-American poets. Tracie Morris and Reg E. Gaines do not just make an easy nod to multilingual expression—they are daring in their willingness to stand before live audiences and speak in Spanish. They speak their feelings in Spanish. When Tracie Morris begins her "Morenita" poem, we are soothingly involved and seduced in her bilingual sensual quest for love and precise definitions in relationships. Nuyorican language is no longer the property of Puerto Ricans speaking in a blend of English and Spanish; it is now more like one of the dialects at the edges of the Roman Empire, which were once called vulgar but are now the Spanish, Italian, and Portuguese of modern Europe.

Now, this is the very heart of the matter. They are both attempting complex intense communications in the Spanish language and are fearless about accents or mispronunciation. They are intent on diving into the endless possibility of multilingual expressiveness. This is new and exciting, and it shows enormous promise for the African-American poetic voice in the Western Hemisphere. Gone are the days when English would remain the only means of expression for North American artists. It is clear that today alternate systems of speech are growing increasingly popular and creatively alluring. Spanish has been present on the North American continent since the very beginning of the Columbian occupation. It is not about to disappear and in fact it will continue to grow in importance as the economic relationship between the Southern and the Northern hemispheres begins to equalize.

The linguistic sophistication and complexity grows further when Holman spots Adrienne Su, an Asian-American woman whose simple demeanor and shy presence belie a poet whose sensibility is made of steel and concrete. With Su, the poetic discourse expands beyond issues of language and race into personal moral dilemmas. She approaches the mike and announces that she will read a sestina. When she begins we're inside a very mild tone, but then the content crosses over, and the audience begins to hear phrases like "You said the last word with your last/breath and I was not there to bury/it" and "What/you didn't count on was writing/the note, dying, and no one coming to bury/you"; the listener becomes aware of a very powerful statement being made about guilt. Su is saying, Don't make me feel guilty about your suicide. She finally drives it home when she says, "You intended/to get what you got. Now get out." Asian-American poets have been central to the Cafe ever since the Basement Workshop and Fay Chiang started to visit us at our 6th Street location. The Asian-American perception of American morality, American culture, and language changed for the Nuyorican poets of the seventies the way in which we talked, the way we used the verb. What was then a relationship of great educational value has grown into an artistic partnership.

The complex moral discourse that Adrienne Su has brought into the room quickly shifts as Bob Holman's keen eye lands on Hal Sirowitz, a poet whose mock-psychiatric plays on family, especially his relationship with his mother, have made his poems extremely popular among Poetry Slam devotees. Everyone is ready and perched for the "Mother said" refrain that Sirowitz has made famous:

> Don't stick your finger in the ketchup bottle,
> Mother said. It might get stuck, &
> then you'll have to wait for your father
> to get home to pull it out. He
> won't be happy to find a dirty fingernail
> squirming in the ketchup that he's going to use
> on his hamburger.

Sirowitz plays with depression, repression, psychological tension, and psychiatric outrageousness has made him the late-twentieth-century homespun Sigmund Freud of Slam poetry at the Nuyorican Poets Cafe. His humor is sharp, and long after you've laughed at what is an apparently simple statement of fact, it keeps on reverberating until you're aware that a great language-smith has been at work. His Jewish-American humor, accompanied by his deadpan delivery, is by now part of the folklore that will be passed on to the twenty-first century.

As Sirowitz takes his applause and the crowd is laughing wildly and madly, Edwin Torres is brought up to the mike, and the crowd is in for yet another mystery tour in the jungle of words that have by now swamped their sensibilities. Edwin Torres, NuyoFuturist, passes beyond all other sound poets and their inventions as he begins to read. Torres depends on the phoneme as the unit of sound. He often begins by hitting a sequence of vowels emitted at an extraordinary range of pitches and volume. This playing with vowels then modulates into vowels accompanied by consonants, and there begin to appear syllables, which stretch from the lower register to the most extreme upper register, a combination of vowel and consonant that leaps between scales and finally can, after a full two or three minutes, reach a point where words begin to appear, not necessarily spoken, but congealing in the ear of the listener, who is surprised by the appearance of a word and then a sequence of words that leads the mind into recognizable sequential language. Is it a stretch? You bet it is. Has it worked? Judging by the audience, who begin to applaud as Torres pulls himself back into familiar noun-verb-object relationships, it has worked. The sound-play begat syllables, which begat words, which begat sentences, which begat a poem.

The poetics that binds these poets is alive and being invented as they themselves evolve as poets and thinkers about their art and their craft. The media coverage that has engulfed these poets has been so plentiful that it is now possible to cull from the endless articles a sense of the poetics that is being created in midair from one article to the other as these poets are made to think about content, quality, and craft. In *Newsweek,* Kevin Powell says "poetry is the quickest way to express what you see and feel," yet Paul Beatty seems worried about the hoopla that may dull the critical edge that poetry should have: "The real hook of poetry is that it turns things inside out, and I'm not sure all this trendiness measures with that." Beatty is expressing a very important reservation, but it is a reservation that is not just pertinent to these poets; it is a reservation that is pertinent to anything today in America, where trends are devoured like ice-cream cones, in seconds. It is clear that Beatty is worried about permanence and continuity.

Allen Ginsberg recently praised Beatty for "his very smooth, good, sophisticated, syncopated ear." He has also read Beatty's poems as "microchips bursting with information." Ginsberg has once again encapsulated the poetic moment, since it is true that Beatty is a condenser and a fine filtering voice for the experience of the late twentieth century. So that by the time that Evelyn McDonnell in the *Village Voice* describes him as perhaps "the first poet to transcribe the language of the telecommunications age onto paper," we have finally come the full circle round, and we have reached what is probably the best description of the poetics of the first decade of the twenty-first century.

IV. THE OPEN ROOM

The Open Room was the first idea. At the beginning there was a well-lit, clean, and open space that received the artistic input of anyone who walked in the door, and from this beginning was derived the complex programming that now goes on at the Nuyorican Poets Cafe. In the early days of the Cafe (1974–1982), the hosts of the room were mainly Miguel "Lobo" Loperena and Lois Griffith. At the end of the bar, Lobo or I would stand with a ledger and a pencil and simply enter the names of the people who came to perform in order of arrival, so that a famous poet dropping in for the evening could be preceded by a first-time poet and followed by an habitué of the room.

Lobo Loperena would handle the room with his gentle and eagle-eyed capacity to move the room from conversational, social interaction/chaos into a listening audience. This transition was always massively difficult, since it was the practice to have the room filled with recorded music right up to the point at which Lobo would step up to the mike to make that most difficult of all transitions: taking people from muscle-body-action (dancing) to mental-ear-repose (listening).

It still remains a magic memory for all of the people present on the night when Lobo stepped up to the mike and, in an effort to make a dramatic transition from recorded music to poetry, announced that the poets of the Nuyorican Poets Cafe had created a Nuyorican chant. He then proceeded, for the first time ever, to perform what was to become the classic chant for our poetry performances and for the room:

La   La   La
Le   Le   Le-e-e-e
Le   Le   Le
Le-e-e-e-a!

Tru cu tum
Cu tum cu tum
   {clave: ///}

Tru cu tum
Cu tum cu tum
　{clave: ///}

Pa' eso te pulla
Pa' eso te duerme
Lo mio no es violencia
Lo mio es dulce

La　La　La
Le　Le　Le-e-e-e
Le　Le　Le
Le-e-e-e-a!

　　　And the first poet is . . .

The deep chest-tone and the sustained vowels of the chant galvanized the audience, which had been sweating and frantically moving to the music; within seconds, Lobo had managed to make the dancers into listeners. He had found a way to move from dance to poetry successfully. The room filled with a cathartic round of applause. Instead of the usual begrudging attitude, often accompanied by boos, that heretofore had preceded such a transition, the audience yielded to what was the room's mission after all, the performance of poetry.

The Open Room had found its ceremonial master in Lobo, and Lobo had found that his Nuyorican chant became an inspirational and practical way to move people into a space where self-expression and poetry can take place.

The Open Room is a gathering place for all kinds of writers and readers who are, for the most part, jittery and anxious about the moment that is coming to them. The poets wait for their names to be called, poems tightly gripped in hand. They are ready to face the audience. It is an audience that is not ready to bear the weight of boredom easily, and people who sign up know that the result can be either crushing or elevating.

The Open Room is the basis for the open, generous, embracing attitude that is in fact the aesthetic of the Cafe, and its continuity through all the years is our root. The Open Room simply must happen every week, since the opportunity to come back the next week is what gives the poets the impetus to write that next poem and allows them to learn how to relax through the nervousness that distorted or destroyed the poem the week before.

It is important that poets know they can always come back the next week, that the audience will be there, supportive or critical but never passive, hungry for the images that the poets have found in the interim. For example, one of the regular poets of the Open Room is Pauly Arroyo. Pauly has been with the Nuyorican Poets Cafe from the very beginning. In the early days he was a martial artist who would get up and perform martial art katas for the Open Room. It was fascinating and riveting to watch Pauly masterfully exhibit the physical control of breath and body as he performed his katas. The audience would go wild, and approval would be his. As the years passed, Pauly moved in the direction of language and began reciting verse. This met with very critical responses from the audience, often disappointing Pauly, yet week after week he would return, challenging himself and the audience again, and the outcome has been an engrossing evolution in which Pauly has reached a place where he can combine his martial arts movements, display his virtuoso control of breath, and engage language that can stir and animate the audience. He has finally arrived at a performance where breath, physical movement, and language have come together, and the audience has given him the recognition that he's wanted. He is becoming a poet who can express experience and arouse the listener:

> And though we play our tunes
> the ghetto still plays the sound with us
> we bongo like madness we bongo our dreams we bongo our tunes
> don't let us be stopped because we won't we will keep tryin'
> and if we are still a rhythm of sound
> let our music bounce from every wall and town
> and if we can play the tune once more
> I play it just for you.

While Pauly Arroyo's development in the room has been progressive and has incorporated many elements, Shorty Bón Bón's poem became a classic hit in the room from the very first moment that he recited it. It was a rainy night, and Shorty came into the room looking for shelter, looking for warmth, and looking for love. I remember spotting him and instantly went to the ledger and entered his name. When it came time to introduce him, he was still sopping wet, with a glass of wine in one hand, a cigarette in the other, and a poem in his mind. The poem was "A Junkie's Heaven," and once he recited it, the room went wild and requests for a repeat began immediately; in fact, it might have been the first time that the room as a whole asked for a poem to be repeated. Shorty obliged and felt proud at the reception of his poem and at the birth of a Loisaida* classic.

> *His sacrifice was not in vain*
> *though he died because of an abscessed*
> *brain*
> *a junkie dreamt*
> *of his lament*
> *When I die*
> *I shall go to a land*
> *where the cocaine is clean*
> *and I'll smoke my pot only when it's*
> *at the darkest of green*
> *here all the angels are junkies*
> *and the Christ is so hip*
> *that for the crime of my bootlegged*
> *wine*
> *he'll demand two sips*
> *yes, come to my heaven where all*
> *the junkies walk free . . . and*
> *remember all you potheads out*
> *there*
> *the smoke is on me . . .*

The Open Room has become the trial ground for "slammers" to practice away from the blinding spotlight of the Friday night Poetry Slams. The greater calm and ease of the Open Room can and does give space for people to discover their poems, to hone their work, and, since the room is so receptive, poets often go for issues that are close to their hearts, or issues that are inspired by political current affairs. These Headline Rhymes are direct, wet-ink-on-the-page responses, the news told as an individual's response, not a

*Loisaida (lō ē 'sī da) (the Lower East Side in Nuyorican, a creation of Bimbo Rivas) 1. That portion of Manhattan stretching from "Houston to 14th Street/From Second Avenue to the mighty D."—Miguel Piñero. 2. The eternally transitional neighborhood known in other incarnations as the Lower East Side (see Ed Sanders's "The Yiddish-Speaking Socialists of the Lower East Side" and "The Low East" [David Henderson]). Also check out the street signs along Avenue C, "Loisaida Avenue," and Bimbo's mural on C between 5th and 6th.

committee's decision. Like the poets of the sixties and seventies told of Vietnam and Cambodia, here you will hear of the War in the Gulf, the Los Angeles riots, natural disasters of all types, and serial killers. Often, too, the personal and political intersect, and you will hear poems on rape, whether it be the reporting of a rape, or the autobiographical revelation of the experience. Oftentimes it seems as if the mind of New York is on display, and that the mind of the poet and the city are one in their concerns.

Carol Diehl takes the question of women and men and their relationships out into the audience in a semiserious comic release that drives the Open Room audience crazy:

> *What if*
>   *the ability to menstruate*
>   *was the prerequisite for most high-paying jobs*
> . . . .
> *What if*
>   *women were always making jokes*
>   *about how ugly penises are*
>   *and how bad sperm tastes*

Since someone in the audience or at the bar will always inform the poet, "We can't hear you," one of the most precious Open Room lessons that the young poet can learn is how to react to a heckle, how to use the mike, how to acquire calm and poise, how to improve the recitation of the poem. The Open Room is where a "virgin" poet takes the first steps to becoming a performing poet. Sometimes, however, a "birthday poem," a poet's first poem, is his or her last. Nevertheless, most poets are willing to come and share in the nerve-racking wait for their names to be called and then face the audience's reaction. You never know who might be in that audience, and it is part of the charm of the Open Room night that many people have found friendship and companionship as they come back week after week seeking people who are listening to others speak.

After reading, a poet can relax and enjoy the heartfelt congratulations, sometimes even receiving an invitation to read in another place. Many poets have gotten their start in the reading circuits around the city in the Cafe's Open Room. Of course, there is always in the Open Room the opportunity to make an absolute fool of oneself and not have to worry about it, since there is a sense of communion and connection and great partnership that comes from a reading that takes place at 2:00 A.M.

27

To be a host of the Open Room, as in the great tradition of Miguel "Lobo" Loperena, you have to have a great sense of balance, the capacity to absorb constant heckling and interruptions of people going to get wine, beer, coffee, and tea, and the sound of people booing, jeering, or approving a poem. The room is in constant flux. The host must be a very centered person. Lois Griffith has been at the heart of the Open Room for the last decade. Now Keith Roach has evolved into the quintessential Open Room host, capable of handling the readers, the audience, and the feel and flow of the room. As Keith says, "It happens, on occasion, that there is a poet who is overwhelmed and done in by the moment. Sometimes vapor lock occurs. These are some of the most engaging moments. Someone will step forward and restore some of the poet's lost dignity. Most poets who undergo this experience realize that there is some more work, some more practice, some more nerve." The success of a great Open Room night lies squarely on the shoulders of the host's resourcefulness, inventiveness, and generosity. The evening's master of ceremonies carries the full weight of the night's success.

And finally, the Open Room contains an ambience so rich in the folklore of Loisaida that readers with national and international reputations have stepped in as surprise guest readers to enjoy themselves, the room, the bawdy atmosphere, and in so doing, by their very presence, they always incite the crowd and heighten the performance of the Open Room devotees. All you can be assured of at the Open Room is surprise, poetry in all stages of gestation, and a simpatico crowd in the wee morning hours.

I.
POETRY
INTO THE
TWENTY-FIRST CENTURY

paul beatty **DARRYL STRAWBERRY ASLEEP IN A FIELD OF DREAMS**

         they raised the price of dreams
blue inked can of del monte creamed corn
where baseball players
are reborn

         in their prime
         to play in modern day times

and not only was the ball white

shoeless joe jackson was white
         his uni was white
         all the dead white players was white
    takin batting practice in white home uniforms
    under white iowa clouds

i squirmed in my seat hopin for a
warm thunder storm
            that would rain down cool papa bell
            and hell would drip off corn stalk blades

pool into a homestead grey
                        inna grey away uniform
flip down flip-up shades
and say   hey now lets really play

                    got to wear your sun glasses
                        so you can feel cool

but its only a movie
and in film school heaven is
where white doctors who played
only an inning and a half in the show
can pray for a tinker everlastin chance to groove the 0-2 sinker

        white boys steady leanin in
    truly believin this is the best movie theyve ever seen
but none of em asked josh gibson to slo-dance
across the color line that
falls in an iowa ball field
                broken but unhealed

fathers younger than their sons play catch
onna mismatch patch
natural grass and james earl jonezes broad ass

        hollywoods black fat majesty
        bellows . . . *and the people will come*

    black people smiled and fell in single file
to pay to watch mel ott run through Fences

and put the suicide squeeze on my mothers mother
whose color
is the same
as a night game infield

30

. . . and the people will come

to see that black fathers to be
   with scars on their knees
      from shinbones split in half
        and knocked off kneecaps
practice the tap dunks they will pump over their daughters n sons

. . . and the people will come

how could daughters n fathers build
wooden bleachers
just to sit and cheer male features

if umpire pam postema dies in the minor leagues
ty cobb'll hook slide into heaven
and she'll call him out

and he will
get up dust himself call her a . . .
brush it off as a tease

is this heaven
     no its iowa

is this heaven
     no its harlem

is this heaven
     no its bedrock

is this heaven
     no its cabrini green

do they got a team
   aint sure they got dreams
   damn sure aint got a field
or crops that yield
       is that the sign for steal
       i approach the third base coach
       and ask is all the movies for real

AT EASE

every morning roundabout nine
the east 2nd street
red fire engines whine

        a shrill drill sergeant
        rousting my mind

                its time to rise and shine   shine
   in the east village
   another dollar draft recruit
      boot camp saloon sambo
             a genesee on tap dancin hambone poet

bivouacs in the groovy lower east side barracks
makin friends wid homespun poet pundit bums
recitin jack kerouac

and for fun i attend
allnight outdoor open mikes
free readings about real people
who seem so lifelike

     last night i bought a stolen bike
     a freewheel three speed
     grew a goatee

camped out on avenue B
and for a change in perspective
went to   A Retrospective of Scatological Abstraction:
               from Popeye to Gillespie

           skeeter ta rebop rap pap debose
                  debang
                 deboom
            i yam what i yam
          and thats all that i yam

b'diddly bop repetitious rot
dont forget to stop at my seddity sop co-op
                                        listen to my loizada
                                                    lambada
                                                tostada
cholesterol-free blah blah blah poppycock

                                                            salt free nuts
                                                            salt free nuts

i just kickback n watch
black combat boots
move thru an east village tour of duty
                                        an in unison death march
                                                    to the cadence
of the ultra cool
hop hop   who
hut-hop hep   who
hut-hop hep   who
hut-hop het   who
                        einey meany miney moe
                        lets go back and write some more

i admit theres an urge
to merge ginsbergs
ice age incantations
with some inspired spitfire monk vibes

                        but no tai chi for me "g"
                        nix on the tye dye

                wont hindu my blues   nor
                                        tofu my soulfood

im gonna be
    the bulimic bohemian

                        eatin up my people
                        then purgin their regurgitated words
                        on the page

                              and the poems
                         become self made
                    little icarus birds

              immaculately hatched
from the multicultural nest eggs
of the east village and west l.a.

                                        born to sing lyric segues
                    while caged

whats the   latin
                    scientific
                              slave name
for pretty peacocks
         whose feathers span the flesh spectrum
                                   but are stuck on with wax
it looks nice
but can it fly

              look up in the sky
              itsa bat
              itsa crow
         no its supernigger/indian/chicano/womanist/gay/asian everything

able to fly through the peephole
in the white medias ozone
                    talk proper on the phone   and act ethnic at home

y know
its like multiculturalisms
the lefts right guard
of truth justice and the american way

                    a spray-on deodorant
                    against the stench of isms

                         Contents under
                         extreme pressure.
                         May explode.

i understand the effort to prevent skin cancer
by removin epithets and fluorocarbons from the history texts

but multiculturalisms
sunblock jargon
                doesnt protect
                against big brother sun rays
                on days when niggas went to the beach
                and wore socks

to cover up the lack of respect for the blackfeet

  not the indians
                but the crusty lizard skin
              two inch thick toenailed
                  curled hammertoes
            knuckled corns *my soul is rested* on

never heard anyone
other than
a black man
utter these words   *man she got some pretty feet*

dont nobody appreciate feet
like we do

           i fell in love with my second grade teachers feet
           her toes smooth n flat   her insteps were all that
           i would drop my pencil alot
           to watch her wiggle her little piggies under the desk

we used to stay after school
to sneak around and smell her shoes
and this little piggy ran all the way home

what you learn in school today

bout how columbus
landed in cuba stuck a flag in the ground

how neil armstrong landed on the moon and stuck a flag in the ground
how rick rubin landed in rap and stuck a flag in the sound

hey you all look what i found

the east village
a human garden   a botanical class menagerie
with its own avant-garde beatnik color guard

that when asked to
present the colors of their flag
                they go   *white and ummm*
                              bob kaufman aaaand lets see uhhhh
                              oh yeah the angry guy

hey leroi

i joined to this peoples army
to seek that quintessential beat freedom
that only white boys seem to achieve

the rest of us
still dream about being so casual
being able to act up
with the bill murray i dont give a fuck   boom shaka laka
                                          boom shaka laka
                                        chief house rocker attitude

hey dude care to smoke a bowl   no regrets hold your breath

dont smoke buddha
cant stand sess
it takes two to make-ah thing go right

so i force a discourse
      wid corporal gregory corso
      his pissed on disciples fix bayonets
      point their self righteous rifles   at my writing

dont get upset but

                    why dont you [blacks and other oppressed etc]
                    write more universally

does that mean write more white
drink tea in the morning
write about flowers n lust and poeticize the dust in the light rays

                      dont pull my daisy

but like paul revere said
at end of his midnight ride   whoa

it never ceases to amaze me
that whenever these jazz crazed

                      surly black berets
                      police the proud grounds
                      of their past

          they always
    mention diane di prima last

                      boom shaka laka
                      boom shaka laka
                    thats the fact jack

          i've heard   elvis   donny hathaway
          and roberta flack rap about the ghetto

but in the village
          i can peruse stacks n stacks
          of used and overdue library books

rows n rows
                of mad magazine paperbacks
like Al Jaffee's   Snappy Answers
                to Stupid Questions

How does it feel to read in front of so many white people

snappy answer #1:   the tompkins sq. park zoo closes at 1:00am
snappy answer #2:   *i feel the earth move under my feet*
                           i feel the sky tumblin down
snappy answer #3:   sometimes i feel like othello in the last act
                           desdemona is thru
                           and now usin modern medieval seppuku
                           heez fixin to spill his noble guts to the public

      Soft you; a word or two before you go.
      I have done the state some service and they know't:
      . . . Speak of me as I am: nothing extenuate, . . .
      you must speak
      Of one that loved not wisely, but too well; . . .   340
      I took by th'throat the . . . dog
      And smote him thus.   352

why you stabbeded my brother in the back
i be got no weapon

doin the hollywood shuffle
here in alphabet city
where the contradictions are so deep
you got

                  white supremacists
                  datin *black chicks*

where the tattooed unclenched fists of anarchists
talk bout if they had money
theyd start the revolution

when if theyd redeem
all the pop bottles

               they toss at the cops
               they could at least leaflet
               all the way to avenue D

but paulo friere multiculturalism and foucault
and the high brow *whats wrong with the world*
handbilled and postered so and so

dont go into the projects

Cuz thats where the for real
dispossessed pink slipped guerrillas in the mist stay at
hangin around   brass monkeys on the buzzards back

and in the middle of my rant
the man said
lighten up jack
straighten up and fly right
cool out and add a white boy to your jazz collection

so i attached gerry mulligans
hook n ladder long-ass sax
fire engine red hair to my wake up solo
this mornin i feel like
a black sideman playin poetic trumpet

                    my my aint that sumpthin

a literary bojangles
inna military band
playin taps
                red black n greens at half-mast
                his bitterness iz dead

while uptowns fife n thumb drum corps
separates the trapezoids from the squares
            the raw from the done

                        i polish up my buttons n buckles

                        check out my reflection

                        fakin the funk

                        im ready for inspection
lace up my doc martens
and im marchin

hut-hop hop hop het-who
hut-hop hep who
lookin' good   lookin' good
      lookin' good like you should

nicole breedlove
AN OPEN LETTER TO MYSELF

I didn't mean
for it to happen
like this
(my life that is)
I don't want it
remembered
that welfare
bought us things
we didn't want
And my brother
joined the army
to get away
from the government
I don't want it
written
that I packed my bags
left them at a friend's
and slept
on the D train
for a month
until I lived
under my friend's bed
I don't want it
mentioned
that I slept
on a floor
in my office
before I moved
to Bensonhurst

ate spaghetti
and ketchup
and slept next to
twelve cats
that lay across
the place
where my spirit
should have been
I don't want it
noted
that I was running
from the mafia
chasing off the ghosts
and hiding from
the landlord
I don't want it said
but I'm telling you
because if it must be told
the D train
really fucked up
my lower back
and if it must be told
make sure the
Library of Congress
is notified

This has been
a brief moment
in Black History

FRONT PAGE OR BUST

Yeah—
well there was
a gay bar
blown up
on April 25
with a pipe bomb
and the police
are listing it
as a "faggot assault"
but JFK Jr.
was on the front page
as "the hunk that flunked"
And in the last week
there have been
two hostages released
from the Middle East
and President Bush
is gloating
about something
he didn't do
but Elizabeth Taylor
in on the front page
as the "ailing diva of film"
and David Aponte
who was set afire
for saying no to drugs
and was burned
over 80% of his body
and is still
in the hospital
with unthinkable
hospital bills
but Mike Milken

was on the front page
for crying
about a 600 million dollar fine
(poor baby!)
And a black man
was killed
while surrendering
to two white
police officers
who were suspended
with pay pending
an investigation
but Donald Trump
in on the front page
as the man who can
buy his cake
and eat it too
And movie stars
continue to take precedence
over the homeless
and politicians'
personal lives
continue
to take precedence
over justice
And names like
Elizabeth Taylor
Mike Milken
JFK Jr.
and Donald Trump
are just
fancy names
for irrelevance

"THERE MUST BE A CONSPIRACY"

There must be a conspiracy
Against the Black Man
Because what's being done
To the Black Woman
Has never been kept
A secret!

dana bryant ## FANTASY LOVER #5

Your scent preceded you
by ten feet
I sensed it well
before you'd slipped
silent beside me
or even turned my barstool to behold
your red-rimmed eyes
"Jamison," it whispered,
"with a twist of Drakkar Noir
or Pouilly Fumé with
early dinner.
Neither one before Five"
I heard the click of
the collar latch on
my neck chain
It was clear your
hands were accustomed
to the leash
You were much too
comfortable in your
role my dear
You did not flinch

When
For a moment
I bared my teeth
I noted your nails
were very finely
manicured
buffed to a subtly
numbing sheen
You have ten thin
delicate fingers
two 18 karat gold cufflinks
and one micro thin Rolliflex
Which I let
brush my cheek
briefly
As your whiskey dipped
pinky passed leisurely
over my lips
for several seconds
Then you asked me
for my name
I, of course,
would not give it
so our dance could begin
Again
Again
Again

HOUSECLEANING

Tonight
I was a mystery woman
who wasn't pretending to be
because I was truly a mystery to myself.

I sucked my teeth in rag
and saw they were
green
from too many
days of neglect
I kicked the door behind you
and found my heels
were
calloused and cracked
from
running
in pursuit
of you.

I sat before
my splintering
wood panelled wall
bits of plaster
on the floor
fallen from the ceiling
which caved in
after the
few short weeks
I was alone
again.

You always said it would.

You always said my
surname was disaster
and that was why
you
split.

I fear for my safety.

Moreoften
I fear my own self
reflected

thank god the only mirror I own
is caked with dirt
I haven't been home often enough
to tend to it
I was too busy
following
you.

I watch
minute particles of dust
resettle on the blanket
I just shook

and yet

I long for you
I want you to take me in your arms
and embrace me like a lover
of really fine things
I want you to taste me with relish
succor me
until the wellspring of my
bottomless desires
has filled up
despite my loneliness
with myself

allow me to be myself
allow me to be separate enough
to love you
properly
unbind me from the weave
of your checkered past
release me lovingly
tell me your name
not Michael or Beau
Sequoia or Jim
or any of the others I've
fallen
in with

46

tell me YOUR name
give me permission
to
clean
my
house
release me lovingly
Daddy . . .

regie cabico   # CHECK ONE

The government asks me to "check one" if I want money.
I just laugh in their face and say,
"How can you ask me to be one race?"

I stand proudly before you a fierce Filipino
who knows how to belt hard-gospel songs
played to African drums at a Catholic mass—
and loving the music to suffering beats,
and lashes from men's eyes on the capitol streets—

South-East D.C., with its sleepy crime,
my mother nursed patients from seven to nine,
patients gray from the railroad
riding past civil rights

I walked their tracks when I entertained
them at the chapel and made their canes pillars
of percussion to my heavy gospel—
my comedy out-loud, laughing about, our shared,
stolen experiences of the South.

Would it surprise you if I told you my blood
was delivered from North off Portuguese vessels
who gave me spiritual stones and the turn in my eyes—
my father's name when they conquered the Pacific Isles.

My hair is black and thick as "negrito," growing abundant
as "sampaguita"-flowers defying civilization
like pilipino pygmies that dance in the mountain.

I could give you an epic about my ways of life or my look
and you want me to fill it in "one square box."
From what integer or shape do you count existing identities,
grant loans for the mind, or crayola white census sheets—
There's no "one kind" to fill for anyone.

You tell me who I am, what gets the most money
and I'll sing that song like a one-man caravan.
I know arias from Naples, Tunis, and Accra—
lullabyes from welfare, food-stamps, and nature

and you want me to sing one song?
I have danced jigs with Jim Crow and shuffled my hips
to a sonic guitar of Clapton and Hendrix,
waltzed with dead lovers, skipped to bamboo sticks,
balleted kabuki and mimed cathacali
arrivedercied-a-rhumba and tapped Tin Pan Alley—
and you want me to dance the Bhagavad Gita
on a box too small for a thumbelina-thin diva?

I'll check "other," say *artist,*
that's who I am: a poet, a writer, a lover of man.

GAME BOY

he buys me a glass of bass draft & asks if i am japanese/
his remarks/
you are the perfect combination of boy & man/

are you the hip, hot, hung 9 inches of fun/ seeking the slim
smooth, smiling, authentically thai-tasting, geish-guy,
on-the-side macho dancer/ looking for his lord-&-master?

i am not a korean dragon lady/ running down avenue "a" with a teapot
between my legs/ shoutin'/ where's my tip?/ gimme my trophy!/ you
wanna play
with me?/

you can/ just quit orientalizin'/ cause i ain't
gonna change my cotton-knit calvins for you or my mother/
if i lose

i ain't gonna fry you an emperor's meal or throw you eurasia/
or butterfly you an opera/
i'm thru givin sex tours of unicef countries/ 3rd world is for hunger/
& fat sally struthers

      i've long been the "it" in a "rice queen phenomenon"/
that's burned faster than gin bottles/ thrown at the black
of my skillet/
games so old as jason & hercules/ men fucking my body like fresh-
golden fleeces/ they ride my boyhood on bikes in the woods/
then rape/ 'n kill it/ with leashes/ spit words/
in personal ads/
those clever written puzzles

for fun/ they blood-brother baptise my emotions/ then martyr
my sisters in the back room basements

i am beyond being poker-faced/ mysterious/ submissive/ wanted-by-you
or a being who's glossy & "g.q."-queen gorgeous

you wanna play freeze-tag?/ i'm frozen already
touch me you'll swear i'm the ice-man's ice monkey
hit me/ & watch where the mah-jongg chips land

play with me then/ if you think/
the sweet that's left to the taste in my tongue is enough & not bitter/
love me for this/ i forfeit the game/ remove my makeup/
& call you the winner

xavier cavazos
LONELY NIGHT IN NEW YORK

Lying on my bed near Mulberry Street
Near the empty crates that once held strawberrys &
A young Asian girl's face i think of you &
Your cat & the food you served for two delicate animals
Lying on my bed near Mott Street & Canal &
Where Italy & China overflow like that soda
You should of never opened i remind myself
How i miss spending time in your room in Seattle
There on Grand Street five stories above Picolo's Pizza
I pretend you are with me & i take your hand &
Wrap it around my cock   like the way my mother's
Fingers must have wrapped around red sheets
In the delivery room   i imagine you hold me that way
Steady like a picture   like the way your tongue
Holds each word before it's sent out in syllable or sound
Before you find my middle name or the color of my last lover's
Back   but i like it that way   the way it feels
When i make love to myself & think of you
So i do it again & this time you're bent over
Like that fetus i never had & i come as hard
As a girl running out of her house
After she found her mother dead
I come again & again & again
I come like mail you never wanted
I come like a period in a strange town
With one tampon & no Circle K
I come like your mother's last kiss
Like your father's kiss he should have never gave you
I come like your sweet name   like your name
Like your sweet name & wrap it around my veins
Like some lovely hum in my ear
Like some lovely hum
Like some humming ear
Like some lovely

Like some ear
Like some
Some hum

AT THE AIDS CLINIC

Men with long bones crossed legs &
Bent hands like 1492 transatlantic
Here nobody knows the name of the land
They're going to   everything could be the West
Indies   or at least the West Indies for awhile
Then the first flush of air   like a pilgrimage
Across the great hall of despair   artwork
Holds the walls with dignity   you think
You're in Seattle but the nurse tells you Soweto
You ask the doctor your name &
He begs you for bread in Spanish
You try to tell him the time on your watch
Before your lips collapse
All he says   lo siento   lo siento
Lo siento

U.N. RESOLUTION

Somalia   i have eaten you
Teeth round on dirt
So hard you think it's cake
Tongue fills with milk like women

With no eggs nursing cattle   i have consumed this
Somalia   i have consumed you
Girls nine with long skin &
Thin bones i have taken in the palm
Of my hand & sucked like a carnival of a
Lollipop   a ferris wheel of blueberry muffins &
Chocolate milk   Dick's deluxe & greasy fries
Cheesecake backed up by more cheesecake
I have consumed this   Somalia
I have consumed you
At three in the morning red eye & baked i have
Eaten the belly of Mohamed Hassan &
Digested him very well thank you &
When i needed help to get to the toilet
I took the leg of his brother &
Used it like a cane of support for comfort or
Nourishment   i have consumed
I'm a glutton of a person
A pile of shit so high you call me
President or U.N. or Xavier
I'm a good american boy
I learned my lessons well
I say my prayers &
Lick the plate clean every time

samantha coerbell
THE ROMANTICIZATION

And when he said to me
"Honey, you will be my only one"
I thought of God, country and
apple pie
All the things I'd been taught
to believe in
so I believed

He would take me in his arms
holding me too tight
"There's a lot of bad out there,
Baby"
a protector of my frail
little body frail
brittle fawn
all doe eyed and
gushing affection we'd
gurgle and coo and promise
each other
"If we do it, it will be
a bond of our LOVE"
"It'll be forever, like
world class lovers"

Water caressed the shore
dawn met a gentle drizzly fog
off in the distance
a trio of blindfolded violinists
played

He "TOOK" me there on the shore
with a kiss
gentle and wet (not too wet)
soft ever lasting
rolling in the sand
we made love for hours
no sweat (really not a drop)
my lover lifted me
my limp frail brittle little
spent
body carried off into the
morn, up to the house
bathing me in scented water
sponging my skin
apologizing for making me
his
his by the flesh

not the ring
When he said "I'm sorry, Sweetheart,
I love you"
I believed

It's always like that
when I remember
blocked shoved back
are the fuzzy green dice
over the rear view mirror
the glimpse of some kids
faces peeping in to see
the car rocking
a seatbelt clasp
wedged up in my shoulder blade
diving deeper into my flesh
each time you dove

I've even forgotten how
"Things just got a little out of hand"
a kiss hard and wet
(all my chin was wet)
a tongue made its way down my throat
without first meeting mine
wherever my top was
as you sucked my nipples raw
telling me I "loved it like this"
I'd lost track of your other hand
the one I could see
muffled my screams with your
flesh between my teeth
until I heard the lock clank
heard the gates open
heard the flesh tear
how it burned just the finger
then your dick
ugly gangly looking
not invisible and
spiritually fulfilling
the glow

the movies promised
not slick long hard
like in porno flicks
ugly mean poking in
missing the hole you dug
instead you pushed harder
like to make a new
fucking hole
pulling out 8 inches
when you only put 5 in
blind gruff bone dry
you kept on
because you were
"almost there, yeah baby, I'm
almost there, you're gonna
fucking take me there with
this tight pussy of yours,
only a tighttight pussy does it
for me"
such high praise
cumming inside me
spilling all over the cracked
vinyl interior of your daddy's
Chevy Impala
parked in the parking lot
by Beach 43rd St.

Sweat dropped off of your skin
into my eyes
it didn't matter
I was already crying
my sweaty stomach
only excited you more
I sweat even though I "wasn't
giving, just taking" from you
my sweat made you mad
crazy mad
horny mad
you were "gonna show me"

"give me a fuck I'd never
remember, it'd be that . . ."
"Good," I thought,
"good, now you'll have to stop"
you couldn't hurt me again
if your, as you said
"little soldier wouldn't salute"
that was too quaint for the scene
too little boy
too dirty old man
not a 5'8", fair skinned male,
aged 17, last seen wearing a gray sweatshirt,
blue jeans bunched around his
ankles

Pushing me "get up and fix
yourself, bitch"
apologizing for not making me
his by the flesh
'cause I "ain't seen nothing yet"
the only ringing
was in my ears
When he said
"Whore, I should kill you"
I believed

Morning came with hesitance
memories are counted in
days months years
for morning to come is to
accept what really has passed

His hugs were always too tight.

malkia amala cyril
BLUES TOMORROW

Bleeding into the sound
of headless hunters splintering the spines
of mules carrying my face like an undue burden
split nuclear and factioned
i am dust to this decaying corpse of civilization
abandoned to set with dusk
west of blood
sucking ozone free carbon dioxide
smoked out lungs
wrestled to a burial with the moon
back streets in the belly of Bed-Stuy
swallow bullets
peace treaties branded in the milky flow
of moonlit blood

then what is blood to you

if my abdomen is stretched inside out
seeping down the length of my tears
blowing in the speed of decapitated orgasms
edges of sun playing in the corners
of my mouth
if i could stop spinning
i swear i would
cement the cracks in my windowless smiles
taste blood sweating off the laughter
of thunder
screaming down the throat of
AK's
and be bulletproof
instead of shot to hell military style shit
instead of skin
the bottom line cranes toward jazz
my hunger is naked

and sleeping with revolution
i am the single drop and lava
wanting to arch my blues toward
the instinct of lonely
colored between silences thick with
Holiday or Smith
anger bled tears sing laughter with a soundtrack
and alive forever shaking this song screaming in my ears
and breathing deep the mountains of Martinique
and
      oh god
i need to burn into somebody's
                         skin
be wild and with a different face for every moon
          shit
             i need to burn

WAIT

Wait a minute longer than
silence lingers on too many
tongues roll first symphonies
drawn down concrete steeped fire
and i know
the coolest base bare toned and full of tears
the way midnight rain
slips
    sorrow
         stark
let it down and you are in the moonlight
                       baby.

alvin eng # ROCK ME, GOONG HAY!

Lose that shit—this ain't the mainland
I'm the Goong Hay Kid hope you understand
Don't do no kowtowing or no rickshaw
So don't be talking no dragons or the Great Wall
I ain't good in math, don't know kung fu
Ditto for Confucius and Fu Manchu
So don't mess with me or call me Bruce Lee
'Cause ain't no one badder than Kid Goong Hay

Rock me, Goong Hay

I only come 'round when the sun goes down
When I cruise the streets of Chinatown
Where the gangs and dolls they all concede
That the baddest dude is Kid Goong Hay
Now I'm too up on things and too down by law,
The defest C-town B-boy you ever saw
So don't dis me as some ping pong, ching chong,
Mah-jongg, egg foo yung, bang a gong, muh fuh huh

Rock me, Goong Hay

Now I'm no quick fix like MSG
Or some exotic treat from column A or column B
You won't find my kind on a dim sum tray
'Cause I'm rhymin' for tomorrow, not just today
A roots-rock-rapper proud of the sound
"Break it up break it up break it up breakdown"
'Cause I'm the rappin' real deal all brains, heart and balls
So how inscrutable is that to you all?

Yellow fever *was* our lot in this country
Now we're the so-called "model minority"
Which really don't mean shit if you think about it
'Cause plenty still despise our slanty eyes

So don't overcompensate for your sorry state
You can't keep us in the laundry or the railroad track
'CAUSE IT TAKES A NATION OF BILLIONS
    TO HOLD US PEOPLE BACK!

Rock me, Goong Hay

Goong hay fat choy!

TWAS THE NIGHT BEFORE CHINESE NEW YEAR'S

for Vincent Chin

Twas the night before Chinese New Year's
& all throughout Chinatown the word was out:
The old man was being hunted down
like the other from another planet.
His believers at the Pagan Pagoda knew he was gone
but they hung out all night anyway,
with hopes that he would return.

Twas the night before Chinese New Year's
& a dirty kind of quiet ripped up East Broadway in search of a storm,
but found only the old sewing woman
taking the moon out for its nightly walk.
The birdman of the Bowery
left his cages wide open but the birds would not fly
for they knew the tedium of surviving on the inside
was much easier than trying to get their wings out
there in the sweet and sour sky.
But how would the old man survive?

Twas the night before Chinese New Year's
& the red noise of the new year had not yet begun

but in a sense had already ended.
Nobody could fall asleep but no one could wake up
as visions of the old man danced in and out of the broken neon
shadows hovering over everybody's bed.
Twas the night before Chinese New Year's
and all throughout Chinatown all the traffic lights stayed yellow
but all the people saw red.

maggie estep THE STUPID JERK
I'M OBSESSED WITH

THE STUPID JERK I'M OBSESSED WITH
stands so close
I can feel his breath on my neck
and smell the way he would smell
if we slept together
because he is THE STUPID JERK I'M OBSESSED WITH
and that is his primary function in life
to be A STUPID JERK I CAN OBSESS OVER
and to talk to that dingy bimbette blonde
as if he really wanted to hear about her
manicures and pedicures and New Age Ritualistic Enema Cures
and, truth be told, he probably **does** want to hear about it
because he is
THE STUPID JERK I'M OBSESSED WITH
and he does anything he can to lend fuel to my fire
he makes a point
of standing, looking over my shoulder
when I'm talking to the guy who adores me
and would **bark like a dog and wave to strangers**
if I asked him to **bark like a dog and wave to strangers**
but I can't ask the guy to bark like a dog or impersonate
any kind of animal at all
cause I'm too busy

looking at the way
THE STUPID JERK I'M OBSESSED WITH
has pants on
that perfectly define his well-shaped ass
to the point where I'm thoroughly frantic,
I'm just gonna go home
stick my head in the oven
overdose on nutmeg and aspirin or sit in the bathtub
reading *The Executioner's Song*
and being completely confounded by the fact that I can see
THE STUPID JERK I'M OBSESSED WITH'S face
defining itself in the peeling plaster of the wall
grinning
and winking
and I start yelling: "Hey, get the hell out of there, you're just a figment of
my overripe imagination, get a life and get out of my plaster and pass me
the next painful situation please."

But he just keeps on
grinning
and winking
he's THE STUPID JERK I'M OBSESSED WITH
and he's mine
in my plaster
and frankly,
I COULDN'T BE HAPPIER.

SEX GODDESS OF THE WESTERN HEMISPHERE

I am THE SEX GODDESS OF THE WESTERN HEMISPHERE
so don't mess with me,
I've got a big bag full of SEX TOYS
and you can't have any

'cause they're all mine
'cause I'm
the SEX GODDESS OF THE WESTERN HEMISPHERE.

"Hey,"
you may say to yourself,
"who the hell's she tryin' to kid,
she's no sex goddess,"
But trust me,
I am
if only for the fact that I have
the unabashed gall
to call
myself a SEX GODDESS,
I mean, after all,
it's what so many of us have at some point thought,
we've all had **someone**
who worshipped our filthy socks
and barked like a dog when we were near
giving us cause
to pause and think: You know, I may not look like much
but deep inside,
I am a SEX GODDESS.

Only
we'd never come out and admit it publicly
well, **you** wouldn't admit it publicly
but I will
because I am
THE SEX GODDESS OF THE WESTERN HEMISPHERE.

I haven't always been
a SEX GODDESS
I used to be just a mere mortal woman
but I grew tired of sexuality being repressed
then manifest
in late night 900 number ads
where 3 bodacious bimbettes
heave cleavage into the camera's winking lens and sigh:

"Big Girls oooh, Bad Girls oooh, Blonde Girls oooh,
you know what to do, call 1-900-UNMITIGATED BIMBO ooooh."

Yeah
I got fed up with the oooh oooh oooh oooh oooh
I got fed up with it all
so I put on my combat boots and hit the road
with my bag full of SEX TOYS
that were a vital part of my SEX GODDESS image
even though I would never actually **use**
my SEX TOYS
'cause my being a SEX GODDESS
it isn't a SEXUAL thing
it's a POLITICAL thing
I don't actually **have** SEX, no
I'm too busy taking care of
important SEX GODDESS BUSINESS,
yeah,
I gotta go on The Charlie Rose Show
and MTV and become a parody
of myself and make
buckets full of money off my own inane brand
of self-righteous POP PSYCHOLOGY
because my pain is different
because I am a SEX GODDESS
and when I talk,
people listen
why?
Because, you guessed it,
I AM THE SEX GODDESS OF THE WESTERN HEMISPHERE
and you're not.

reg e. gaines PLEASE DON'T TAKE MY AIR JORDANS

my air jordans cost a hundred with tax
my suede starters jacket says raiders on the back
i'm stylin . . . smilin . . . lookin real mean cuz
it ain't about bein heard just bein seen

my leather adidas baseball cap
matches my fake gucci backpack
there's nobody out there looks good as me
but the gear costs money it sure ain't free

and i gots no job no money at all
but it's easy to steal fresh gear from the mall
parents say i shouldn't but i know i should
gots ta do what i can to make sure i look good

and the reason i have to look real fly
well to tell ya the truth man i don't know why
i guess it makes me feel special inside
when i'm wearin fresh gear i don't have to hide

but i really must get some new gear soon
or my ego will pop like a ten cent balloon
but security's tight at all the shops
everyday there are more and more cops

my crew's laughin at me cuz i'm wearin old gear
school's almost over summer is near
and i'm sportin torn jordans and need somethin new
there's only one thing left to do

cut school friday catch the subway downtown
check out my victims hangin around
maybe i'll get lucky and find easy prey
gots to get some new gear there's no other way

i'm ready and willin i'm packin my gun
this is serious bizness it sure ain't no fun
but i can't have my posse laughin at me
i'll cop somethin dope just wait you'll see

come out a the station west 4th near the park
brothers shootin hoops and someone remarks
HEY HOMES . . . WHERE'D YOU GET THOSE DEF NIKES
as i said to myself . . . i likes em . . . i likes

they were q-tip white bright and blinded my eyes
the red emblem of michael looked as if it could fly
not one spot of dirt the airs were brand new
had my pistol knew just what to do

followed him very closely behind
waited until it was just the right time
made a left turn on houston pulled out my gun and screamed
GIMME THEM JORDANS . . . and he tried ta run

took off fast but didn't get far
i fired (POW) he fell between two parked cars
he was coughin/cryin/blood dripped on the street
and i snatched them air jordans off a his feet

while layin there dyin all he could say was
please . . . don't take my air jordans away . . .
you think he'd be worried about stayin alive
as i took off with the jordans there were tears in his eyes

the very next day i bopped into school
with my brand new air jordans man was i cool
i killed to get them but hey . . . i don't care
cuz now . . . i needs a new jacket to wear

THOMAS THE BURNT ENGLISH MUFFIN

you son of a . . .
Georgia sharecropper the
brand nubian showstopper
flip floppin from left to right
afro/saxon fly by night and we know
your wife's white
woulda/coulda/shoulda
been like Thurgood a . . .
man who took a stand so
don't be mistaken
achin truth is Thomas:
the burnt english muffin
wants to do his bojangles shufflin
on the supreme court
but Homey don't play that
Judge Bork shit so the
muffin's gonna have a fit
tryin ta git in
raised as a . . .
new hope pope lover
Mother Theresa was his
holy rollin visa out a poverty
claimed he pulled up his own bootstraps
"perhaps"/but ivory hands helped push
Bush appointed him so something's wrong
all along claimin his disapproval of quotas
not one iota except when it fits his needs
leads one to believe . . .

the burnt muffin is least qualified
or are the president's hands tied
"GEORGE . . . confide in me"
has C.T. ever made a decision

check him out on colorvision
with his mouth wide open
gropin for words not there
so where is he comin from
sum total of the disenfranchised
american success story
wavin old glory frantically from
sea to shinin sea of
red blood flowin knowin well
this racist system
condemns his people to hell
as he half smiles and replies "no comment"
this satan sent disguised as a catholic
triple pick six does no good and much harm
as alarm clocks rock the boat cuz
we don't need another judas goat
and a vote for you who straddles the fence
makes no sense as you
rinse your hands of the
nonaborted bloodbath charade
parading down fifth which you must take
baked in white ovens burnt to a crisp
speak with forked lisp mind confused
if you're appointed black people lose
and will Thurgood's shoes ever be filled
grilled cheese and tomato
on burnt english muffin
huffin and puffin when it finally hits
DAMN!/i ain't what i thought i was cuz
i turns my back and hears black nigger
and just can't figure it out
no doubt you've been brainwashed
your people squashed
hated frustrated while you've been
checkmated by George
and not the one from valley forge
but that low life ass wipe lizard
who seriously considered
the former grand wizard of the

KKK can you say . . .
David Duke of pearl white satin
and even if you don't speak pig latin
you'll understand his . . .
"OINK OINK BOINK BAM" the royal scam
another black pawn gone as
crosses burn on the white house lawn
and supreme court justices sing along
to this free expression of
racial muck and mire . . . so Thomas
you burnt english muffin
smell the smoke wake the fuck up man
your ass is on fire

JUST ANOTHER MISUNDERSTOOD
BROTHER

labeled psychedelic though we called it noise
you could never be one of the boys playin' that
granite . . . shit/
too black to be white too white to be black
yet clapton townshend mccartney and big/ lip/ mick
longed to suck your dick cuz you was the man
gave us all the tickets to ladyland but we refused
to go didn't know . . . bout axis—weren't experienced

nappy heads hard as the rock you sling shot
through our ears but/ we didn't hear/ so you left
stratocaster in hand to a strange gray land of
cockney royalty and . . . L.S.D. soon to be a legend
you had no friends just parasites flyin' high
as kites/
pluckin'/ suckin'/ duckin' fame comin' off as a
lame . . . motherfucka . . .

as we torched our altered states hatin' you
for kissin' frosty's behind we was . . .
ray charles blind to where you was comin' from
never checked out third stone from the sun or
machine gun 'til you was dead . . .
took one look at your white boy styled head
of hair knew you was nowhere didn't care
you were a part of us resented the fuss

honkies made over you some nigger from seattle
who couldn't even play and today/
twenty years later . . . prince's hair is even
straighter than yours and we act like the
doors were so slick/ yet . . . they've all stolen
your licks your clothes your wild shows prove
you can teach new dogs old tricks

but you paid your dues playin' blues on the
chittlin' circuit takin' shit cuz you . . .
wanted to jam told to scram by threatened
veterans who saw those liquid brown fingers
on your magic left hand command that strat
to speak at will cry/ moan/ shriek/ shrill
you was . . . bad/
miles knew . . . little richard did too
but most of us had no clue it was like . . .
fallin' asleep watchin' the late show and
even black radio wouldn't bring your noise
refused to excuse you while you kissed/
the sky said it was your tie-dyed hair fryed
wind cried mary thought you was a fairy but/
you was just shy . . .

all the while worryin' what we thought you
sought our support yet few of us bought your music . . .
failed to help you through those wild times
hard as the symbol you'd now become not drum
but phallic a quick prick fix to a dyin'
industry dominated by young white boys who

stole old black men's songs . . .
couldn't play couldn't sing and along the
watchtower came the wild thing/
abused/ confused/ destined to lose

but you saw the light the first ray
tried to break away from that acid rock
back to bebop band of gypsies you'd
set us free . . . and/ with a single song
screamed to america how wrong/
the war was . . .
and the blue-black abstract givin'
patriotic americans a heart attack manner
in which you played the star spangled banner
shook/ the world . . .

while we concerned ourselves with the
skin color of the girls you dated frustrated
peabrains who failed to realize the train
you took traveled at the speed of sound
but we knew every verse of . . .
hound dog by elvis shakin' his pelvis
better than we knew your songs except
purple haze a simple phrase barless cage
from which . . . you'd never escape

repeatedly raped by fakes and snakes taken
advantage of you were merely lookin for love
and when you needed us most we weren't there
scared to claim you as our own now you're
stone free-history jimi/ we done you wrong
waited 'til you was long gone before we
listened to the songs you played emotions
displayed like depression/ pain and sorrow . . .
but you pegged us all square when you said
think i'd better wait 'til tomorrow/

eliza galaher NO. FUCK ME

You in the evening town
Lost in lust lost
Turn around in your bicycle gown
Your white-jeaned black-booted
Pedalling flight.
Turn down Ludlow Street
To the neat little rows of
Chicken bones cold knishes
Max Fish flashing
Hydrant falls splashing down
Upon El Sombrero hills o' beans
In black plastic bags.
Lock up your bike
Better yet
Carry it up the three flights
Work up a sweat
A glistening glow
Showing through my peephole.
Knock the knock
The three-knuckled tap
Topped off with inquiring calling of my name
And I open the door the same
Way I've been practicing—
Just enough for you to catch
My beauty-marked cheek
My long slender neck
Then swing open fully O!
It's really not so
Your bike's on St. Mark's
We've both stopped for coffee
We'll fuck on a sack
Of water-processed Colombian beans.
O to fuck a lesbian
To fuck another woman
A dream a dream!

Yet you ride your bike down ABC
First Second and Third Streets
Too cool to be cruised
Too caught up
Chanting
Fuck Jack fuck Joe
Give me fame glory fortune
And a good strong fuck.
But no
Fuck me!
Glory to me the lesbian poet!
I am the fucker to be fucked
The Amazonian plucker
Of the straight girl puckering up
Her luscious lips
For the unavailable kiss.
No Jack no Joe!
Just the poet on her Ludlow
And the fading back fender
Of a straight girl's Schwinn
A no-win situation
But fuck me nonetheless!
Have you ever tried?
Ever applied your hand
To the inside of my thigh?
Fuck me so!
Just a little lubricated slip
Of your tongue and your lip
A little sliding of the little finger
Make that the index
Make it a complex combination
Of index big and ring fingers—
Take off the ring please—
But O the pleasurable squeeze
Round down and up again
Coming
Across each other
At Sin-é Cafe
Refuse to acknowledge me!

But fuck me anonymously
I won't tell a soul I swear.
Rip off my underwear!
Rip my jeans with your chain
Ride me off in the pouring rain
I'm good for the bumpy
Good for the go
Swing me over your shoulder
Carry me up your stairs
Throw me down on your canopied bed
Spread my lesbian legs
Behold!
A treasure!
High Sierra!
El Dorado!
Lost arc!
Yahweh!
Your way's no good
My nymphian juice
Here here
Here's the fruit!
Looted duped and dumped
No more!
I'm your apple plum banana!
The casserole of the sea!
Eat me!
Delight in a cup of coffee
After me . . .
And after you—
After you
Don't get your boy
And you get on your bike
Do you ever once think
Of fucking a dyke?
Fuck
Me!

YOU KILL MY LOVE FOR YOUR LOVE FOR ME KILLS ME

My mom's a maniac
And she's making me one, too
Three four
A while I thought things might
Be getting better
Not jump the gun
Bang
Don your carapace, Mom
'S baby sent a photo
At your request
Pretty little snapshot
S in the air
Over oceans
Landing in your bougainvillea
Bush plucking
Petals for a lei
For my arrival
Is delayed
Mom
Mom?
Mom?!?
A kiss and a hug, Mom!
A kiss and a hug!
A kiss and a hugging
The curves of 80 East
On my way back from Lancaster
Just under
One year
Since I've slept with another
Woman to woman
Talk Mom
I'm in love
I'm in love
I'm in love with her

Poetry
Is the way
I want to say
Something to you
Her
Voice is beautiful
Postcards
Sent from Brooklyn
Could not compete
With the way you
Love me
Please
Just love me Mom
Where'd I go wrong
It was the haircuts
I gave you
A photo
'Cause you
Asked for one
More move like that Eliza
And you'll kill me
Mom
You'll kill me with
A postcard
Sent from Brooklyn would be nice
If she could write
One short note-
Ing my haircut
She said
Can I touch
Your hair
Falls onto the porch
As I snip snip
At your request
The closest we get to touching Mom
Is your scissors in my hands
Ache for human contact
Lacking that I fill my days
With errands to the photo

Booth
Two dollars for you
Asked me for a photo
And I consent
Twirl the stool to
Eye level
With me Mom
You're scared to death of Eliza
Smiles a good smile
For Mom
I wanted her to call just to say hey
You know what?
I think you're beautiful
Women fill my mind
If I send you a photo
Of me Mom
Mind if I show you what I
Look like
A concentration camp victim
Like a dyke
Like a man
Starts singing as I walk by
And I hit her
And I hit her
And I hit
Her one hour of kindness is more
Than you've given me in 28 years
Old and you still don't look like
Me
Me
Me, Mom!
That's me in the photograph
S lay sprawled on your floor
Is covered with photographs
Lay sprawled on your floor
Is covered with photographs
Lay sprawled on your floor
Is covered with photographs
Of a baby

Smiling for the camera.
She is sweet
She is two
She is smiling up at you
As you take the shot
By your daughter
You don your carapace, Mom
I only wanted you to
Love me Mom
I only wanted you to love
Your baby
'S 28
Years old and I
Keep waiting for some kind of sign-
ed my letter
With a snapshot
And sent it off to Hawaii
'S filled with beautiful flowers
Bougainvillea
Jacaranda
Oleander
Birds
Of Paradise
Is a word gone sour
Over used
To think
You loved me for who I am
Going to see her
Soon and maybe she'll love me
In some kind of way
Before I knew I was a lesbian
I knew I loved you
Love me way
Before I knew I was a lesbian
I knew I loved you
Loved me weigh
The pros and cons:
Love me and I'll love you
Don't love me and I'll love you

Never knew
That baby
Did you?

christian haye SENDIN' OUT A P.B.

if the people can't use it
            you been overmusin' it
                        or overdoin' it

putting out an A.P.B.

Avaricious Poets Buffet

this one's for all the hungry motherfuckers in
                                    the house

somebody scream

no I don't take no goddamn cream in my coffee

the fee is one billion dollars for anybody who can bring to me the
hiphop and you don't stop beatin' up on faggots and wimmins in your
rhyme
ain't got the time to take two steps forward and three steps back

in the daze before the hood

I was the sum of the bodies
            united in unconfronted stand of cargo and captain

if you go-go beyond that the whole thing was fucked up when the
captain stopped givin' demotions in favor of promotions
    should've learned some sort of lesson when the first sign of
    affirmative action was the appointment of a house nigga.

somebody scream

i fire hiphop this time
because it wasn't doin' the job right
just wingin' it.

Meanwhile M.C. Mickey Not-Maus
was blurtin' out that
I shouldn't be.

some sistah was gettin' raped
by a bottle of Colt 45
and at the same time she
was instructin' her man to
bash that lesbian bitch
before he came back for her.

Something happened two seconds before hiphop got experienced
uh-huh experienced

in a grandmaster klanmaster flash a lightbulb
    popped up over hiphop's head
    and that shining lightbulb said
    let's make a lot of dough
    and I don't mean whitebread

Born to breed was hiphop's creed

happened sometime after hiphop left the separatist safety of Queens
    and the all-night jammies of uptown
    gettin' down with the mo' money around town
    read midtown and green

Hiphop made a stop
    to drop off the security deposit
    at the bank

Buyin' into the green machine
Bypassin' soca and soukos and Hoocan Doo that

to all in need of real leadership without four
eighth back beats

I forgot the tree growin' on my back
was the rap and even poetry forgot to tap its feet

Dunbar still did us in
ass forgettin' motherfuckers who ripped on two turntables
when the tables turned on the trip.

Hiphop moved in for the kill

uh-huh experienced.

Yeah right, like the new kid on the block whose parents felt they
had some kinda new experience
uh-huh experience

sendin' out an A.P.B.
Any Position Bought
or sold when the white man
is signin' your checks
or puttin' you in check
if the record don't go gold

chained to the profit margin
March right in young fella and play me your demo
mo'moneymo'moneymo'money
i'm stuck on the sugar hill
waitin' to get ill
and rock the party to the break of dawn
like the dawn of a new day when they say
it's o.k. to wipe out the gays cuz they
only expressin' white man's oppression

The hiphop nation was news to Richard Bruce Nugent
going down on hues
or Zora scorin' on the back of a black woman's other
side.

The poet wasn't supposed to be stuck in class
but graduated and left back with the mass
of people not preachers (read warriors)

with silver-lined tongues
which aren't guessin' where
the next meal's comin' from.

I need a record without an umbilical cord.
I need a record with experience uh-huh experience.
That turns the blues into azure indigo and especially Sapphire.

You don't stop

Sellin' out the records and with it the style E.
Posturin' and Frontin' with the best of Profile E.
Fallin' off the cliff with the swiftness of Wile E.

Runnin' off the road and I need to know why B
You say you never tasted a Vanilla Ice E
Ignorin' this you say cause you can't get the time E.

Said yuk when reggae rocked the U.K.
But it's o.k. when hiphop does its European Tour
P.E. on the floor of the Louvre
sharin' the platform
and the poet's oeuvre
is the standin' O' O' O' my god

gospel put a spell on the beat
time to rhyme with the c-r-i-m-e

somebody scream

when hiphop sticks the mike in the chest of the oppressed
dressed up like a sunday turkey turncoating on the underdog

standin' up on its hind legs
hiphop assumes the position.

the gilt without you circles itself
around the ring finger or ankle.

somebody scream

sendin' out an A.P.B.
Anti-Police Beating
when the King is queening
on the enslavement freeway
sayin' hey man this is for the betterment of black folk
don't take it personal
and Paolo Friere is doing 9.8 triple somersaults somewhere under
Brasilia

But still
it doesn't stop
and the final drop
is in the token box
as the musics jumped the turn style
and bought a cap with an
x

why?

if hiphop can't break out of the box of the c.d.
for all colored p.'s
who needs an unknown soul-jah?

uh-huh experience

if hiphop misses the boat from Port-au-Prince
I'm convinced the party
won't rock rock to the planet rock.

somebody scream

if hiphop goes for top 40 instead of last 400
it can x out another's other
and lose the red from its veins?

Sendin' out an A.P.B.

Another Poet's Bankrupted
on the shores of P.C.
I.B.M. or the pedophile's creed.

When sexuality and gender 101
is left off the agenda
one's bound to trip on the
marketer's floor flaw.

To Anybody Pointing Backward I'm
Sendin' out this A.P.B. cause
Another Poet's BankErupted.

Joans' in ya on a personal aside
it took gettin' your ass burned to realize
you were dancin' with the devil.

For T.M. it was as quick as slam-bam-thank-ya-mam

I'm puttin' out an A.P.B. to the B
                    on the Lower E.
who sees it all as two-faced
            not multi-faceted.

to all those who think multi-kulti
is the ultimate high
and try it for fifteen minutes.

somebody anybody scream.

indigo　**HIS VICTIM**

At first there was no pain.
Bright light flooded the room
with sterility
no warmth, no protection,
just light.
Absence in comfort
let me know I was living,
but I was not scared.
A curtain
ran along my bedside
alarming in pattern,
vinyl brick
yellow
orange
a look of bulk purchase
attempting disguise.
The time and day
opened into obscurity,
I was breathing
that was my reality.
Concern and worry
for separate injuries
would come curiously in vanity
cautiously in weakness,
on that day I was numb
waiting for my next cue.
It came carrying a metal chart
and a cheery disposition,
". . . keeping you for observation . . ."
were some words I grabbed onto
"head trauma" and "more tests"
were others.
I tried my best to listen
but fell into my memory.

I met him in a men's room,
there were no urinals
so I emptied into the bowl
nice and loudly.
I knew he'd like the sound,
unembarrassed,
racing out forcefully in the beginning,
increasing in pitch towards the end.
I let him picture
the jerking and readjusting
as I buttoned up my pants,
I added a few seconds for drama,
that's all it took.

He hated seeing himself in me
or maybe it was the way
he needed me so desperately.
At first he seemed like the rest,
one of many to tell the truth,
but it was very different for him.
His actions spoke with non-verbal communication
I must be his first I thought,
the way he rubbed my face against his stomach
awkwardly,
maybe he wanted a blow job,
maybe I wanted to give one.
My representation frightened him,
brought back years spent in denial,
blocks of days,
months,
calendar years building,
waiting for a change in desire,
a change in society.
To him I was more than a man,
I was the first girlfriend that found out,
the Calvin Klein ads in magazines
and the guilt of not turning those pages
as quickly,
I was all the times he said "fag" to the world,

nothing to himself.
With each punch I could feel his consciousness,
his sister's tea parties,
his need to linger in locker rooms.
But the greater hurt I felt
was my need to be punished,
a suffering that satisfied,
that made me a victim,
his victim.

PEEPHOLE

curved with distortion
   my view,
he becomes my clockwork victim
or maybe I am his
the only way I could be his
   on a chain like keys
turning sometimes with pressure
   slamming
other times quiet
   doesn't want to wake the wife.
complicated keys
   he slides me into his pocket
   deep and every time,
coldest metal
   to his
   wrinkled vulnerability.

tito lespier   I HEARD THE BIRD

It came to me
In a mellow tone, in a softly hued vibration
Almost mysterious to the human ear.
I wasn't sure . . . not certain if I should
Respond to such an emotional cadence.
Then all of a sudden SKIDDIDLY-OOH-BOP-SKIDDIDLY-BOOP
Yeah! As abrupt as that might have sounded
Man it was okay, I mean, how was I supposed to
Understand what Sassy Sarah was saying?
I wasn't old enough for romance the way she
Sang it. Oh! But I heard . . . then Ella came to me
Fast, without warning, in tiskets & taskets with
Scatfilled baskets . . . intelligible syllables
Made me smile as a child and I haven't stopped
Since. What more do you need to appreciate
A jazz singer's deed? Listen to Anita baking emotions
Or Bobby McFerrin with his 501-don't-worry-be-happy self.
I'll never forget Bird, and so glad that I heard
The rainbowfilled magic of the jazz singer's word.

It came to me
In a series of rapid salt, peanuts, salt, peanuts
Rhythm go 'round and 'round
Honk, trap drum cymbal bass line
Straight from the kitchen to the table
Fusion, bebop willin' and able to
Withstand MUZAK . . .
Let's go back, dip into the link that
Led to the words, "THE BLUES HAD A BABY
AND NAMED IT ROCK & ROLL," and Jelly told
You so, but you still misbehavin'. If you're
Hip and you hop remember what gets
You to the top. Look back, and check it out.
Don't bury the wings that brought us
This far. Let a yardbird fly high
I'll never forget Bird
So glad that I heard . . .

MAMBO IN "T" MAJOR

We glad to merengue in
Full regalia no matter how
Strong the opposition to
Boogie in other flavors.
You know our neighbors are
Always hospitable to the
Cause of causes, meaning
Carnaval will always be
The order of the day in
La Isla del Encanto or in
São Paulo, Port au Prince, etc.
We glad to replicate the
Dance of El Occidental
Not accidentally, not by way
Of some fad, you've seen
Us before on travel pamphlets
On commercials, prime time . . .
Give these days on the Chittlin'
Circuit, Cuchifrito Circuit,
American Bandstand a break

Be real about the feet
Don't compromise the
Natural beat of the cuero
Que te llama.
Damas y caballeros we
Have for you tonight el
Establecimiento de rumba-bembe
Con todos los motetes that
Have given us (Indigenos) and
You the Public the right to
Dance in your seat, run out
Of toilet paper or not this
Is the unlimited, unconditional
Do your thing moment pass it
By and you don't get to fly

And recuerdate you don't
Have to eat Rice and Beans
To walk on salsa because
Africa has been giving you
Permission since the first slave
Was sold, might I be so bold . . .
Rid yourself of stale/pale
Guilt and get busy where
You stand to lie down this
Is the chance of a lifetime
If you've always wanted to
Be inside of yourself let
The ABACUA take you
There . . . The chains have
Been broken. Uhuru para ti.

tony medina NEW YORK CITY RUNDOWN (EUROPEAN ON ME)

fat beer belly
deadbeat
flat foot
nightstick wielding
trigger happy
pistol whipping
hooligans,
flat butt wannabees
yellow imitation whities,
the sold out beauty parlor
ken & barbie greazies,
the 42nd St. 2 live crew
pornographies, obscenities
& speak easy sleazies,
the cokehead african fleshy nose

buried in white powder
wall street white ass sneezies,
Don't look at me, I got a real job.
I work for the man
& he got his hand
right up my skirt!
Aunt Jemima Oprahs,
prime time mammies of the
rotted airwaves
breast feeding
old white ladies
suckin on her
big bourgeois boob
tube test tube stupidity
& self-hatred individualistic
bootstrap token success story
of the 1st one only one racist
pick & choose role model gory
glory, a horror show
with all the teeth & lies
of arsenios & geraldos
& lucianos shuffling about
in perpetual fraud
redlipped sambos
on the back of Japanese
toothpaste
bought & sold
in america
packaged & sold to you
in living color
corporate coon
scam & scheme of
i had a wet dream
that i was on my
knees massuh please
massuh massuh please
suckin the white
man's cream for
mo' money mo' money

mo' money
get rich quick
jump on the pale pruny
dick of corporate
american lies &
briefcase choke hold
ties, subdued distorted
homeless cries drowning
& gurgling & gasping
in the quicksand
cesspool jive of funky
fat white whore
rats sellin your
mother for a dime
handcuffing your history
& dreams to fit
their crime,
democratic republican
white liberal hypocrites
nothing but a political
pogo stick jumpin
& jammin you in
your eye to make
you do their dirty tricks,
white aesthetic
manufacturers
of the ho hum
dull drum
of copped & lifted
ideas transformed mutated
to fit the alabaster
mask of white middle american
acceptance & privilege,
get the fuck out of
hollywood
off the t.v.
giving my mind
V.D. LSD
herpes

psychological slave ship
auction block plantation
shit you can't get rid of
less we get rid of you big
ass white monkey
on our back
jap slap attack,
is your hair
straight enough
are your lips
thin enough
is your skin
light enough
is your ass
wide enough
to fit the
mx missile
wrapped in
the american flag
or are you gonna
align your mind
with the times?
We don't need to be
in no beauty parlor
wasting our money
& time
our women
got it goin on
all you gotta do
is show an inch
of leg or something
& it's like michael jordan
slam dunkin
in a white woman's face!
you got it goin on
while white women
fall back centuries
into cesspools of their
own narcissism

& vanity
your beauty is a parlor
you don't need to go some
where to change shit or
put shit on
you already got it
got it goin on
Take your money &
produce & manufacture,
buy books & weapons
build schools &
institutions, publish papers
& letters & books,
make art for the people,
clothe & feed the
people, teach the
people to love themselves
& each other
so we could stay
off them corners
out them bars &
beauty parlors
lookin ugly
& phony
with plastic smiles
& plastic hair
while our babies
get raped in school
& go hungry
only to be fed
stray bullets &
lies
like raquel welch
a mexican latin
woman of color
passing for white—
hollywood loves her
white america adores
her, their tongues hanging

to the floor, check out how
dark she is; they're
copping a cheap feel
off our natural beauty,
she's considered a
white sex symbol
& they only accept her
cause she chooses to pass
for white
But if she ever accepted
her mexican latin
roots, they'd
down play her
in a heart beat!!
& so here we are again
in this great big toilet bowl
addressing the flusher:
   America! America,
aesthetically
european on me
psychologically
european on me
mentally
european on me
socially
european on me
economically
european on me
hey, teach!
european on me
hey, teacher, bold faced liar
collaborated, cohort & co-conspirator
with your hand in the cookie jar of history
with your hand in the piggy bank of imperialism
& cultural annihilation!
tell the truth, motherfucker!
tell the truth!!
european on me
hey, big fancy

movie star,
hey, new jack
hustler small time
pimp & gangster
leanin on a corner
sippin st. ides
european on me
hey, big time politician
thief, pocketing
creep distributor
of false dreams
& lies
european on me
hey, jesse jackson
sittin on a fence
thumb in the mouth
& thumb up the ass
tippin to the left
& tippin to the right
don't know which
tip is the best,
european on me
hey, miss america,
yoo hoo tweet tweet,
miss white american barbie doll
of duped plastic wishy washy
cultural depravity,
aesthetically lame
tired skank ho
carpetbagging scallywaggers,
european on me
don't include us in no contest
cause there ain't none, baby!
hey, mr. talkshow host,
mr. horse teeth bart simpson
of the airwaves, crushed klondike
rollie finger mustachioed romeo
flossing w/ white hos pubic hairs
european on me

hey, ray leonard
wanna endorse & sell
$150 sneakers
when our kids go hungry
& get killed for such warped &
distorted status symbols & illusions!
sell this
bastard louse criminal
fuck you, die!   your
image is poison & poisoning
it must be destroyed
shut off!
shut out!
cop out creep
european on me!
We don't need to be
dried up tulips in
somebody's garden box
only to be pissed on
by the gardener & his clumsy
trained mutated son, we teach
we learn, we study,
we create, we build
we plant our own garden
& nourish it &
watch it grow
trees among dry bushes
& corrupt weeds
We are multi-colored
flowers, we bring beauty
to the world
we need to be
mad militant gardeners
of love, caring &
severely critical of
ourselves & outside
antagonists that
don't let nobody
fuck with our garden!

A TREE GROWS IN BROOKLYN?
A TREE GROWS IN BROOKLYN?
A TREE GROWS IN BROOKLYN?
  FUCK THAT SHIT
A BIG ASS GIANT MULTI-COLORED
      GARDEN
GROWS IN THE WORLD
     AND WE MUST
       SAVE IT

(Peace.)

ed morales   REBIRTH OF NEW RICAN

for Eddie Figueroa

As soon as I found you, gasping for breath in the projects on 114th and
  Madison
I knew you were passing a living tradition on to me
"We are a deep, dark story," you groaned. "Our people are a secret unto
  themselves."
Eddie they might think you're crazy but you taught me
What the New Rican destiny will be
Five centuries of miscegenation finally set free
The blood of time-traveling espiritistas and Yoruban existencialistas
Los moros que no se han matado and the Borinquen aesthetic comiendo
  bacalao
Young Lord agitator, Central Park acid dealer,
Joseph Campbell revisionist, phony plebiscite exorcist!
You held on so tightly to our belief in magic, in simultaneous eternal time,
  in *botanica* awareness
You made me believe that our culture is the future, that our thoughts don't
  proceed in straight lines,

That we can take back control of our lives, that we are no longer colonial
  subjects
That to be Puerto Rican is to be fuckin crazy
That the weapon that's going to win is right here.
The revolution is right here, man.
The groove that's in our hearts
Con esta situación, culturally unique
Tu sabes la cuestión de usar las dos lenguas
New and revolutionary communication
Comes into being
Porque only a multiculture pueblo can understand
El adentro y the outside of the dynamic
Culturally, we possess ritmos y sueños que no se
Pueden sacar de our essences
They are reflected in our speech and our manner
No matter what language or banner we choose
Freeing us from being aquí o allá, here, there, everywhere
Mixed race is the place
It feels good to be neither
It's a relief to deny racial purity
We're amused as America slowly comes to see
The beauty of negritude and the Native American attitude
We've been living it day-to-day since 1492

THE LAST HISPANIC

I'm Snow White and you some bitch in the mirror
Saying can't you see you're a person of color
I was brown when I stared
Black when I walked
And some of them said I was white when I talked
Not Hispanic, not his panic
That sounds too Germanic
You're a vowel-laden savior,
Latino's the flavor

I scream Lucy, I'm home
So I'm sucked into the mirror
It doesn't get much clearer
Drawn into the shape of my face
And the fullness of my nose,
My Asian eyelids elide any trace
Of purely European poetry or pose
Staring deep into the pores and the pockets of my cheeks
I gasped as my foreskin started showing streaks
Of my yellow-black brownness,
And I'm out with this
I was hearing the plea of Carabali
Running through the fields of sugar cane,
And into the tropical growth in my brain
What white was erased from my Celtic refrain?
What Spain was left in my mambo mouth stew,
What Hebrew grew in my Portnoy point of view
What gypsy Moor had vanished so completely
How was it that Desi begat Little Ricky?
Latino, Latino,
You spic the truth
So my last trick
Is disappearing the Hispanic
Beams of an eerie, otherworldly light criss-cross
Jump jump everything shakes like a Cali quake
And as I sprawl across a bookshelf holding every last mistake
Of vile volumes falling to the floor with me
Jokingly invoking the death of Jimi Hendrix
I find myself vomiting all over my copy
Of the *Princeton Encyclopedia of Poetry and Poetics*

tracie morris   PROJECT PRINCESS

Teeny feet rock layered double socks
The popping side piping of

many colored loose lace-ups
Racing toe keeps up with fancy free gear,
slick slide and just pressed recently weaved hair.

Jeans oversized belying her hips, back, thighs that have made guys sigh
for milleni-year.

Topped by an attractive jacket
her suit's not for flacking, flunkies or punk homies on the stroll.

Her hands the mobile thrones of today's urban goddess
Clinking rings link dragon fingers there's no need to be modest.

One or two gap teeth coolin'
sport gold initials
Doubt you get to her name
just check from the side,
please chill.

Multidimensional shrimp earrings
frame her cinnamon face

Crimson with a compliment if a
comment hits the right place

Don't step to the plate with datelines from '88
Spare your simple, fragile feelings with the same sense that you came

Color woman variation reworks the french twist
with crinkle-cut platinum frosted bangs from a spray can's mist

Never dissed, she insists: "No you can't touch this."
And, if pissed, bedecked fist stops boys who must persist.

She's the one. Give her some. Under fire. Smoking gun. Of which songs
are sung, raps are spun, bells are rung, rocked, pistols cocked, unwanted
advances blocked, well-stacked she's jock. It's all about you girl. You go
on. Don't you dare stop.

MORENITA

for Gramma Cat, Patricia L., Marta and Carmen B., and especially Julio Dalmau

  . . . Morenita, morenita men have named you . . .

Not Latina. Morenita.
Negrita chiquita
de Estados Unidos.

Ese país.
Same world, different word
Black. A compliment or curse.
I, a girl from this country
at peace with one identity.

Some freedom.
The same means.
Global beans and rice
Combination.

Assimilation of old and new.

  . . . You're so like the lady with the distant smile . . .

Not negrita,
the Loot,
same boat.
Das Boot,
Root of all evil.

Brought over to screw.
African girls have more
corpses per load over.

But too many Blanches
took advantage.
The Man saw what

was happening
and here we came.
Used to blame.
Abused/maimed for baby fodder.
This alloy, a solder
that made America
Become Morenita.

    . . . many dreams have been brought to your doorstep . . .

Which old world colonizer
made you? And India tú,
Morenita?

Both my grammas had that
Black hair.

One Pocahontas, fair.
Then there's Gramma Cat
who knew me.
Eyes almost slant.

Wide flat hips and backside
that sat on jet black hair.
Wanted and feared by nappy girls
her small lips curled to grin.
She received compliments
even when old.

"Look how it grays and stays straight!
What do you use, Catherine?"
"It's the way it's always been."
Her name Mestiza in another place.

In Brazil (not Bahia)
There was query of my parentage.
"*Pardo,* uh, pardon me.
Whose genes are you wearing?"

(Let me get to swearing
and we'll see what comes out!)

No doubt the skin on
my cinnamon back
is Morenita's.
There is no question for me
or LAPD if I'm speeding.

   . . . they just lie there and they die there . . .

Which racist did you come from?
Asks the lingua local,
(not quite that way).
I smile and say,
"If you have to ask,
It don't matter" in English,
Español or *Portuguese*.

Negra. No Latina.
Pardo? Mulata? No. Africana.
From Savannah and other places
of the state in GA.

Mmm, Mmm, Mmm. Ay, Dios,
I say, Unexplained.
The same Morenita way.

   . . . Do you smile to catch a lover, Morenita? . . .
   . . . or is this your way to hide a broken heart? . . .

Nice ta meecha, Morenita.
Ofays want a taste.
No matter what aspect
of the prism's your place:
"Is it true what they say?"
"You can make me a man."
"I don't understand your rage."
The sages say.

"I ain't tryin' to relate to you <u>no</u> way."
Is what Nina's Peaches would scream.
Third eye sight recalls
the origin of this
Spectrum of complex-shuns.
There's no womb at this in
Race memory fac sin nation
Base Integration.
Face value my
grocer mistakes for
one of the niñas
who buy malta.
They ask everyday
what was the cost.

"Cuanto e'?"
I say like the rest
blurring my heritage
in the South U.S.A.
aligning self with
the world's colored girls
Don't consider
suicide.
Know which side I'm on.

> . . . *Are you warm, are you real, Morenita?* . . .
> . . . *or just a cold and lonely, lovely work of art* . . .

MTV glows to booming systems
international emission.

Morenita B-girl style
gives no more away
than, say, ample lips
or hands on hips
narrows a region.

Geechie coast my
most immediate possession.

Ceremonial tied lessons
where bi-lingual means
tongue-speaking
no one had to teach.
Ones sung on beaches
thought faraway.
Reaching freed drums
in advance
of Simon Paul's
rehashed dance.

Morenitas sing,
Remembering.
Roots of blues,
Yoruba, Kongo.
So much more to Morenita
than this side of the sea.

Me.
From this country.
Negrita chiquita
little Black girl
de ese país.
Morenita of the world.

> . . . *Morenita, morenita.*

THE SPOT
for superficial people everywhere

Cross your heart and hope to die
should be why you wear the gear.

The year to make the concept fly
not just the hype hat to comply with other guys
and compliment Michael's 360.

But that would take a bit more time
than stopping by the five and dime
to pick the color, match the size
with your new shoes and new name—"Wise."

So Bet. You check out the display
at the Korean store 'round the way
they even got <u>leather</u> and every shade.
Oh, yeah. The pickin's fat!

The black one with the Red X goes best
with your new high tops.

Run to cop that one or if your woman's by your side
slam dunk $9.95 to show her you got paid.

But never laid down a buck fifty for a bean pie
much less stopped by even Barnes and Noble to get
Haley's paperback down the aisle from this week's Jet
with "Cos" on the cover.

Brother man, it damn sure ain't
about a fashion statement
but how many platelets
you willing to let go.

Setting yo'self up for COINTELPRO
It'd behoove you to check out what
J. Edgar did.

They keep a lid on that shit in
Negro His-story class. The last
thing wanted is to turn you Black men onto
the situation, to be like him—
know the real deal—be aware.

So when you wear that gear on your head backwards
it won't make the spot easy
for someone's target practice.

Right now it just marks the place
you should be smacked in whenever you commit
some heresy like being a drug-dealer
popping each other off or in other ways
disgracing his legacy.

You say "Damn, Sis, Peace" and back off.
But the issue is closer to Power.

The hour for monosyllabic answers is over.
A gun don't mean a damn thing unless you read books
(minus that Perry crap) speak to enough Black folks
who were there or attend rallies to know where to focus.

The point for us to know is the nature of how you livin'
and what that X's actual significance is.

Or else what you wear don't mean a damn thing.
Just brings you closer to the brink of destruction.
The X, a symbol once used to instruct Black men's upbringing
is now seen as a means in the production of tin soldiers.

To boldly go past our elders is seldom where fashion leads.
Not a fad but deeds put Malcolm between the crosshairs
and allows you to wear his red X letter
and not bleed.

dael orlandersmith
POEM II FOR ANNE SEXTON

The curve of my Pluto sister's back
is crooked
as are her smiles
which are interwoven w/cigarette smoke &
glitter dust powder

Her perfume is the bathwater
of faded party girls
w/broken heels & hearts to match
& their once seductive dances are now
Comic poses
& toothless smiles lie underneath
cheap, loose lipsticked mouths
& their once glittering gowns are
shabby dresses

The curve of my Pluto
sister's back is due to
benzedrine and young boys
that holler obscenities & the
alcohol content in a glass
of gin & the
voices in her head that
Scream, "Kill yourself!"
& my sister,
She heeds this call &
Sprawls
w/broken cocktail glass in hand
dismembered
rather like a shattered, painted
baby doll

SHE'S COME UNDONE

As her eyes bulge w/water
& pencil-thin fingers
grab my wrists, she
tells me what was stolen
in Massachusetts
in dark corners

where little girls keep secrets
under sheets soaked in semen
& blood
under shower water that didn't
seem to wash her clean enough &
there weren't enough powders & perfumes
to smother his smell
maplike cuts lay on bone white
wrist — (self-inflicted)

She said it was particularly cold in Boston that year. That year being the
first attempt at suicide and the year young boys & young girls ran hand in
hand up & down Massachusetts Avenue & she

lagged far behind
his smell on her fingertips
& between her legs no
matter how hard she washed

Her mother gave no
explanation & there
would be no husband or
children to fill her house &
at night in her bed
where fitful dreams attacked her,
she always screamed his
name . . . "Papa, Papa!"

MOTHER LOVE

Your belly
swollen
obtrusive
quivers like spastic jellyfish
The grease from your mouth is extracted from 4-day-old food

cooked & recooked which you offer to me slurringly and
generously after your weekly intake of scotch
And as you embrace your bottle,
I am to pamper you
        to cuddle your bulk
which alternates between sloven women stances &
baby poses sometimes w/a cradle voice to match
        In bed when you desire to hold me close and
whisper wife/child confessions in
my ear w/my small head
pinned to your breasts,
I know it is not my
place to bathe you
in maternal/womb hugs
or
massage you w/masculine cologned hands
or to give you consent
because
I am not your lover

My name is daughter
I am your child

willie perdomo
NIGGER-REECAN BLUES

for Piri Thomas

Hey, Willie. What are you, man? Boricua? Moreno? Que?

I am.

No, silly. You know what I mean: What are you?

I am you. You are me. We the same. Can't you feel our veins drinking the
same blood?

—But who said you was a Porta Reecan?
—Tú no eres Puerto Riqueño, brother.
—Maybe Indian like Gandhi Indian.
—I thought you was a Black man.
—Is one of your parents white?
—You sure you ain't a mix of something like
—Portuguese and Chinese?
—Naaaahhhh . . . You ain't no Porta Reecan.
—I keep telling you: The boy is a Black man with an accent.

If you look closely you will see that your spirits are standing right next to our songs. Yo soy Boricua! Yo soy Africano! I ain't lyin'. Pero mi pelo es kinky y kurly y mi skin no es negra pero it can pass . . .

—Hey, yo. I don't care *what* you say—you Black.

I ain't Black! Everytime I go downtown la madam blankeeta de madeeson avenue sees that I'm standing right next to her and she holds her purse just a bit tighter. I can't even catch a taxi late at night and the newspapers say that if I'm not in front of a gun, chances are that I'll be behind one. I wonder why . . .

—Cuz you Black, nigger.

I ain't Black, man. I had a conversation with my professor. Went like this:

—Where are you from, Willie?
—I'm from Harlem.
—Ohh! Are you Black?
—No, but—
—Do you play much basketball?

Te lo estoy diciendo, brother. Ese hombre es un moreno! Míralo!

Mira yo no soy moreno! I just come out of Jerry's Den and the coconut
spray off my new shape-up sails around the corner, up to the Harlem River and off to New Jersey. I'm lookin' slim and I'm lookin' trim

and when my homeboy Davi saw me, he said: "Coño, Papo. Te parece como
un moreno, brother. Word up, bro. You look like a stone black kid."

     —I told you—you was Black.

Damn! I ain't even Black and here I am sufferin' from the young
Black man's plight/the old white man's burden/and I ain't even
Black, man/a Black man/I am not/Boricua I am/ain't never really
was/Black/like me . . .

     —Leave that boy alone. He got the Nigger-Reecan Blues

I'm a Spic!
I'm a Nigger!
Spic! Spic! No different than a Nigger!
Neglected, rejected, oppressed and depressed
From banana boats to tenements
Street gangs to regiments . . .
Spic! Spic! I ain't nooooo different than a Nigger.

REFLECTIONS ON THE METRO NORTH, WINTER 1990

Saturday night
I'm on the 8:40
to New Rochelle
and points North
I'm running away
with my woman
running away from
El Barrio, New York City
Fast playing games

113

symbolic names
Slick Rick
Big Money D.
Hey you!
Who me?
Yeah, you.
On the green—WALK
On the red—DON'T WALK
Stop! Freeze! Don't run.
Cuz you might get shot
for looking like
the wrong Black man
And whatever you do—
please
please
don't sniff dope
3 days in a row

Train is ready
steam whispers
a slow drag
out of Grand Central
through dark tunnels
where foot-long rats
swim in puddles
of leftover rain
Tanisa
my woman
lays her head
on my shoulder
I'm suppose
to be here
I'm doing the
right thing

Like a bullet
the iron horse
will shoot out of
the hole

on 96th St. and Park Avenue
We never see
how the rich really live
with gardens
in the middle of
the street
Doormen hailing taxis
in the rain
for poodles in fur coats

Soon we'll see
where Papo's from
I can never forget this panorama
of the other Park Avenue
Papo's Park Avenue
sounds like
a million hands
clapping in
guaguanco time
Elevator in my stomach
where I stash
dark secrets
starts to rise
I'm ready to get off
on 125th St.
so I could go dive
into those hands
The streets
can kill you
It's true
Clanging cuchifrito pots
compassionate curses along ho' row
my sirens are calling, baby
I got to go
Forget our weekend in New Rochelle
Sunday paper
bagel brunch
sleeping in
after loving all night

Home is where I like to
find myself
when it's cold

110th Street
History of El Barrio, Spanish Harlem
and salsa
street legends
manteca bombs
many a bad muthafucka
done laughed and cried
ran and died
in the swollen arms
of this street
life and death
Boricuas in Nueva York
celebrate with this song
forever
para siempre, mami
para siempre

116th Street
LA MARQUETA in glitter
I don't need books
My culture
My history
is in the aisles
of bacalaito
ajecito
sofrito
pulpo
mi pana
I stretch my neck
to see
if I see
Carlito and Marc
walking toward Madison
to buy a bag
half-n-half all the way

for the rest of the night
all right
a dripping leak-leaky bag
of Purple Rain
so that we can tranquilize
our souls
time
confusion
heartbreak
let's get blind
so we can forget
all the bullshit
Is that me
I see
looking for a familiar dance
to a warm boom-box boogie
writing a mad poem
to a sad drumbeat because
the guns
we play with
don't squirt water or make
that simulated machine gun rattle

Tanisa is sleeping now
she might be dreaming
about our future
and how happy we gonna be
when god blessed the children
that got their own
don't have to struggle no more
If it wasn't for her
my girl
my woman
my wifey
my main flame
my baby
always and forever
with a smile
from Harlem

moreno Harlem
same beat
like my Barrio
soul y salsa
if it wasn't for her
I would be standing on the corner
thinking about the world I've seen
drinking blackberry brandy
keeping a cold hustler company
with stories from back in the days

"Damn, Papo. You right. Back in the days we
use to run through summer nights, laughing, dancing
in the night, swimming in the morning, telling wild stories
later on. Word, I remember those days, kids. We use to
have real fun. . . ."

125th Street
Harlem, USA
I'm ready to jump off
before the doors close
have a nice day
and if this poem is too long
I really don't give a fuck
Because my heart is beating
I'm alive
You know what I'm sayin'?
Can you hear my sirens, Tanisa?
Shhhh. . . .
I could tell her that I got some business to take care of
but she'll look at me with those sleepy eyes
and that soft, mellow voice
and she'll say

"I am your business, Will."

And that's it
Apollo Theater to the West
Willis Avenue Bridge to the East

A river waiting at both ends of
the boulevard
Poets and dead gangsters
chillin' at the bottoms
Nothing for me to do but jump
or turn back
cuz it ain't my time yet
I close my eyes and clench my teeth
I ask my grandmother's spirit for the strength to say no
I kiss my woman
careful not to shake her awake from her dreams
Doors close
steam whispers
a slow drag
away
I'm running away
with my woman
and I can't turn back
the El Barrio, Harlem night
is no longer mine

A Wall Street brokerbanker
in a blue pinstripe suit sits back
and reads the Sunday Business section of
the Sunday Times
Big sales
tall tales
lies
lies
making the world spin
on its head
He glances out the window
sighing and shaking his head
in silence
no prayers
just happy
to have a home
and a son
who's not a Harlem shadow

looking for home
in a glass dick
Hope the market stays healthy says I
in silence
But I wouldn't bet on it
like I would bet on the wrong Black boy dying tonight
The bankerbroker is happy real happy
he don't live in Harlem
like the kid who's sitting next to him
me
Papo
who's running away
who's running away
who's running away
with my woman

kevin powell   TWINS
for Ni'Cole

one last cry for the lives we shed to be born. again
i feel your grandmother's touch   a hand on the ceiling
(she's in the room . . . i know she is)
fanning a desire to be you
love you so much   i
can't recall the death of my sins when i believed
life and love were evil twins stoning my bubble
dreams   pop! that's the way love goes: a catchy
something for the radio   hook the rhythms to your
heart i know you will be sincere forever, a colored
girl who knows this colored boy don't want no
suicide or fire   this time we want it to be right
more than a wo/man we are two peas in a pod like
my ma use to say

PUNKS JUMP UP TO GET BEAT DOWN

& down again.
        butt-naked . . .
                butt-naked . . .
        & living w/ 7 people
a sequel—for the strangers
colliding kneecaps
rigid, fossil-like, past
stories like the glory story
of a lovely lady . . . the youngest one in curls . . .

i could pretend the year was just
another teevee show, a mediocre sitcom
w/ a bedrock twist twist twist:
a brooklyn brownstone built on
layers of dynamite & class differences
(the colored artist's dilemma: am i petty bourgeois
or
a bourgie petty thief?)

nope. the real sitcoms cum as they are
burgundy liquid (that real sticky shit!)
drippin' from an itchy trigger finger
        as balloon-size lips mouth
"whassup dawg! you dead yet?"
& i pretend that east coast niggas
can understand the west coast tribe
but hands on the pumps make you wanna
jump! jump!
to a beat, like paul beatty,
scribble agitprop poetry that splatters
the acid trips of the cultural elite
                        (do we really care if they eat
                unseasoned $12 hamburgers in beverly hills?)

& oh shit what am i doing there? one
nigga toad deposited into a charred existence
but rumor has it that punks jump up to get beat down
& learn to turn rhymes, drop dimes, and sip the hein'
lovetrap
hey, i luv u—the wind yes
she blows me off
(so much for a romance made in brooklyn)
and u saved me in a nick of time
watch those razor hickies! shit!
& must we shave w/ him in the bathroom 2?
(i'm a lover; have always been; feel most comfortable
alone in a stadium full of screaming, foul-mouthed
beer cans)

it is so hard to breathe w/ a plastic nose
my nostrils   here   pull the whiskers out . . .
the blood reminds me of the bell-bottoms &
black power afro picks:
feeling kinda retro
i want to make a triumphant return
          to audubon park
play in the dark on the monkey bars
                    me and my cousin anthony
fall off
          scrape knees
                    remain free
to collect baseball cards & stuff
them into my shop-rite truck
          that george brett rookie card
                    reggie jackson as a yankee
                         (ah, the political possibilities of fragile youth!)
& the mudpies
me and anthony used to make mudpies
& eat 'em 2
bang! bang!
you dead
we killed each other before
b.m.p. (read: black male posturing)

was en vogue
& after grandpa pearly's casket yanked me into the world
unzipped
& you know i don't recall exactly when bob marley
swam into mister rogers' neighborhood
it's a beautiful day to . . . get up stand up . . .
but it must've been around the same time
my
pubic hairs
descended into
a cave
&
i became a slave
2 da rhythm
knockin' the boots
off my wartime fantasies . . .

kathy price LA NEGRA

el mercado
is blurred with color, raised voices
squirrels
worried hens, veiled by cages
and relentless heat
children laugh but do not
run   it is far too uncomfortable
to move the body quickly
beggars squat in the shade
with pieces of tortilla
and black beans stuck to their clothes
the mayan women
sit on narrow streets
it is high noon   the hottest
part of the daylight   we negotiate

              shade, heat partition
        light from our eyes
              Julia, Maria and
        Carmen sing songs loud on this
           block of sounds   songs to
                tilt the pavement   and
        roll the sun backwards
        shift the mirage you seek
        in a breeze or passing fragrance
        of scattered purple flowers
              they pick at the holes
        in my faded jeans   ask
        questions about michael
        jackson, t-shirts, walkman
        radios—whitney houston, and how much
        money do i earn
              am i willing to purchase
        all that they solicit   and it's not
        even the goods on their backs
              they balance these questions with bites
        of soup   bits of squash   and
        pieces of chicken   floating like
        broken islands, shredded hands
        sucking a bit of bone poking thru
        the yellow water
        they
        pass a spoon
           with vegetables
        and the chicken that looks like
torn hands sliding over the edges
        yo soy una vegeteriana
                        relieved
                        no sharing mouth
                        utensils
        they sit close
        point   laugh   a
        reason to do something
        other than an ordinary
        thing—a silly gringa

who won't eat chicken
   who tears holes
in her jeans   and
although she is the
color of soft mashed
yams   will
tell anyone quickly
that she is black
         Carmen touches
my hair   strokes my
skin   merino, mija
mestiza brown
but not black
      black Katherina is the
      color of your sack   it's
the dark place
         under your
      shoe   it's the shade
of our teeth
   from too
      much drink   and
not enuf food   ashes
      from cocaine
      or marijuana
   the chorus of
      daughters slinging
stained glass
         between their
   legs   it's
   the smell of
   dried blood under
our fingernails
      it's the crack
between stones
         the fragrance
of living bodies
         searching for
      a tomb
      it's space between

hope and none
        the devil's
    laughter   tedious
    living crosses
wiping dirt
    across our
    face   and
    you are
    not
        black
    i know she's
not my daughter
    lying bleeding
in the
    street
                that's
why   you   make
    me
sit   with   you
    when the rain
comes heavy
    to feel the
cold and wet
    even when
the sun has
    loosened
the dirt and
    dried all
the water
    you smile
when i weep
    because i'm
american as if
    i know
what that means
    even in
    my own
        country   and
    yes i am black

                black
        black the night
                whispering to
        yr children tucking
comets in their
            fist   when you
close your eyes and
            still drink
                rainbow thru the
        lashes   when you feel
        in the dark for
            a candle and touch
a memory
            i am the tiger's
dark stripe—the zebra
            whisper   tundra
            the african veldt
        your kenya
                your ethiopia
            your river
                niger the
            cool squish of
            mud between
        yr toes
            and
            black
        not   the
            answer   to
                not
                    being
                        white
            simply
        the
            answer   to
                being

                                          127

CELIBACY

para Olivier

olivier, este   poema
                uno   para   ti
                mijo

                                                          this is a poem for you darling
                i took my earrings off
                              to
                                            taste
                you
                              tonite
i   am   dead
      a   dead
                    girl
      in   jerusalem
                a wandering
                              jew   an
                african violet
in the inner
city   deflowered
                                      and pulsating
                              wet in your
                open psalm
                                            a red winged black bird
                blood on her shoulder
feet trussed in circles about her broken neck
              blue notes falling
from her curved beak
        red dust particles
from her dried blood you
    fall between your
fingers
in   the   winter   heat
with   that   herman   girl
straddled and kneeling

between
                    your
          legs
the way you weave your body
in a s over her, spineless thing
movement like water the way
you mix your seed with other
women for me to swim   swim   swim
there now mijo mi cariño
i've spelled your name backwards
and now i am so cold
                    only yesterday solamente ayer
          there was heat
                    and hot
               water   and
          beans and rice, y sopa
                    what
          you french call
                    the sad wine to
          ease a nite swollen
                    gently
i remember i
               was there
          wasting once as
               a woman   someone
once said i'm always someone
i'm someone
          else someone
                    else
          inside of me   something
               i wanna ask you about me
                    those nites i curled
          stuffing crucifixes into
my pretty thing mi cosa cosa linda
          a jungle of bones trailing the hour between
                    dogs and wolves.

carl hancock rux GENEVA COTTRELL, WAITING FOR THE DOG TO DIE

Some haunting blues/and violets weep/from corner to corner/wall to window/call for soul simplicity/before we cut our flesh/and bled on life/some haunting sound/round the mid of day/vapor midst/and first kiss/ago/where we lived/without our nipples sucked/or daughters split in secret/a mother looked into/the crystal of her ball belly/and fathers reached deep inside to catch hold . . . then let go/what gulf or ditch or narrow way/stands between soul simplicity? What holler/hurt/or stingy love/ transcends or sends us there/in border line/manic thought and tragic art/come from our swollen eyes/the crowds applaud/some haunting blues/critics rave/while violets weep/people run from corner to corner/wall to window/to see the sick and dying mind/the rats maze and poets frenzy run/some rock and smoke/or hate themselves/some write or joke/or bait themselves/one comes and goes/with pain and woe/and stands on stage alone/whispering for soul simplicity . . . before we cut our flesh and bled on life/without disguise or careful talk/we walked across the line/as our mind saw a vapor midst . . . first kiss ago/nipples sucked and daughters split in secret/a life of art and tragedy/nihilistic haze and yester-ways soul simplicity.

SAVE THE ANIMALS

I

They call me a dying last breed,
dark, and dangerous who stalks the night/
untamed, uncaged
"Let him die! Kill him quick! Chain him fast!"
If the breed is dying, who's gonna save the animals?
I got gums that sprout gold teeth
An onyx neck to sport my name—

Benz parked outside the projects
and I'll die for the coat on my back!
My gun comes from my hip/
I call it Eve, my second half,
Cuz a woman can bring a man life
but she sure can't save it . . .
The eleven o'clock news has got my mother afraid,
my sister's givin' up
my woman cryin' rape
and my daughter seekin' refuge from me.
While society blows the water hoses
Throws the firebombs
And cracks the whip to tame me—
What book are we in now? *Daniel (in the lion's den)?*

II

I got a name
call me nigger/negro/negritude
black boy/bastard child
african/afro-american/afrodesiac
young buck superstud.
So how do you "make love to a negro without getting tired?"
You don't make "love" to him at all . . .
I got rhythm—
Call it ghetto dancin'/pimpin'/prancin'
untrained free-form break dancin',
sexist/racist rappin'
Watch me snatch your bag and keep on tappin'!
They say I ain't got no form.
They say I ain't got no theory.
When did God give them the patent?

III

I found form and theory in my fists—
Maybe they don't get the gist!
Ain't I got no art?
To pull outside of me and call my own?

Without bowing to their "School of Art" throne?
There are no heroes in this country for me,
'cept the ones who died—
but nobody taught me about them.
My first pain was a white Dr.'s hand across my ass,
My second was a white teacher who taught my class—
lies about who I was in history,
if she told us anything about black men at all!
Anybody know what time it is? *A time to live, or a time to die?*

IV

At least give us three snaps for resurrection power.
Give us a standing ovation for all of our
Dying brothers without friends or family.
Nobody could afford to keep us alive
But everybody grabs the shovel to dig our graves
and keeps on laughing/keeps on ignoring/keeps on moving.
This country of colors is so busy being white—
Everybody's a visionary but nobody has sight!
Our fathers sleep on sidewalks and ask themselves why
Their own sons and daughters do the "Dionne Warwick"
and "walk on by."
Yes! My nails are dirty when I hold out my hand—
Sorry, I skipped my weekly manicure.
Yes! The train car empties during rush hour upon my arrival.
Hell yes! My body stinks.
Damn right! I'm on the brink
of a nervous breakdown, and no therapist's gonna *give*
me analysis.
So I'll mumble to myself/till somebody listens/I'll walk
naked/till somebody sees/I'll jump in front of rushing
cars/till somebody cares/
that it's a black man who might spill his blood . . .
But then that would be a first for history—
Should somebody care? Naw, let's do the "Peggy Lee" and
ask, "Is that all there is my friend? Then, let's keep dancing."
Anybody know what chapter and verse we at now?
John 3:16, "For God so loved the world. . . ."

hal sirowitz   I FINALLY MANAGED TO SPEAK TO HER

She was sitting across from me
on the bus. I said, "The trees
look so much greener in this part
of the country. In New York City
everything looks so drab." She said,
"It looks the same to me. Show me
a tree that's different." "That one,"
I said. "Which one?" she said.
"It's too late," I said. "We already
passed it." "When you find another one,"
she said, "let me know." And then
she went back to reading her book.

DEFORMED FINGER

Don't stick your finger in the ketchup bottle,
Mother said. It might get stuck, &
then you'll have to wait for your father
to get home to pull it out. He
won't be happy to find a dirty fingernail
squirming in the ketchup that he's going to use
on his hamburger. He'll yank it out so hard
that for the rest of your life you won't
be able to wear a ring on that finger.
And if you ever get a girlfriend, &
you hold hands, she's bound to ask you
why one of your fingers is deformed,
& you'll be obligated to tell her how
you didn't listen to your mother, &

133

insisted on playing with a ketchup bottle,
& she'll get to thinking, he probably won't
listen to me either, & she'll push your hand away.

ONE THING LEADS TO ANOTHER

While I was putting your underwear
in the wash, Mother said, I noticed
some brown stains, which can only mean
that you're not using enough toilet paper
when you go to the bathroom. And when
you leave the house & get a wife,
she won't be related to you, except
by marriage, so she won't be as tolerant
as I am about dirty underwear.
You don't want her to do separate washes,
one for her clothes, another for yours,
because that'll get her into the habit of doing
other things separately, like eating. And
once she realizes how much more enjoyable it is
not to eat with you, & not have to hear you
chomp on your hamburger, she might try not to
live with you too, which means divorce.

SONS

We're Jewish, Father said.
So we don't believe in Christ.
If God wanted us to worship Jesus
he would have arranged for us to be born

into an Italian family. I have nothing
against Him. He was probably a very nice man.
You have to give Him credit for trying.
A lot of people still believe He's the Son of God.
I don't know what He had against His real father.
But if you ever did that to me,
said you were someone else's son, I'd be insulted.

paul skiff

the smiles of two over
 -aged hookers on
Central Park South walking
into the St. Moritz hotel work

like the teeny pink see-through
dress on the guy with great
legs crossing Amsterdam at
72nd.—the more a person can

flash of what they do not
have the more you will put
utopia on so tight inside
your head the word

fuck will come out of
your mouth in a whisper of
freak beauty

JUNE 15, 1990

Pounded on to the door of my building:—
QUIEN HABLA POR LOS NIÑOS?

I wanted to come out and
play but i have
to go to the grocery store because
the price of beans has doubled
in a year.

What's the most confusing day in Harlem?
What do spaghetti and women have in common?
What do you get when you cross a Mexican and an Italian?
Why was the Gay fired from the sperm bank?
What's long, black and smelly?
What's black, has white eyes and knocks on glass?
What do you call two Vietnamese in a Trans-Am?
Did you hear about the Polish Lesbian?
Why are Jewish men circumcised?
What do you get when you cross a Japanese lady with a Chinese lady?
Why did God invent women?

yeah, well
What do you get when you cross government with TV?
Why is Free World just a market term that means get-it-while-you-can?
What do you get when you cross sex with public discussion?
What do you get when you cross justice with a bank account?
Why do Hollywood and Disneyland want to be seen as major industrial
sites?
Why does everything in the food store have poison in it but they
put louder slogans and brighter colors on the boxes?
Why do rich people think that if they get together at a party,
eat roast beef, drink champagne, dance and pay money to a charity then
they will not have to really do anything about poverty and disease?
Why can't the largest manufacturer of jail cells pay any attention
to foreign buyers?
Why do Republicans and Democrats spend money and lie to each other

while the right-wing throws bombs at women's health clinics and
decimates culture to show government is not in power?
Why is public education a war of attrition?
Why is the scene a place where people wear sprayed-on personality?
Why are criminals the only people who believe in law?
Why is the only punishment for original sin this fucking government?
Why have inalienable rights moved from the seventh to the eighth
planet from the sun?
Why do famous babies have no names, they are just descriptions of
the end: beat by mother, stabbed by father, fallen out
the thirteenth floor, starved and deprived of sunlight, stolen,
dumped in the trash,   born high on freebase,   sold.
Why don't they call it   the statue of   Equality?

i wanted to come and stand in the crowd on Astor Place and
block traffic so a mad-flash of a youth could pump his skateboard
fast enough to hurl himself over four trashcans. i want to hear
the smeared clack of the wheels. i want to see him mid-air, knees up
to his ears. i want to hear the voices jeer, coax and scream as
his legs unravel past the fourth can and rip the waiting board
from stillness.

i want to catch the three-year-old bumbling on 3rd street wrapped
in heavy coils of Christmas lights that turn him into a tiny
constellation, a zodiac of untied sneakers, scratched knees and
one hundred and fifteen volts—neon niño brown skin twinkling,
tiny, fragile, courageous festival of miniscule ignitions celebrating,
unguided and wordless.

i wanted to see the grease-caked men edge out of the trash hauler's
garage to have their faces stretched by the girl who is dancing up
3rd street wearing only a man's jacket. i want to hear her laughter
split the street, hear her singing drain the weight from every stone.
i want to see her steal the men's shadows. i want her smile.

i wanted to come out to play
but they are closing the Nuyorican's because
the Government wants them to put in another toilet—?

yeah, right

keep us underserviced and then
shut us down for it.

Put in my mailbox:—

Planafiquemos juntos para luchar contra el abuso del casero y el
desplazamiento y poder defender nuestro vecindario para la gente
que vivimos aqui!

yeah that's what happens when language
has a landlord.

we're the future
  We're the future
we're the future
  We're the future
no we're the future
  no We're the future
we're the future
  We're the future
we're the future
  We're the future

Well, i don't know about that—
you can fuck that future shit.

ALL I KNOW IS
WE ARE FREE BECAUSE

THIS WORLD IS
STILL UNFINISHED

peter spiro   # WE ALL NEED

Franky needs a fix.
Danny needs a fuck.
Denise needs to fuck a trick in a truck for a fix.
Danny's in a fix cause Denise wants to fuck Franky.
If Franky got a fix from Danny he would fuck Denise.
Denise would fuck Danny
if he'd unfix Franky
who ain't fucking no one till he's fixed.
Danny needs a fuck to be fixed.
Franky needs a fix more than a fuck.
Denise fucks for a fix but she needs neither.
We all need
to get over the bridge.

Tommie tried to get over the bridge by taxi cab.
He pulled out a shiny .38 and beat the fare
all the way to Sing-Sing Penitentiary
for a six-year bit.

J.J. tried to get over the bridge with a bottle of Four Roses
and a handful of seconals.
Word is: he went through the bridge
instead of over it.

Poochie's shootin cocaine.
He don't even know the bridge is there.

Ronnie tried to get over the bridge by robbing Poochie.
All he got was a handful of lint
so he lit Poochie on fire.
Donna tried to get over the bridge by selling her brand new baby
for 30 grand.
The day she got the money she ran into Ronnie.
Ronnie made a B-line to the bridge with 30 grand in his pocket.
That was the same night Poochie got outta the hospital.

Poochie bought 30,000 dollars worth of cocaine.
He floated all the way to the bridge and when he got there
he just kept floatin up

                  and up

                      and up
until he was outta the picture completely.

Joey worked hard and went to night school to get over the bridge.
He graduated
put on a new suit
and when diddly-boppin
with a diploma in his pocket
up to the bridge.

When he got to the bridge there was a sign across it that read:
"Let me make one thing perfectly clear:
No trespassing!"
So Joey went back to the block.

Franky needs
Denise needs
Danny needs
Tommie needs
J.J. needs
Poochie needs
Ronnie needs
Donna needs
Joey needs
I need
they need
we all need
to build our own goddamn bridges.

WORK

1.

They say,

      What would you like to do

or where would you like to work

      they chop my solid twenty-four into segments.

You get two hours for waking, showering, eating.

One to two traveling then at least

eight there.

One to two more traveling home

supper a quick fuck or three beers

then sleep eight and

wake up again to shower, eat, travel, work, travel, quick fuck,

sleep, wake, shower until they merge and flow like

molten lava and I say,

         Yes, but I get two weeks vacation

         per year, ten holidays, twelve

         sick days and one floating personal

         day to live and I feel

like the negative space between the bars of a jail cell

that farts freedom in your face.

         These men, shelling out salaries

         of death sandwiches

         for my half hour lunch break.

2.

They say,

      What would you like to do

or where would you like to work.

      I think, Earth. I'd like to work

      on Earth, third in from the sun.

Does the bear say,

         I work in this section of forest.

Does the eagle say,

         I work in this part of space.

Does the shark say,

I swim only here.
Does the air work or the wind.
           And what kind of work do I want to do?
I say,
    I want to eat and sleep and explore
        like the bear and the eagle and the shark.
I want to speak like the wind and breathe air
                   period.
I want to hang a sign on my door:
        Do not disturb while I'm at work
           dreaming.
They say,
     this is lazy.
They say,
        you are worthless.
They say,
        you have no ambition.
And I tell them,
           I am an unambitious worthless problem
like the air and the wind.
I will sleep and dream like the air and
move in passion like the wind
when it pleases me and for
no one.

    3.
They say,
        What would you like to do
or where would you like to work.
They tell me,
        Do something you like to do,
        life is wonderful when you
        like your job.
I tell them,
        It is an oxymoron to like
        your job
        as if a convict ever loves
        his cell.
They say,

Learn to drive a tractor trailer or fix
automobile transmissions or
learn to weld or fix toilets
or serve drinks with paper umbrellas to people under the
shade and I think,
No one likes to work
the name itself implies
contempt, a comfortable
contempt like the old convict who
after years
accepts his cell as home.
Some people like their jobs,
they say
and I think,
Who?
Who likes their job?
Does the garbageman really like picking up shit all day?
Do tellers like to sit all day behind a bullet proof
glass wall?
Even poets don't really like to teach workshops.
(I have heard them say this.)
Fill ketchup bottles, stuff sausages, clean pots
or sell hot dogs and cigarettes.
And if you say,
Doctors love their work or dentists love
their work or lawyers or engineers or stock brokers
then why,
why do they value their
vacations as much as the
garbageman and the teller and the sausage stuffer and
the pot cleaner?
Baseball players like their work
some actors and poets and
all sleepers
who dream.

4.
What kind of things perpetuate work?
Cancer,

yes cancer makes work.
It makes work for surgeons and people who run
self-examination breast programs.
It makes work for social workers and therapists
and nurses and chemical manufacturers and the people
who clean the floors in hospitals
and those who make the paper cups in hospital
bathrooms and makers of
high fiber cereal
and companies who advertise for
high fiber cereals and

          morticians and casket makers and
          people who supply the metal for
          ash carrying urns and for the miners
          of iron ore used for metal
          ash carrying urns
and for florists and greeting card companies.
     It makes work for
       wig makers and sellers of wigs
         and for plastic tube makers
           and journalists and typesetters
            and single parent rap group organizers
             and ecologists and environmentalists
             and lab technicians
              and surgeons and people who run
               self-examination breast programs.
Oh, I've said that already.

   5.
Factories would close without
        workers
but plants would still grow
wind would still blow
mountains would still fold.
       Without prison guards there would be
no prisons.
And doctors could not work without
       orderlies and secretaries
       the dry cleaners

                    the house cleaners
                    the supermarket stock boys
                    the tellers
                    the mechanics and the fixers of
                    automobile transmissions and toilets.

Armies could not function without
foot soldiers.
We have set this nightmare into motion and
                    we can stop it.
                              Quit!
Fighting for full employment is not the answer
                    Fight for full
                              unemployment.
Everybody,
          set your alarm for noon or turn it off and sleep
until you want to get up.
          Bears do this, cats do this, birds do this
so why should we be any different
inhabitants on this third planet in
from the sun
somewhere spinning and revolving in the
universe
yes, the universe is not up there
it's here
and we are in it.
                    Quit and sleep.
                    Sleep and dream.
                    Stop it
stop it
          you're killing me.

CAUSE AND EFFECT

Cause you are poor
you go to public school.
Cause public school is free
you get a lousy education.
Cause you get a lousy education
you are uneducated.
Cause you are uneducated
you are treated with contempt.
Cause you are treated with contempt
you are contemptuous of others.
Cause you are contemptuous of others
you do not abide by the rules.
Cause you do not abide by the rules
you do not have a job.
Cause you do not have a job
you steal.
Cause you steal
you go to prison.
Cause you go to prison
your life is wasted.
Cause your life is wasted
you are angry.
Cause you are angry
you are dangerous.
Cause you are dangerous
you are a bad effect.

And you are destroyed

cause you were a bad effect
cause you were dangerous
cause you were angry
cause your life was wasted
cause you went to prison
cause you stole
cause you didn't have a job

cause you did not abide by the rules
cause you were contemptuous of others
cause you were treated with contempt
cause you were uneducated
cause you got a lousy education
cause you went to public school
cause you were poor.

adrienne su
THE EMPEROR'S SECOND WIFE

I light the extra room and stay there nights
when I'm not called. I curl in the empty quilt
and know she's with him. I pull the blankets tight

and hope I won't remember how she goes
to him in nothing, original and dank, denying
little. She understands his need; she knows

I'm filling in the nights when she's unwilling.
She knows I'm twelve years old and only starting.
But I'm the one whose sleep is shallow, spilling

into day. He's everything to me but lover.
He tells me, if we don't make love, it's right.
It's best my spirit stay intact, all over.

No one else must know. They think the two
of us are fucking all the time we're here.
But we just talk. The rustling girls who do

my nails are scared for me. They think I'll swell
before the winter. But in the chamber's privacy
he only wants to hold me, kiss me, touch, and tell

me I am gracious. He won't do violation
—that's how he calls it—so we lie beside
each other, tumid with desire and the patience

of two statues. *It's wrong,* he says. *You're young.*
You should be learning grammar. I cover my face
when he says these things. I ache. I've just begun

to see the error. He thinks girls happen slower,
that as long as we're unopened, we're immune
to breaking. He imagines I'm intact all over.

That lady must go. When I learn magic,
I'll erase her, have her put away for stealing.
But she doesn't hate me back. She brings elastic

ribbons, ties my hair in twists. She comes
with plates and pastries. She gives me stockings, pins,
and slips, and asks me if our husband's won

me over. I tell her he is all a girl
could want, and more. She snickers when I say it,
then agrees. In recent months our emperor's revealed

another side. He can't be still. She likes
my work. It's clear she thinks I do the service.
We talk about his mouth, his hands, his eyes

and feet. She says, when I'm a few years older
I'll be deadly. She thinks I never cry,
that I'm serene, divine, immune. Intact, all over.

ELEGY

You said the last word with your last
breath and I was not there to bury
it. You spent your life writing
the note and intended
to go alone; you knew what
to say but *poof!* you were out

of breath—the night went out,
the chills passed, the last
gesture stopped. What
took a little longer was to bury
you. Everyone thought you intended
to stay; you were writing

me letters and though I wasn't writing
back, you said you had risen out
of despair and intended
to forget the last
ten years, in which you had buried
so many skeletons you didn't know what

you were born for. Anyway. What
you didn't count on was writing
the note, dying, and no one coming to bury
you. The police didn't check out
the shed until the last
of the month; they intended

to go home by dark, then opened your untended
grave at dinnertime. What
gets me is not that I was your last
woman, nor that I was off writing
term papers when you walked yourself out
of the world, not even that they'd bury

you and not invite me, but that you buried
your body where you intended
to be found and were sniffed out
belatedly, faceless, unmanly. What-
ever threw that wrench, I'm writing
you out of my memory as fast

as I can. The last word's been buried
but it's in your handwriting. You intended
to get what you got. Now get out.

ADDRESS

There are many ways of saying Chinese
in American. One means restaurant.
Others mean comprador, coolie, green army.

I've been practicing
how to walk and talk,
how to dress, what to do in a silk shop.

How to talk. America: *Meiguo*,
second tone and third.
The beautiful country.

In second grade we watched films
on King in Atlanta
and the ships at Old Gold Mountain.

They said we had hidden the Japanese
in California.
Everyone apologized to me.

But I am from Eldorado Drive in the suburbs.
There may be spaces
in the wrong parts of the face,

but America bursts with things it was never meant
to have. Take the fevers and accidents,
take the dark kitchen workers, crawling rafts.

But save the names, like mine.
It's different because it fits on a typewriter,
because it knows,

because it is Adrienne.
It's French.
It means *artful*.

edwin torres   # DIG ON THE DECADE
("glue perpetuatin' myth" . . . so said Shakes-Pois)

chilleeeee-moholeeeee-eddieeeee-yahhhhh-GO! GO! GO!
Gusting, weeping, sorrow, sweeping, boyeeeee-gooooo-YAH! YAH! YAH!
Go-Gopher Slash - tuff cyber kick - ruffle-tuff-f-f-f-f-f-f-f-f-f-h-h-h-h-h-h . . .

These are my sweeping visions of exactitude, dude!
Dig on the decade, Mother Cycle/Motor Rever, brother blow the b-boy
   down with bebop.
Move-on-OTHER! Over-revved REVVER!
I gotta maddening pace to keep, do you *get-so*, the vision of my sweep . . . ?

Seek three thicknesses of mist.
But give it up on the one . . . nine plus the one-oh, I ni-ni-nine-one oh, tie
   my eyes blind,
both down plus one minus one, mine one, one oh ni sweep this cycle, past
   visions reved-isions.
Dig on this decadence—shooting by infant mortality's roaring motherhood.

Swerve by screaming baby air-sirens, baby air-moans. Give it up on the one
    one,
oh, I ni ni, gotta gotta, fligger that Mau-Mau, mommy's gotta Gun-Gun!
    Royal Badness, Dude!
Sweeping sapling exactitude! A mule . . . afloatin' in the mist, follows:

> Yo, Sap! The burro giddy, ap-ap, chappy-pap-pap . . . Gopher Slash,
>   Pop tuff cyber kick it
> higher. Tufted-ruffle-f-f-f-l-f-l-f-h-h-h! SWELL-mire, through
>   FLANKS-falloped,
> through FIELDS-allopian. Mother Horse Barreled Brightness, your
>   kickstart's gonna
> eat me alive if I let it . . . and we all want to be eaten alive
>   sometimes, don't we?
> Well do not, I repeat, DO NOT look now, because I know the guy
>   with the big eyes
> who's been looking at you   . . . *I s'eem m'eyes inna temple . . .*

I reached for your eyes, with one hand.
Holding on to the HOUR of the word, with the other.
The pow-Pow-POW-OW!-Ow-ower of this, sweeping blindness.
This fire that breeds contempt for sparks stillborn.
This countryscape.
This decadence of soil.   . . . *fire breath in the shiny rain . . .*

Vision becomes a blur to society.
"A BUTT-WAG . . . TO THE FACE OF SOCIETY!"
He is her BONER to society.
NINE becomes a rounded tail . . . *bone-thrown-to-dog.*
ONE becomes a hounded throne . . . *ohhhh . . .*
Let round *GO* to tail, oh, one ni-nine twice over-revved-revving-OTHER!
Your revved-isioning reach, comes to each one. Fall into that brightness
between silence and sun.
Step off, on the girl-up down, on the one . . . . on the decade,
    Mother Cycle . . .

> *Chilly Moholy, ten to the one and oh.*
> *Mo-Fa-Si-Bro down, with calendrical no-no.*
> *Chilly Moholy, twelve to the one and two.*
> *Donkey gone down, with elliptical boo-boo.*

Explodable choo-choo, go to town GO-GO-MEZ! Mex-Crispies.
Olive peas plodding explosivity pits.
A reverb-down with Cousin It—it's so *(whoosh)* . . .

I GOTTA MADDENING PACE TO KEEP! DO YOU *GET-SO* MY,
SWEEP!?!
Look at me! LOOK AT ME! Take-my-thumb-out-of-your-mouth-and-
LOOK-AT-ME!!!
'Cause I KNOW the guy with the big eyes who's been lookin' at you.
    bare . . . skin . . . back . . . . my patience . . . . . . your bridle . . . . . .
    . . . riiiiiide . . .

My blood-color-roar looks good in t-shirts. But I haven't the muscle to
    wear, on my sleeve,
a tattoo of love-philosophy that suckles my gorilla-zit-knuckle-monkey-
    wrench despair . . .
a testament to this "Decade of Androgo-Me" . . . forever, for all to see.
My country on my skin, etched in mother-land-hot-rod-blood-red . . .
    that . . . I don't have.
Dig it, I don't have that *lip-dangle-exhaust* that spurts out shaved-head
    gyzmatics.

I don't have that *swagger* that shows I've been working on a '58 Flyboy-
    Blackeye-Turbo-Heart
that jumpstarts like Black-on-Eyed-Peas.
My hair *doesn't* grease back *that* way, it's too thick, too Latin.

Mo-Fa-Si-Bro-Holy-Yo-Soy . . . AMMA-RICAN,
diggin' on this SWEEPIN' vision.   . . . *ojo mio motro mio ho* . . .

When you talk to me, I can hear the light that comes from your ears.
When you look at me, my glasses become perpetual goggles,
AS IF I were trying to achieve that "look" of Cycle Revving Decadence!
Mine eyes have seen a wall . . . between the gory and the home,
and my blindness gets in the way of your sight . . . and I like that.
My poem becomes my hot rod.

OOOHH, *Gopher Cy Kick, gets clocked by a dis!*
    Rev-revving Rev-Revver into Body-Sweeping-Kiss!

Get down on the one, (kiss, kiss, kiss)
Get down on the one, (hummm, hummm, hummm)
Get down on the one, Girl Up, on the NI-NI-NINE. Slow, slow,
    stop. YO-YO
STOP . . . I GOTTA DRINK THIS IN . . .
I gotta lather you up with my, acetylene-torch sincerity.
A blur of liquid coming down, decades' ladder.   *. . . water feels up*
    fall your legs feel . . .

I gotta believe in this God. E. Dog world.
In the hideous gesture of unrealized dreams,
and the should've beens that never will *because* of their dreams.
I gotta dig on the decade, 'cause the year was a blur.
Mine eyes have seen . . . the chapped lips of void kissing areola's
    perception, I think . . .

Cycle Mother Horse Barreled Brightness,
diggin' her spurs into my vision, again.
I reached through the mist, for the dusk of your sweat,
and found that I fine-tune poems better than hot rods.

I soar . . .
hawk-estic virtues that swim butterfly strokes formed by filly-whipped talons.
Saplin' Burro-iddyap o'er me, homey! It is the east, and Chilly says it best:

Chilly Moholy says, *"Love that culee culee."*
Chilly Moholy says, *"Love it all the time."*
Chilly Moholy says, *"Love that culee culee, 'cause there ain't no*
    other booty
    that can boop like mine, boop-boop like mine,
    boop-boop-ba-boop-ba-boop-baba-boop-boop . . . ."

Baby Air-Moan Siren screams for his "two am" feeding his, "who-I-am"
    feeding,
as he rides that donkey, hoo follow the flicks of fluff floatin' his eyes, s'eem?
Whacha'kin toll, fitchit ciant floa' a devil winnga polamina-annjell.
S'eem, wi coll hiim a-floater. Iin hees eyes, he follo the fleeks 'n fluff 'n tuff-
    ruffle-fluff-ov hees eyes . . . . as heem *ride-dat-ASS!*

Baby Air Siren . . . . we call him a floater, riding on that ASS!

Hey, behhh-boo-baba-baby, POP That Jazz!
BRIDE that Ass,
Is the put-together, A-meeee-rica, A-meee-rica!
My country tis of me!
As is the put-down id . . . Amma-rican, Amma-rican!
And MY country is full of me's!

Y'see . . . yo soy speekin' HOMO-*SAY*-P'EON, Psyco-Sexual Satis-
FAC-SHON!
Giddy-YAPP-ON Hetero-Traction . . . Chilly-Foal-Filly-Hill-Coal-
Muzzle-Stang-Breath-Nostril-Beast-Witha-Big-Eyes-Been-Lookin-At-You,
Sweet Beauty Caballo . . . Mi High-Steppin-Abuello-Steed, NINE-Hands-
Tall-BIG-Balled-Chapped, LIP-Is-On-Stalin, I-Flipped-On-The-Battle-
An-Weeped-On-The-Sapien-*SWEEPING*-The-Sapien-Down-To-The-
Ground. Clocking-One. Killing-One. Gusting-To-Gust-In-Nomadic-No-
Matter . . . I gotta maddening . . . *(whoosh)* . . .

. . . and I just wanna hold you . . . I reached, round your neck . . . to, you
know, fine-tune this, poem . . .
. . . *so the mother s-i-n-g-s* . . .

WHEW!!! I just had a **Super-Psypo-Hyper-Mono-Filetero-Meeo-Trilly-**
Yac-Psyche-Out-Sapplin-Burro-Giddy-Mundo . . . Pom-Pom-Home-
Home-Ni-Ni-Gotta-Gotta-Fligger-that-Mau-Mau-Mommy's-Gotta-Gun-
Gun . . . De-JA-VOLT!

Dig THAT decade, Mother Cycle!
GROOM THAT MARE!! BRIDE THAT ASS!!-homey, Ah kissed that,
ASS The only NOT what you can do,
where only the put-down-put-put-choo-choo GO to town.
Baby, My country is a "tis of me," and I can grow up to be what I want
to be!
And I can believe in a GOD.E.DOGGY.DADDY if I want it to be.
And I can bow-wow the people into the pow-wowing vision, of my sweep!
The ow-OW-HOUR of the word, is upon us . . . perpetuatin' myth, so said
Shakes-pois:
M'lady, Doth Mi Romp Ingcite Ye? . . . P'WAAAAN!!! . . .

Doos Mi Cycle TWAANG Fantasies 'Pon Thou Whip-ped, Strap-ped,
   Leather Boot-Butt?
Wouldst Fire Breathe In Misted Shine? Couldst itchit phlegm noggitt in
   dissin' thine?
   Gopher Cy Kik, Askin' Ye DIS Quere:

"How many ruffle-tuff-fuckers-inna-motherfuckin-woodchuck-chuckin-
   truck-chuck-woolerin
wooly-paaaaaat-say-jackin' . . . *(whoosh)* . . . BAAA-AA-AAW-AAW-HEE-
   HAW-HEE-HAW—YAHOOOO—
ALL ABOARD!!!!"
YAHHHHH . . . GO!. GO!. GO!.
MO-FA-
SI-BRO-
HOLY, *YO*, ALGA-RIN*DO*, HOL-MANOL*O*-ISANDO,
NE-ANO, PRA*HA*-SIN-SON, PA*IS*-AÑO, PA*YA*, PATRA, RINC*ON*-
   NNNNN . . .

   . . . hmmmmmmm . . . hmmmmmmmm . . .
   . . . hmmmmmmm . . . hmmmmmmmm . . .

      S'il viento se presenta vani . . .
      co viento siempre sensa vani . . .
      co supre sopla sinz facil . . .
      supre sopla sinz facil . . .
   . . . hmmmmmmm . . . hmmmmmmm . . .

e herra mi bodi fi two . . . hear nine tunes fine . . . thres thri
   thicknessi . . . o . . . mi otro . . . smia patre . . .
n I hear a fine-tuned hummm . . . in the mist . . .

      sun
      he risks risin'
      sings one
      in seeks
      in comes
      sun
      seekin' one

Holdin' two thicknesses of mist,
Gopher Slash Tuff Cyber kicks it into high NI-NI-TWO—but gives it up
   on the one.
3 minus ni to the *oh mine is ni-i-ice* . . .
Wavin' a *"LATER"* he passes
the herd grazing in the mist and splits, a gusting whoosh of his own
   tomorrows.

And like loins on cool safire, you bride the wind.
Like that Girl Up Souped Up Hyper Shot BIG STUFF Boy . . . .
   you come . . . to reach one . . .
      water
      the water feels
      your blur
      falls

The sweep of my vision . . . riiiiides, afloatin' een the eye-fluffs offa bloody
   mule.
Dig on the burial of decadence . . . *33 crystalmassen das dappybeat* . . .

Groom the ass with beatiletto heels, Mother Cycle . . . Epic Mecca . . .
   Terra Revver . . .
Your revved-isioning-reach, comes to reach one.
Silence the brightening fall, my sweet one.
Quicken the quieting dark, by sleep.
One leaps and hopes to keep one reach.
By sweeps, my sweat, for you, grows deep.

      forever
      for all to see
      my body sings my
      culture swings
      in me

      . . .

The frenetics of an energy   *The symphonias of a moment*   *The artsism of a*
   poetrics

The language of the incoherents   The understandings of a naivete sophisticat
    i-ching

The lunatic musics of bug   The plain folk   i-wonder

The realization of a cinematics   The arm   The clockwatch   The donkey
    The baby

The portals of all things   The falling of all dreams

The eyes are in the temple   The eyes are in the temple

I.E. Seducer

i.e.'DUSA'
me USED-TA be young
NOW
DUSA-me-DUSA-no-COSI-fan-TONGUE
SOY < COMMUNI-GATO >

DAS A *BAAAD-DUSA*...Mister *R-R-R-R-ATTO!*
SPEAK to these *CATS*...Mrs. *ALL-R-R-R-R-IGHTO!*
Can / YOU / ME / ca / to ?
Communi-*GATO* ?
hmmmmmm ? purrrrrrrrrrrrrrrrrrrrrrrrrrrrrrrrr-meow

E E E E E E E E E E E E E E E E E
I. **E**
S E - d u c e s - M E E E E E E E E E E E E E . . .

I.E. SEDUCER: me-**DUSA**-me
INTO
two-GATOS-de-*prrrrrrrrrrrrrrrr*

communi**gatos** -de
communi**cacion** -de
communi**gods** -de dos - two dos - you lost ?
Myth-Ology ?
Mithuth... ?
ALL-R-R-R-R-RATTY ?
hmmmmmm ?

prrrrrrrrrrrrrrrrrrrrrrrrrrrr
dos dios / two gods / two zeuses... < *ZEUS, DUSA-ME-DUSAS!!!* >
two sides / the IN and the OUT / AUDIENCE -BACKSTAGE

<u>ONE:</u> speaks

truth-*deuces* through *doses* / of truth

speaks

herra-*that-that-that* tongue

me-USED-ta-*feeeeel*-young-juices

hmmmmmmmmmmmmmmmm

me-USED-ta-be- *YOU*...once   (one)

<u>TWO:</u> speaks

through psycho-babbling MYTH-sters

through HIP-STER'S placenta

through COBALT-PIG'S surrender

of the GENTILE'S-INTELLIGENTSIA—

<see-I-hear-this>

purrrrrrrrrrrrrrrrrrrrrrrrrrr-meow-as

I. E E E E E E E E E E E E E E E E

SE- d u c e s - M E E E E E E E E E E E E E E . . .

<see-I-*feeeel*-this...

...*prrrrrrrrrrrrrr* >

and it shines as it listens...

to-voyeuristic-chainsaws-that-cut-your-peep-

SLEEP!

O MY DARLING...e.i.e.i.e...and

DUSA-me

like ya-USED-ta

SPEAK THROUGH ME...COMMUNI-GATO DE DOS DIOS,
GODS OF THE TWO:

the JAH of Inside,
and the NUH of outside.

and these gods will MEET-*one day* ::: and do we go through LIFE-*one day*
to get our inSIDES-*one day* ::: to meet our outSIDES-*one day*?
e.i. e.o. e.a, *my darlin'*

—————————— purrrrrrrrrrrrrrrrrrrrrrrrrrrr

meeeeeooowwww

The gods that travel through you and I
communicate through these cans-you
c o m m u n i c a t e ?
through these CANS-YOU
COMMUNICATE?...THROUGH THE
FEARS?   THE BLUES?
The carcass of ooze? And the Wizard of
O   z   ?

Through the blatant refusal
of insensitive truths,
and honesty's promise,

and reality's noose.

SEDUCER!?!

[-*si UNO! si DOS...es un "i.e. Seducer" Dolores?*
...me-Dusas! -Si dueno...solares de rosas! -Dolares,
senoras? -One dollar, rose pesos!]

one dollar / juantala / juantala / one dollar

juantala HOLD ON...YOUR
DEAR
LIFE >>> else-SHE-
felches,

psyche-SEE-nosis,

prog-NO-sis,   psyche-DO,
        YEAH-
bro,
                my
        GOD!!!
Jacking over jism hill,
and wondering *uncontrollably* of your jism's newborn kill!
<SNAP>-ooooooooooohhhhhhh...
        das-a-*BAAAD*-STILL-TIME quiet, **bro!!!**
Can YOU / ME cato ? Communi-GATO ? *hmmmmm...?*

        SPEAK THESE *CATS*
        YOU MANY GATOS!

_____

communiCA-*ting* and *prrrrrrrrrrrrrrrr*SING-*ing* and *ttttttttttttttt*TING-*ling*

        pssssssssssssssssssssssssssssssssssssssssst...**by threadbare**

you whisper...I said - *THERE* go two gods who seduce us:

the **JAH** of inside / and the **NOH** of outside   and the **YOU** / and the **I** / and that

        you and I
        are the zephyrs of thousands that suffer within us
        and zephyring wishes will i.e. forever
                oh my darling oh my darling oh my darling i.e.
                just breathe believe and be true to you
                it's there forever
                to take you far   and watch you   fly

MISSION-FUCKIN'-IMPOSSIBLE

(. . . H-E-E-R-R-E-E-'S . . . H-E-L-L-O-O-O-O . . . H-E-E-R-R-E-E-'S
. . . H-E-L-L-O-O-O-O . . .)

Hey . . . Spank-Fuckwheat & AlFuckya.

Hey . . . AbFuck & Fuckstello.

Hey . . . WilFuckma, Fuck, BetFuttyFuck'n-ArneyUck.

Hey . . . Nort'n-Trick-Fucksie-RalphFuck.

Hey . . . MurphFuck-Illigan's-I-Fuck-Alloping Ouurmet, Fulia Child,
Joyce Frothers,
The Fockra WinFuck Show, Peter Fuck as Fuckalombolo-Fuck,
Mutual of Fuckahas Wild Fuckdom, The Carol Fucknet Show, Ob-
NewFuck, L.A. Fuck,
Ed Fuckivan, Lawrence Fuck . . . m-i-Fuck . . . k-e-Fuck . . .
FuckFuckFuckFuckFuuuuck.

Hey . . . Clar-Fuck-Kent-Uper-Man-Fuck-Ois-Ane . . . . . . Uck.

Hey . . . Petticoat Fucktion, The Fucky Bunch, Fuck In The Fuckily, My
Children . . . Fuck'em All!!!
My-Mister-Fucker's-Neighbor-Hoo-Fuckame Street, Magilla Fuckilla,
Fu-peed Racer,
Fockeye, Hey . . . Olive FuckOyl, Fruto, Captain JackFuck's Funny,
Fucker Fudd,
Forky Fig, Fucky The Menace, Fuck The Fuck Cosby Show, Different
Fucks, Fuck Squad,
Fuck Search, Star Fuck-The Fuck Generation, Sixty Fuckits, The Six
O'Clock Fuck.

Hey . . . Dan Ra-Fuckather, Fuck Eutell, Faity Tong-Urrent-Af-Fuck-Air,
Eter-Fuckings, Ted Fockell,
Farbra-Falters-Falter-Fucktite, Felix The Fuck, The Fuck Is Right, Let's
Make A Fuck,
Fuckanne Fuckannadanna, H.R. PuffenFuck, RomperFuck-aFooby-
Dooby-Fuckoo,
The Fuckship Of Eddie's Fucker, DarrenTabaFuckAntha Stevens, My
Three Fucks,

I Fuck Of Eanie's Fuckoop, Eople-'s-Ourt-Ivorce-
     Roop . . . Hey-Hey-We're-Fuck-Onkies.

Hey . . . Curly, Moe & Fucky.
Hey!

mike tyler   THE MOST BEAUTIFUL WORD IN THE AMERICAN LANGUAGE

Why 12 Steps
why not 11 steps
or 39 steps
howbout 1 step
I've heard that first step's a doozy
        humane beans
        are unlike the street of bending trees
        they fall quick
if that 1 step is
revolting, sickening, bullying, damaging enough

you only need the one

I've heard that first step's a doozy
            thru the arches of trite self-examination
            witnessed by nodding fiends
            a pudgy baked complicated marshmallow
            is machine rolled into flat dough
            and cookie cluttered
            on a grey tan ton tin pan
            alley waste of flat little bitter
            crunchy duplicate yellow xeroxed spills
            faux sugared treats
            with pathetic stiff hands

                reaching out in exactly same position
                to pathetic stiff hands
                reaching out in exactly same position
                to
fingers never bend
touching is only
abutting

        Abutting we will go
        But isn't it a good thing
        to stop the demon drink
        to turn winos into whiners
        boozers into bozos
        to remove the grape from the expectant gape

        to put a towel over the tv set

        ("My friend is thinking of putting
        a towel over the tv set. Doesn't want
        to get addicted.")

        what's willpower and personal freedom
        to a dead person
        but that's *my* point

What's the most beautiful word in the American language

            donut
            tire
            tornado
            spasm

            rally
            fret
            nose
            fodder

            farm
            stamina

element
hose

fill in four words here

feast
love
warm
kind

drink
sing
snuggle
fuck

tumor
kidney
cancer
death

bunny
breakfast
sleep
purr

noodle
nightmare
work
will

damage
death
(already said it)
drink
(already said it)
stop

What's the most beautiful word in the American language

> clumsy
> target
> erase
> checkers
>
> evil
> evolution
> alternative
> upsidedown
>
> kite
> dumb
> munch
> elephant
>
> satire
> hedge
> orange
> fast
>
> believe
> fight
> aware
> resist

What's the most beautiful word in the American language

She used to listen to Joni Mitchell albums

she knew me as a baby
and hammocked me gently in her arms
she knew me as a kid
and protected me with sophisticated teenage charm

now her original tone is a busy signal

What's the most beautiful word in the American language

When the weapon wants you
when the cross hairs meet at your heart
when the butcher's massage is bloody and forever
when it rains inside

When the toupee is amplified
when feeling good is a pin-prick of intense anti-self
when groups are formed by groups
when language is shallow and compelling

When the noise is quieter than the silence
when all you can hear is yourself telling yourself to be quiet
when dripping is a function of turning the faucet off
when you hate you

When magic is explained
when the magician claims mystical powers
when love is stuff
when beauty is a sawed-off personality

What's the most beautiful word in the American language

She used to listen to Joni Mitchell albums

Resist

Resist

Resist

Resist

The most beautiful word in the American language is

Resist

7:00 AND THE TULIPS ARE RED

and the underground doesn't have to be materialism's mirror
why go into a tunnel if the searching scoring sun can still sore
an indirect hit is language the tool of the tongue or the snake
'round the bunny heart unattaching laws to engage the full fur
fluffiness hope falls infernal when you do something you always
meet up with something that wants to do something else does
that mean you should change your behind stick it out someplace
elephants are running hot and cold scared and the bee timorous
beastie feastie buzzing on us for over a deadage is hovering
whipping helicopter wings the gravel

the gavel gave grave diggers somethinc to dug justice the buryer
in an unjust ice age the frozen deserters see-thawing out on splinter
unKemp playgrounds suddenly all of a sudden no forget it i'll try
to swing it with one chain dragging from a dead bar the lions were
right eat what you don't understand

oh where oh where have the lying tamers gone is the geometry of
softness all the triangles circles and squares are parallel telegrams
beeping out retorts of atrocities exactly as they happen dee dee de
deep doo doo reports from the back are that stabbings are occultant
at dreadular intervalves

to sum down quilt me the whole in the donutin i want to stare into
stasis faces of facts so sensual oohs and ahs orgasm the air the rich
got richier the poor got poorier the snore got snorier heavy hands can
lift heavy problems so let's get heavy handed you were bad bad bad you
hurt hurt hurt us you imprisoned us in your sentences and hated us with
malignant cunning sign that cunning control bill misty mystics miss
running away you meet up with your enemy that has never moved never
move because the earth is moving and you look silly walking on a walking
sidewalk euphoria it now how?! how now frown coward mausoleums
have mouse in leotards negating the guards so the new can get out

THE BAKERY HAS NO BAKERS

The bakery has no bakers
instead
behind the steaming muffins
auto parts salespeople lounge with unfamiliarity in sugary smocks
the auto parts distributor has no salespeople
instead
leaning on the formica desks
zoologists stare uncomprehendingly at catalogues of carburetor screws
the zoos are without experts
instead
pacing cages littered with disappointment
bank tellers try desperately to get the various species' calves to suckle
the banks have no tellers
instead
flanked by imposing fake marble pillars
dentists get flummoxed by electronic dollar bill counters
the patients have no dentists
instead
trembling in garages
neighbors prepare to extract teeth with force over flair
the people have no neighbors
instead
in empty houses filled
hate groups burn welcome mats and upturn hospitality carts
the hate groups have no members
instead
during clandestinely chilly meetings
ordinary citizens try their best to work up an outrage about someone very
   much like themselves
the ordinary citizens are extra-ordinary
instead
at proms with "pows" and "bams"
superheroes vie for the girl or boy next door by displaying increased
 tolerance
   of kryptonite

the comic books have no superheroes
instead
framed in garish printing greens
presidents spew lying thought balloons
the presidency has no president
instead
taking charge of the state of affairs
a country feels in its pocket for change

II.
POETRY
OF THE 1990S

alurista ROMA ROJA RAJA TABLA

roma roja raja tabla
i las sonrisas abundan
en el silencio nocturno
mientras los vidrios
translucen los fuegos
los leños las llamas
por tele fono u grafo
copado de carcajadas
neumáticos italianos
un alemán no hace ruido
cuando saca su matraca
y chisquea los dientes
para escupir vellos púbicos
sin embargo los chicleros
rajan árboles erguidos
con las frutas de la tarde
y los huesos africanos

tumbalean congas cueros
cinturones y aceitunas
on thee, average your
feet together looking for
a partner musically
waltzing a salsa 'n'
frijoles negros on your head
manifested, man infested
thru thy sweater how's
the weather, honey?
bee u busy being buzzy
being born b thee average
or a person bursting forth
b a verb above, below
make u rattle, rock & ramble
i slip thru the asphalt meadow
plucking melodies in marble
flapping tongue across your eyes
yes past vigor bigger
imagination warmer
pointed funk florida
roma roja raja tabla

VORAZ LEÓN

voraz león, voraz urano
verás sobre la sala del crimen
lo que le pregunté al presidente
que si de piedra ha de ser la
cama no me escama a mi
la muerte serrana susana
que candela que caminé
caminé y caminé sin
pisar lineas ó quebrantos

pero, que te cuento, gira vira
vuélvete tú a lo que eres
divina escucha tu duende
que la luna zapatea libertad
justicia, hermandad, besos
abrazos despeja venganzas
calma tú que la lucha es
nuestra como aztlán también
como nuestros vástagos como
nuestro pueblo, libre y ké!

FOOLISH RITUALS

foolish rituals haunt my nervous system
        a moon beholds my offer
                to be one with
        or without
                the sun prevails
dawn is near, como los esta dos uni dos
                equality is far, as far
        as dios, dos
                the u.s. of a. has
                        bullets or bread
god has only questions
                man wonders still whether
                        to be or not 2
        claras lunas anuncian
                        presagian el ser
el sol se impone, know no nothing
                darkness gone
                dia logue prevails
                        it b logos
                solution, dia logue
        remains

the sheath of eros
         promise of life
                 with violence
removed, renounced, resigned & absent

jimmy santiago baca
DUST-BOWL MEMORY
for Abaskin

My ancient neighbor, Mr. Abaskin,
was born in Russia, roamed Europe,
and when the call came from America,
he boarded ship and came.
Seventy years farming this land.
Every morning he walks the dirt road
with his aging wife, reminding me
of two solitary mesquite trees
rooted high at the edge of a rocky cliff,
overlooking a vast canyon gorge.
Hands hardened, yellow claws
from farming tenderly pocket candy
in my son's pants.
He scolds his shepherd Kiki
for exciting grazing sheep or scaring
Rhode Island Reds. We meet every noon
by the fence where our feed is
and small talk
conditions of fields,
how he and his wife could buck
three hundred bales an afternoon
when they were my age.
His memory an old dust-bowl town,
he remembers who lived where
before we came, who was born to whom,
when Williams' Packing Company started

stealing people's cattle, when people
started locking their screen doors,
and a time when only Spanish was spoken in this valley.
"Didn't have to go to town. These Mexican folk
had the finest gardens in the world,
why tomatoes and chile you wouldn't believe. . . ."

BELLS

Bells. The word gongs my skull bone. . . .
Mamá carried me out, just born,
swaddled in hospital blanket,
from St. Vincent's in Santa Fe.
Into the evening, still drowsed
with uterine darkness,
my fingertips purple with new life,
cathedral bells splashed
into my blood, plunging iron hulls
into my pulse waves. Cathedral steeples,
amplified brooding, sonorous bells,
through narrow cobbled streets, bricked patios,
rose-trellis'd windows,
red-tiled Spanish rooftops, bells
beat my name, "Santiago! Santiago!"
Burning my name in black-frosted streets,
bell sounds curved and gonged deep,
ungiving, full-bellowed beats of iron on iron,
shuddering pavement Mamá walked,
quivering thick stainless panes, creaking
plaza shop doors, beating its gruff thuds
down alleys and dirt
passageways, past men waiting in doorways
of strange houses. Mamá carried me, past
peacocks and chickens, past the miraculous
stairwell winding into the choirloft, touted
in tourist brochures, *"Not one nail was used*

to build this, it clings tenaciously
together by pure prayer power, a spiraling
pinnacle of faith. . . ." And years later,
when I would do something wrong,
in kind reprimand Mamá would say,
"You were born of bells, more than my womb,
they speak to you in dreams.
Ay, *Mijito,*
you are such a dreamer!"

CHOICES

An acquaintance at Los Alamos Labs
who engineers weapons
black x'd a mark where I live
on his office map.
Star-wars humor. . . .
He exchanged muddy boots
and patched jeans
for a white intern's coat
and black polished shoes.
A month ago, after butchering a gouged bull,
we stood on a pasture hill,
and he wondered with pained features
where money would come from
to finish his shed, plant alfalfa,
and fix his tractor.
Now his fingers
yank horsetail grass,
he crimps herringbone tail-seed
between teeth, and grits out words,
"Om gonna buy another tractor
next week. More land too."
Silence between us is gray water
let down in a tin pail

in a deep, deep well,
a silence
milled in continental grindings
millions of years ago.
I throw my heart
into the well, and it falls
a shimmering pebble to the bottom.
Words are hard
to come by. "Would have lost everything
I've worked for, not takin' the job."
His words try to
retrieve
my heart
from the deep well.
We walk on in silence,
our friendship
rippling away.

BLACK MESA

for Rito

The northernmost U-tip
of Chihuahua desert
infuses
my house
with its dark shadow,
and leans my thoughts
in its direction
as wind bends a row of trees
toward it.

I want to visit
it
before winter comes,

and balance myself
across culvert that connects
my field
to Isleta Pueblo.
Strings of water trellis
from rusty holes
and bubble scum and black moss weed
below.
Branches barrage the passage,
and draw blood at my shoulder
as I crouch past,
then climb No Trespassing fence.

I don't know what this year has meant to me,
but I've come here to find a clue.
Up Black Mesa's east side,
'dozed in '68
to run I-25 south.
Sky showered stones
at children playing
on ditchbanks,
dynamite blasts cracked porches,
foundations, and walls
with shuddering volts.

Rito was murdered here
by sheriffs,
brown beret Chicano activist
who taught children in the barrio
our own history,
tried to stop
them blasting Black Mesa.
And now, under my hiking boots his blood
crossbeds minerals
and forms into red crystals,
ceremonial Chac-Mool plate
on which Aztec warrior Rito
sacrificed his heart to the Sun.

Rito believed in a justice
whose history
is without margins.

To my right, a steep downdrift
gush of cutting boulders,
the jagged edges of a key
that opens my dark life
and gives it a certain meaning
of honor and truth.

I re-imagine myself here,
and pant the same breath
squeezed from these rocks 1000 years ago.

Etched on slabs,
wolf and coyote wear
skins of stone,
watch me pass, silent
at the shortness of my life, at my
brief visit here on earth.
I finger the rough braille
of each drawing
in the cool crevice slab,
and discover in this seeming destruction
a narrative of love
for animals and earth.
I go on,
climb boulders drained
down a rip gorge,
and stand on the flat cap rim
of Black Mesa, fuzzed
with chaparral, cacti and weeds.

In lava cracks,
I learn to read, smell and hear
the darkness again 'til black depths
lighten slowly to twilight
and the old man who lives

in stone
offers me a different view
of life and death.

I believe that whatever tragedy
happens in my life, I can stand on my feet
again and go on.

I lay on a slab stone
and nap in sunlight
unafraid of snakes that plume stones
around me.

In sluggish revery
I am in a small café
in Española.
Seat myself at a round wooden table.
A man approaches me,
sits across from me, and states,
          "Thank you for the stone in my mind.
          It sings to me and I still listen to it."

I rub sun glare from my eyes and look around,
as if he sat next to me,
then walk over to the black-lipped rim rock.
Languid whitewashed adobe houses below are
obscured by lush branches.
I bend
and pocket a lava chip as token
of my ascent from stone,
                              and go.

I have a vision of mountain range
proportions,
to speak the heart's language.
To write the story of my soul
I trace in the silence and stone
of Black Mesa.

My hope breaks this hour's crust
and ferments
into tomorrow's darkness, into
another year of living,
to evolve with the universe,
side by side with its creative catastrophe.

catherine bowman   1-800-HOT-RIBS

My brother sent me ribs for my birthday.
He sent me two six-pound, heavily scented,
slow-smoked slabs, Federal Express,
in a customized cardboard box, no bigger
than a baby coffin or a bulrush ark.

Swaddled tight in sheaves of foam and dry ice,
those ribs rested in the hold of some jetliner
and were carried high, over the Yellowhammer State
and the Magnolia State and the Brown Thrasher State,
over Kentucky coffeetrees and Sitka spruce

and live oak and wild oak and lowland plains
and deep-water harbors, over catfish farms
and single-crib barns and Holiness sects
and strip malls and mill towns and lumber
towns and coal camps and chemical plants,

to my table on this island on a cold night
with no moon where I eat those ribs and am made
full from what must have been a young animal,
small-boned and tender, having just
the right ratio of meat to fat.

Tonight outside, men and women enrobed
in blankets fare forth from shipping crates.

A bloodhound lunges against its choke
to sniff the corpse of a big rat and heaps
of drippings and grounds that steam

outside the diner as an ashen woman deep
in a doorway presses a finger to her lips.
A matted teddy bear impaled on a spike
looms over a vacant lot where a line of men
wreathe in fellowship around a blazing garbage can.

Tonight in a dream they gather
all night to labor over the unadorned
beds they have dug into the ground and filled
with the hardwood coals that glow like remote stars.
Their faces molten and ignited in the damp,

they know to turn the meat infrequently,
they know to keep the flame slow and the fire
cool. From a vat of spirits subacid and brackish,
they know to baste only occasionally. So that
by sunrise vapor will continue to collect, as usual,

forming, as it should, three types of clouds,
that the rainfall from the clouds, it is certain,
will not exceed the capacity of the river,
that the river will still flow, as always,
sweet brother, on course.

MR. X

                         All my Ex's
live in Texas, so the country song says and no excuses,
it's mostly true for me too that the spade-shaped extra
big state with its cotton lints and Ruby Reds holds the crux
of my semi-truck-I've-never-had-any-kind-of-luck-deluxe-
super-high-jinx-born-to-be-unhappy-if-it-ain't-broken-don't-fix-

it loves, for example, there was the snakebit mudlogger who fixed
himself forever diving off that hexed bridge, and that foxy ex-
patriot who imported exotic parrots, he'd pump me up with his deluxe
stuff, the salesman who felt so guilty for the wide-eyed excuses
he told his wife that at the Big Six Motel just outside Las Cruces
he spent the afternoon hunched over *Exodus,* bemoaning the sin of extra-

marital sex, and the harmonica player, his mouth organ could extract
an oily bended blues, on sticky nights we'd hit the 12th hole pond with a
    fix
of Dos Equis and a hit of Ecstasy and I'd wrap my legs around his lanky
    crux,
as moonlight cut through the water like a giant X-ray, his Hohner ax
glistened in and out. And then there was the feckless shrink. No excuse
for his fixation, the tax man, the cute butcher from the Deluxe,

the Kilim dealer, the defrocked priest. So what if my mother was a deluxe
lush, my father Baptist and weak, I can't blame them, I was born just extra
affectionate. Don't ask about the abortions, and who can ever make excuses
for the time I spent holed up with the Port-O-Can tycoon my friend fixed
me up with, or the Mexican sculptor who made cathedral-sized onyx Xs,
twisted crucifixes. Art, he quoted Marx, was history at its crux.

Then there was the Ph.D. who took me to Peru and showed me Crux
(the Southern Cross), Centaurus, Musca, Vela, Lupus, and another deluxe
equatorial constellation that I forgot. For fun I ascribed each sparkly X
a name and date, so now I have a star chart to exalt each of my extra-
ordinary, heavenly bodies. But that night I dreamed the stars were fixed
on stacks of pages: pica asterisks to indicate omissions, footnotes, excuses,

explanations. I stood there, Ms. D. Giovanni, with a million excuses.
Now in exile I journey on the Styx with Mr. X in our boat the *Crux
Criticorum.* I wear an aqua slicker, he a sharkskin suit. He's non-fiction,
never incognito. We've got our sextant and spy manual open on our deluxe
waterbed. I can just make out the tattoo above his boxers in this extra
dark, there's the curve of his back. Now we'll break the code and go
    beyond X.

DEATHWATCH BEETLE

You are my dog. Your teeth are white. Your tongue
is black. You are my circling sea fish. Behold,
the circling of the planets are nine. Three times
nine the moon comes full

circle. Blind night snake, here in this narrow space
we shed our skin again. Taste the air, it's like
milk. I love this part of the river. We are
two night snakes kissing.

You are my mastiff bat. Your fur is cocoa.
You fly with four long fingers. The fifth, the thumb,
is free and clawed. You are my bearded pig. Rain
grubs and roots the swamps.

You lick and eat the ground. Why didn't they tell
me of your filthy habits? Your penis is grooved
and you have two sallow tusks and there are scent
glands in your anus.

You are my sable antelope. Horns like carved
storms, face piebald, ears two blue cloudlets, your back
a Niagara of brilliance. Now my desert
woodrat. I find your

stick rooms filled with forgotten objects. My arms
and legs are cut and bruised from chasing over
the cactus. And now you're my deathwatch beetle.
All night you tap, tap,

tap on the window. There's a luminous spot
on your thorax and your nostrils open and
close like fans. You say there's no need to worry
you have an extra

set of eyes for the water, enough air in
your wing case to keep us alive a long time.
Mammoth cumulus trundle the hemisphere,
now as we're churning

in the icy Atlantic, the wind a blue gray
aphrodisiac dug up from the Fire
Island mud. Fever yellow burns on the sky.
Darling, this is our life.

diane burns   # SURE YOU CAN ASK
ME A PERSONAL QUESTION

How do you do?
No, I'm not Chinese.
No, not Spanish.
No, I'm American Indi—uh, Native American.
No, not from India.
No, we're not extinct.
No, not Navajo.
No, not Sioux.
Yes, Indian.
Oh, so you've had an Indian friend?
        That close.
Oh, so you've had an Indian lover?
        That tight.
Oh, so you've had an Indian servant?
        That much.
Oh, so that's where you got those high cheekbones.
Your great-grandmother, eh?
Hair down to there?
Let me guess—Cherokee?
Oh, an Indian Princess.
No, I didn't make it rain tonight.

No, I don't know where you can get Navajo rugs real cheap.
No, I don't know where you can get peyote.
No, I didn't make this—I bought it at Bloomingdale's.
Yes, some of us drink too much.
Some of us can't drink enuf.
This ain't no stoic look.
This is my face.

ALPHABET CITY SERENADE

Once they built the railroad
the buffalo split
past the horizon line
once they built the railroad
now it's done.
Brother, can you front me a dime?

I'm down and out in Loisaida
I'm out of smoke in Loisaida
I'm out of tea in Loisaida
I'm out of luck
I'm out of mind
all at the same time
in Loisaida.
Oh East Village ai yi yi yi yi yi yi.

I'm American royalty
walking around with a hole in my knee
I'm a hopeful aborigine
trying to find a place to be
Oh East Village ai yi yi yi yi yi yi.

Back home now I'd be at the pow-wow
I'd be drinking herb tea and eating deer meat.

Maybe smooching in a blanket with a Potawatamie.
But here I am on Avenue D.
Sacrifice of Manifest Destiny.
Oh East Village ai yi yi yi yi yi yi.

I'm not your steppin' stone.
Hey man, can you spare a cigarette?
Do you know of a place to sublet?
Do you know where I can cash this check?
Do you know, do you know that
I hate Chevrolet
I hate Doris Day
I hate Norman Bates
And I'm at war with the United States
Oh East Village ai yi yi yi yi yi yi.
East Village ai yi yi yi yi yi yi.

Oh, so you want to talk about gentrification, huh?

PEÑA'S SON

A friend in Zimbabwe
called and said
"It's just like Long Island
only every once in a while
you look out the window and see
a rhinoceros."

wanda coleman # TOUGH LANGUAGE

for the head baker

he complains i don't play it hardball enuff. he
wants it slammed to the table like sirloin gouged from
a fresh kill still bleeding onto the hardwood. he
wants me to spike it in deep until shrieks
erupt like Krakatoa and rent white flesh gives way
lava running toward ocean's edge/steam and villages
burning and the women children even the men running for
shelter. or cold as that blue arctic beast that
cracked and numbed the Titanic sinking all-American
hope. he wants to kick back and watch them all
shiver/head for the useless lifeboats. he knows
there's a soulblack sub off the coast loaded with
relentless torpedoes—a one-woman lynch mob marauding
thru the streets of his mushy pampered academic boredom
robbing and raping her 1-dimensional way across town
to shoot the sheriff and liberate him from himself

AMERICAN SONNET

rejection can kill you

it can force you to park outside neon-lit
liquor stores and finger/the steel of
your contemplation. it can even make you
rob yourself

(when does the veteran of one war fail to
appreciate the vet of another?)

the ragged scarecrow lusts in the midst of
a fallow field

and the lover who prances in circles envies me
my moves/has designs on my gizzard/kicks shit

this is the city we've come to
all the lights are red all the poets are dead
and there are no norths

DREAM 7219

the nutmeg brown brother his loss of
pigmentation blotched pale skin signaling
transglorification hands melted down to stubs
the fingers disappearing into a maw of scaly
skin and bone long thin arms and thinner legs
becoming the son his semi-kinky sandy brown bush
his tight shorts his legs white as balsa his
final moment's moaning towards me "mother!"
he cries and i grope for the space in which
to bend and cradle him to heart's last sleep
at the end of his barely 30? years the dancer
who only danced once

martín espada REBELLION IS THE CIRCLE OF A LOVER'S HANDS (PELLÍN AND NINA)

for the 50th anniversary of the Ponce Massacre

The marchers gathered, Nationalists
massed beneath the delicate white balconies
of Marina Street,

and the colonial governor
pronounced the order with patrician calm:
fifty years of family history
says it was Pellín
who dipped a finger
into the bloody soup of his own body
and scratched defiance
in jagged wet letters on the sidewalk.
Around him stormed
the frenzied clattering drumbeat
of machineguns,
the stampede of terrified limbs
and the panicked wail
that rushed babbling
past his dim senses.

Palm Sunday, 1937:
the news
halted the circular motion
of his lover's hands
as she embroidered
the wedding dress.
She nodded, knew
before she was told.

Years later, with another family
in a country of freezing spring rain
called Nueva York,
Nina is quietly nervous
when her son speaks of rifles
in a bullhorn shout,
when coffins are again bobbing
on the furious swell of hands and shoulders,
and the whip of nightsticks
brings fresh blood
stinging from the scalp.

But rebellion
is the circle of a lover's hands,

that must keep moving,
always weaving.

TWO MEXICANOS LYNCHED IN SANTA CRUZ, CALIFORNIA, MAY 3, 1877

More than the moment
when forty gringo vigilantes
cheered the rope
that snapped two Mexicanos
into the grimacing sleep of broken necks,

more than the floating corpses,
trussed like cousins of the slaughterhouse,
dangling in the bowed mute humility
of the condemned,

more than the Virgen de Guadalupe
who blesses the brownskinned
and the crucified,
or the guitar-plucking skeletons
they will become
on the Día de los Muertos,

remain the faces of the lynching party:
faded as pennies from 1877, a few stunned
in the blur of execution,
a high-collar boy smirking, some peering
from the shade of bowler hats, but all
crowding into the photograph.

LATIN NIGHT AT THE PAWNSHOP

Chelsea, Massachusetts, Christmas, 1987

The apparition of a salsa band
gleaming in the Liberty Loan
pawnshop window:

Golden trumpet,
silver trombone,
congas, maracas, tambourine,
all with price tags dangling
like the city morgue ticket
on a dead man's toe.

jose-angel figueroa
SATINLADY BLUES

The Life and Times of Billie Holiday

She was a good high-yellow woman
with almond-shaped eyes
born to sing how the nights
sometimes grow old and then untold
like an accolade quite blasé
of beautifully ugly problems
whispering mornings may never come
like a sabotage of the mind anchored
to confusion in a bottomless stream
overflowing with elusive times
and bittersweet melancholy
with life as a one-night stand
shipped and sealed for despair
reaching nowhere to be treated

half-home or lacking words and far
less time without any everything

"And Momma may have Poppa may have"

But bless the child who becomes his own
beyond that blink and sigh blemished
with tears while singing to survive
and masquerade the streetwise
waving pride to zigzag through these
swaggering changes when pushed or
haunted by shattered moments
feeling discarded and diffused
like a slow saxophone solo fading off
into obscurity as the piano player
mellows down this war that's never
quite the same the morning after
when a child becomes a holiday for pain

Yet in voice and skin Lady Day traveled
the whole night once ever more
to subside or blend in and sing
of these self-concerns to comfort
the trifled spirit in a subdued rage
weighing more than her legend to mend
each wound as the darkness descended
by approaching the microphone with
redolence showing how it really feels
being a maid and mistress to fiasco
between the new-man cures and cold turkey
or stray dogs and desperate revivals

Blaring the spirituals with
heartspinning blues to put new wings
on expectations and turn anticipation
into gold with dignity while
holding on to a piece of time
and stuff shadows into silk dreams

with maybe this or maybe that
perhaps today and why not

Living her songs without regrets
to cross over and burn this pain
out of loneliness while improvising
a tonality for chilled laughter between
the Honky-Tonk or rap-talking times in
Tin Pan Alley with top hats and tails
and away from the sun-splashing
sidewalks or hot biscuits to kill
the shock from bad whiskey and put on
a new ensemble of self-respect
to sing with pleasure why sadness
puts a tag on you: and clean out
the sky of its strange fruits

Asking who really knows and if you care
of how southern poplar trees bleed
and agony embodies the air
of subtle prayers that rot in gloom
and dangling bodies cannot compare
how far-in can grief close these eyes
and scream updated with the times
when death brags and never changes
and these processions are combined
with minds now broken into danger
when in the thick of all-in-all
first-rate hatred makes a brusque call
of more half-tones and deeper shadows
and exclusively from across the tracks
where corn whiskey succumbs to sorrows
while crocodiles mingle in rough dance halls
riffin' this outrage before tomorrow's
when spinning the wrong way on poplar trees
and far past backwards with this breeze

But Billie Holiday always kept bouncing
right on back to confront all these

absurdities and understand what rhythms
such ways and times entrapped before
winding down and becoming a prisoner
of her own great myth: remembering
never to forget love could ever be over
when you can wake up singing

With white gardenias in your hair

BORN TO ACT OUT

A theatre of poets-of-poets
gather to emblazon *Short Eyes*
with a final glimpse before
the midnight blues closed shop
for the hereafter when quietus
moved in with its own no-frills
no-deposit/no-return attitude
for some ice-cold bitter ass.

These epic versifiers came
to mix with the minors
the majors and poet laureates
wolfin' with the good
the great and self-proclaimed
that writing is a coffee
drinker's dream of a pink pig
with wings selling the best
bullshit in town with
weekend editions for deaf
insomniacs drunk on amnesia
to demystify help-wanted ads
in alphabet city amidst
greater shadows of poetry.

They gather in the heartburn
of Loisaida where the love
of kissing poetry in its mouth
is a suicide mission.

Yet *Short Eyes* had no need
for these split-second memories
caged in a few moments of silence
for he was born to act out
that damned loveable poet-thief
enchanting and cruel
love-loving and deathful
outrageously addicted to both
with the sly smile of a saint
singing do-wops in harmonizing
with hell while kissing angels
in the basement to deflower
youth of wild scattered ashes.

Until all came to be
dead with life at 41

writing high crazy happy poetry.

hattie gossett   PUSSY & CASH

it all comes down to pussy & cash
i don't care what you say
thats what it all comes down to

everybody wants some pussy
everybody needs some pussy
for one reason or another everybody needs some personalized private pussy
    they can call their own

a private pussy of ones own is a great status symbol cuz it means you can
     play pussy on parade whenever you wanna like when you be steppin out
     in the world with yo private pussy on yo arm or invitin yo friends over
     for a party hostessed to the mostess by yo personal pussy whose face
     body & mind have been beaten within an inch of life for the occasion

in another form of pussy possession people get surgically & psychologically
     madeover complete with paris pout in order to conform to a wildside
     fantasy of what pussy looks & lives like only to find themselves lost in
     that endless gap between ideal & real when it comes to the true drama of
     being an everyday living pussy

of course theres an endless pool of pussys on reserve waiting for you to
     bring them in
to run yo household take care of yo kids or grandmama or run yo business
if you know the secret password—whar da hoz iz?—you can get some clean
     freelance pussy to help you through the night when you got to be
     farfarfar away from yo regular pussy

when you aint got nothing else goin for you at least you know you can
     always fall back on yo personal private pussy

if you cant git no respect from the big boys out in the world you can
     always displace that rage youre too scared to direct to the bigboys by
     fuckin with yo pussy
you can send yo pussy out for sandwiches & coffee or lock it up in the closet
     for a week or you can refuse to put through for a raise or refuse to pay
     child support or you can stick broken soda bottles into it

you can impregnate or sterilize yo pussy
you can even put yo pussy out on frontstreet in a 3pc corporate suit
sensible pumps & crotchless panties
                         money honey
              money honey if you wanna git along with me
                    cuz pussy gits cash
          oh yeah & everybody needs cash aint that right
                    pussy sho nuff brings cash
                         good gawd!

cuz people will pay cash for just the illusion of pussy over the phone pay
    cash to look at pictures of pussy pay cash for an inflatable rubber lifesize
    doll with an artificially moistened pussy between its legs or for a dis-
    embodied lifelike artificially moistened rubber pussy that comes in a
    velvet box

everyday all day long people pay cash for detergents automobiles floor
waxes booze hi
fashions insurance policies ballet classes political clout fur coats cosmetic
surgery
front row seats tanks & bombs & expensive vacations when these things are
displayed
(or implied) on tv or in the movies or the press in close association with
pussy

some people pay exorbitant private school fees mortgages carnotes tennis
    lesson fees credit card interest & countryclub membership fees to say
    nothing of loanshark & shrink fees so their sons are exposed to the better
    quality pussy & so their daughters can learn how to act like the better
    quality pussy & both of them can marry somebodies with some cash so
    the grandkids wont have to hustle so hard

people will break their necks to say nothing of the law in order to go all
    over the world & do all kinds of lowlifed things to other people in order
    to get more & more cash to keep all their personal pussys living in a
    manner to which they have so lately become accustomed
                    & then & then & then
                when the cash gits low
              when the cash gits real low
      i say when the cashflow gits so low till it runs clean out
                  who feels it the most?
              there ya go—the pussy!
            hard times hit the pussy hardest of all!

last hired first fired do not pass go right to the unemployment line & stay
there even after the benefits run out
then hit that welfare line with yo babies
then the shelter line
cuz the pussy is the bottomline
pussy can stand all kinds of stress pain & strain & bounce

200

right back so they say never been nothin else like pussy
& never will be pussy primeval raw material dont control
nothin causes cash to flow pussy sweatin to create cash
dont be no pussy like pussy aint nothin dont control
nothin cash you cant beat it theres nothin like pussy
nothin in this world like pussy without cash or
control pussy aint listed in the revolutionary
handbook or the feminist dictionary cash
pussy cash pussy cash pussy dont control
nothin pussy aint nothin like it dont
control nothin cash pussy on parade
brings cash pussy spits out babies
bounces right back brings cash
dont control nothin aint
nothin like it in this
world let me tell you
cash nothin like
pussy cash pussy
cash pussy cash
pussy cash
it all comes down to pussy & cash

SUN RA!
performance poem for jawole

    1.
ive been dancing all my life
probably came out of the womb doing a little step
ive danced on 4 continents plus several islands
in places hifly la la la & lowdown lowlife ummmph
i got a dance major masters degree
someones even doing a thesis on me
danced solo duet trio quartet & ensemble with my own dance company
with music

without music
even got rave reviews in the new york times
but more than anything else ive always wanted to dance with sun ra
now hes left this planet
guess i gotta wait til we meet somewhere over there on the other side of
space is the place space is the place space

2.
voice of the universe
sun ra speaking:
                    "there are other worlds they have not told you of
                    somebody elses idea of how the world should be
                        aint necessarily how its got to be
                    there are other worlds they have not told you of
                                    them
                                    folks
                                    been
                                a walkin
                            they a walkin
                            a walkin up
                            on the moon
                        if you wake up now
                        if you wake up now
                        if you wake up now
                        it wont be too soon
                        if you wake up now
                        it wont be too soon
                take your first step into outer space
            like a little baby who never walked before
            if you fall down get up & walk some more
                    like a little baby
                go on & walk some more
                walk some more
            traveling the spaceways
                from planet to planet
                rocket number nine
            second stop is jupiter
                rocket number nine

from planet to planet
traveling
second stop is jupiter
rocket number nine
second stop is jupiter
rocket number nine
from planet to planet
traveling
second stop is jupiter
second stop is jupiter
second stop is jupiter"

3.

sun ra & his myth science arkestra
live!
from the universe
the entrance will last 2 centuries at least
just the entrance alone
imagine the costumes
cant you just see all those singers elephants capoeraistas birds lifesized
puppets giant lizards mimes musicians & tigers all working together for
"precision discipline & beauty" cant you see sun ra with all his sequins
glitter feathers jewels gowns & crowns doing the space walk walking space
spinning infinitely spinning spinning spinning infinitely spinning the
universe spinning & somewhere among all that "precision discipline &
beauty" will be lil ole bow-legged
jawole willa jo zollar from kansas city
me
dancing with sun ra & his myth science arkestra
yes

4.

when i was in paris & spoleto i did it like this
in brazil & chicago they screamed when they saw this
in boston & new york i whipped it on em like this
in jerusalem & miami they were speechless when i did this

in jamaica & los angeles they couldnt get enough of this
in berlin & new orleans there were encores galore for this

      4a.

sun ra speaking
the voice of the cosmos:
                    "this is the creators song of tomorrows world
                              cosmic paradise
                            its springtime again
                        song of tomorrows world
                              cosmic paradise
                          the creators song
                        song of tomorrows world
                            springtime again
                        song of tomorrows world
                            cosmic paradise
                        song of tomorrows world"

      4b.

me & sun ra
when we do our duet
just me & sun ra
i am gonna do it like this
thats good for the duet dont you think
then when i do it with the arkestra
with sun ra & the whole big myth science arkestra live!
& me
i am gonna do it like this
"from planet to planet"
& like this
& like this
& then "from planet to planet"
i am gonna
gonna
gonna
"from planet to planet"
gonna
"from planet to planet"

204

4c.

voice of the omniverse
sun ra speaking
excerpt from a cosmic musical:

> "lets go slumming
> please
> take me slumming
> lets go slumming
> on park avenue
> lets hide behind a pair of fancy glasses
> lets make faces when a member of their classes
> passes
> lets go smelling
> where theyre dwelling
> sniffing at everything the way they do
> they do it
> why cant we do it too
> lets go do it
> lets go slumming
> please take me slumming
> lets go slumming
> on
> park
> avenue"

5.

s u n   r a
sunny
a/k/a herman sonny blunt
earliest known earthly manifestation date: 22 may 1913 or 1914
bir
ming
ham

al
a
ma
bam
a

earthly transformation date: 30 may 1993
at his sisters house
bir
ming
ham

al
a
ma
bam
a

    5a.
sun ra speaking
voice of the universe:

        "if you not suitable for the future
          you probably wont make it in the present either"

    5b.
danced on 4 continents
plus several islands
in places la la la & ummmph
with music
without music
more than anything i always did want to dance with sun ra
now hes left this planet
guess i gotta hookup with him somewhere space is the place space is the
   place space

    6.
sun ra speaking
voice of the omniverse:

      "this is the song of tomorrows world
        you cant just play the notes
         you gotta feel the spirits

> 4/4 time point 2
> fractions in rhythm harmony melody
> spirits dont need to count"

7.

listen i gotta go now cuz i dont want to be late for my gig in the omniverse
with sun ra & the myth science arkestra live! with me
the original urban bush woman infinitely spinning spinning
spinning the omniverse infinitely spinning the entrance
alone will last 2 centuries i am gonna do it like
this "from planet to planet" & like this & like
this traveling & then "from planet to planet"
traveling gonna gonna gonna "from
planet to planet"
"from planet to
planet"

note: all material in quotation marks is either a direct quote or paraphrase from sun ra. some quotes are
from songs by sun ra. some quotes are from the 4-hour interview between sun ra & phil schaap originally
broadcast live during the sun ra festival on radio station wkcr-fm at columbia university.

jessica hagedorn
LATIN MUSIC IN NEW YORK

made me dance with you
tito   eddie   n ray
somewhere with plumjam eyelids
i danced with you
in a roomful of mirrors
in miss harlow's house

the white girl's in town
and i smell death
the poet dying in a bar

body shaking in time
to lady day's song
      he's dying in a nod
      in a lullaby
      of ambulance haze
      and chloral hydrate
      they burned his brain

somewhere
i saw the white girl smiling
la cucaracha was up all night
hiding her spoons   her mirrors   her revolutions
in the morning
         the trace of vampires
         still there
         in the blood   even after a bath

you can't wash it away
you can't hide it
again and again
i looked under my bed
    inside a perfume box
        in the argentinian dagger
           the baby wolf gave me
              in your eyes
                in a furtive smile
                  in a good fuck
                    in the boogaloo i do
there's no escaping it
  somewhere   with plumjam eyelids

i danced the tasty freeze shuffle with you
the reds   the blues   the tango con tu madre
it's there
in town for the night
a guest appearance   a quick solo
death gets hyped
and i'm in love again

latin music in new york
made me dance with you
azúcar y chocolaté
the alligator dream
of a tropical night

death makes a quick run
to las vegas
trying to take the poet
with him

latin music in new york
made me dance with you
tito   eddie   n ray

revolutions are creeping out
from under my bed!
and i sing a song for you
     and you
         and
             you

SKULL FOOD #2

This city is demented.
There are big holes in my head.
Sunshine works in Times Square
Tamboo drives buses for the MTA
takes my money
tells me
you look pretty too.

Thank you,
I say.

There are big holes in my head.
My memory has become too selective
and I hate this city.

Sunshine meets her
man Psycho
in the park.
Sunshine is a beauty
thick ankles
albino ringlets
a nose for trouble.
I remember hundreds of
fifteen-year-old girls named Sunshine
in 1967.

Sunshine
I call out
from the back of the bus
is that you?
She doesn't hear me
of course
she only has eyes
for her man Psycho
but Tamboo hears me
though I'm mute.
*"Say, can I eat your pussy
for ten bucks and a bag of groceries?"*
RIGHT NOW?
I am amazed.

Sunshine
gets off the bus
ahead of me
disappears into the dark
city park
calling to her drifter lover:
"Psycho! Hey Psycho!"
She sings.
De de dementia

I whisper back,
half in love
with her melody.

It's the same girl
twenty-two years ago
but now the escalator works
in the underwater train station.
The city's submerged,
but everyone asks me for directions.
How should I know where you're going?
I'm from New York.
Liar.
You smell like you're from Oakland.

De de dementia
Ferdinand Marcos sits
two rows ahead of me
and at the next stop
Imelda rushes in.
How would you want to be remembered?
How would you want to be?
How would you want?
Dan Ackroyd interviews
Jose Napoleon Duarte of El Salvador
animal torture
animal abuse
animal neglect
in Norte America

For us
it's not a question
of slaughter
it's a question of torture.
I've got big holes
in my head
big lapses
and polka dots
of memory.

As for me,
Duarte replies,
I am a fighter
who confronts
destiny.

kimiko hahn
THE DETAILS WE FALL FOR
for my students

Shifting to fifth and swinging behind a Harley
he could be you: black helmet, gloved fists—
on that spin down some LA boulevard,
the heat of February sweating the streets,
my hands around your waist in our first contact
since I married a second time still not to you.
What were those weird trees,
Dr. Seuss illustrations, cocktail mixers?
and what about all that pink—
bungalows, latex buns, tanning billboards—
details instructing the interior landscape
we ride through even, or especially in sleep.
I'm back in New York.
So to the driver behind me:
don't tail the woman behind the guy on the motorcycle.
She's working on a rough draft.

THE HEAT

Did you watch women collect red seaweed
in the white foam
and think of afternoons in your apartment
view of fire escape and brick wall,
smell of everyone's cooking,
taste of each other's mouth and extremities.
Did you listen to their work song
and think of the radio in the alley blaring:
undying love, love, undying love.
The air was full of air,
the heat, heart.
From Sei Shonagon
we know one can travel in dreams.
The difference between the dreamer
and the dream traveler noted in
a broken twig, footprints in the garden,
or the doormat muddy and askew.
Yes.
Any effort at love
resolved itself in fucking and crying.
I imagine you turning away on your Harley
toward the urban blight.

*

It was Danceteria in December.
I think I leaned over to tell you
I wanted another drink
but licked your ear to my own surprise.
More in the taxi.
We couldn't believe it:
discovering the edge of heat
that makes a person lie to everyone
yet never admit it even as the words unravel.

I could play *mother* with you:
a naked baby I'd nurse and rock

then suddenly we were adults again
on top of an orgasm.

Hours of refusing to disrobe
until finally, hand up my skirt,
drenched and crying
we'd give in to bludgeoning throbs.

Or the little hand mirror
held like a key hole
as we watched something in another room
distant and glistening.

Even rising to leave for my husband
the blood could not calm.

                    *

Sometimes I don't know I'm writing a poem.

                    *

Meeting a year later
I could barely look at you.
Now I have enough distance to ask questions
beyond ember.
What was my need to leave the nuptial bed
for a single, dark in the afternoon?
A need akin to leaving father?
That departure we think makes me, me.
One looks up from a newspaper
and knows some chest or ass
is it
then goes beyond imagination
and still doesn't call it wrong (was it?)
calls it *need*—
as absolute as a child running across the schoolyard
away from the figure in herringbone tweed.
There are times
when I think existence
could not be without the excruciating melt

of reason
or the acute sorrow of separation.
Is the self so persistent,
her self,
one thinks she doesn't look for mother
even at the point of telling some bitch to fuck off
he's mine. I said mine,
honey.

*

This summer fishermen catch enormous fish,
fins rotting from the diseased waters
we vacation in,
syringes stuck in the sand.

*

I have to admit I miss your letters
pungent from the chin-pei-mei
you crack and roll around your mouth,
the waitresses I know you lean against,
the quotes from Wittgenstein,
and somehow from the whales;
your letters, letter perfect from the rewriting.
I know you too well—
down to the angle of your hard-on.
Yes, the texture.
But why did I risk everything for the heat?
Was it because there was an alternative *everything*?
One that included hours of quoting Donne
instead of eating and drinking?
One where pleasure included difficult questions
about our individual futures and American literature?
As I write I lapse into—
here, here is my envelope, baby,
send me that letter.

*

Say it. Betrayal:
1.) springing from the uterus,

2.) rejecting the breast for a view of the world, new tastes,
    society,
3.) demanding the babysitter,
4.) demanding daddy,
5.) and later, replacing daddy with boyfriends.
Of course it's all point of view:
betrayal to one
development to the child.

*

Whenever I ask the neighbor's little girl
if she wants this or that
she says, *I want something else.*
Of course.

*

It's a relief, though not a conclusion, to visit you now
and not taste desire from teeth to gut.
To know we've come full circle:
to ensure tough standards in one another's work
even as I recall the afternoon I said no
and you threatened to tie me to your desk
then kicked me out shouting: save it for your fucking
    poems—
what was that strange music?

*

I could go on.

david henderson **EVERGREEN (A CHANT FOR THE TROPICAL RAIN FOREST)**

for Bob Marshall

EVER green evergreen Ever green EVER green evergreen evergreen
evergreen evergreen EVER green EVER green *evergreen evergreen*

for land developer's dreams
mahogany breakfronts   toothpicks   chopsticks

EVER green evergreen Ever green EVER green evergreen evergreen
evergreen evergreen EVER green EVER green *evergreen evergreen*

the death of deciduous broadleafed evergreen
for pastureland to graze diseased beef for export
for sleepy named housing hamlets   bowling alleys   7-Elevens
hamburgers as far as the eye can see   *evergreen evergreen*

tidy clusters of new england style homes   parcels and lanes
along the pan-american highway from amazonia to surfeit
economies of the northern mainlands
the same route as the slave ships
slave cattle slave land   slave trees slave citizens
endeavoring feverishly
evergreen

evergreen Evergreen
Ever Green Ever Green
Ever Green Ever Green
Ever Green *evergreen*

On the green stalked forest of the eternal rain
outside Fordlandia-Belterra   the ancient Amazonian
where conquistadors and free-market entrepreneurs
merge in history   destroying wealth for profit
destroying Indians for workers   destroying a planet for fortune

EVERGREEN Ever Green evergreen *evergreen* evergreen EVER green
broadleafed deciduous evergreen *evergreen*
broadleafed deciduous evergreen *evergreen*
sheltering the climate of the earth plane
sheltering the manatee, the jaguar, the spirits of the Arawak

Broadleafed deciduous evergreen *evergreen evergreen*

sheltering the Otomac of the lower Orinoco River Delta
sheltering the Conibo Indians

broadleafed deciduous evergreen
sheltering the Kuikuru, the Warao

broadleafed deciduous evergreen *evergreen*
sheltering the Bakairi, the Aquaruna

broadleafed deciduous evergreen *evergreen evergreen*
sheltering the Lacandon Maya Indians in Chiapas, Mexico

broadleafed deciduous evergreen *evergreen evergreen evergreen*
sheltering the Panare of Venezuela
sheltering the Chacobo of Bolivia

broadleafed deciduous evergreen evergreen EVERGREEN *evergreen*
sheltering the Banjaresco and Batak peoples of Sumatra,
                            the Penan of Borneo
sheltering the Binga pygmies, the Biri and Budu of the Ituri Forest

broadleafed deciduous
EVERGREEN evergreen evergreen *evergreen evergreen evergreen*
sheltering the campesinos of Amazonia
sheltering Henry Ford as he destroyed millions of acres
for Fordlandia, a rubber plantation that would never pay off
sheltering the successor to Fordlandia-Belterra, the beautiful earth
sheltering old Henry Ford ever greed *evergreed* EVERGREED

broadleafed deciduous evergreen
evergreen   evergreen   evergreen   evergreen   evergreen

and in every town city and hamlet of America rain forest homes
rain forest beef   fast food mahogany   6 football fields of rain forest
pastureland burned every 60 seconds to clear parcels for export
wood for charcoal for toothpicks for chopsticks for 99 cent
hamburgers as far as the eye can see football fields of fast food beef
rotting in the waste disposal systems of innocent towns and hamlets
along the roads and highways of California that wend high into the
North among the timberlands—redwoods conifers broadleafs
deciduous I see moving before me, beside me, behind me forever
evergreen   evergreen   evergreen   evergreen evergreen
EVERGREEN   EVERGREEN   EVERGREEN   EVERGREEN
EVERGREEN

POEM—MIGUEL PIÑERO

there is a procession for departed poet-playwright-santo
Miguel Piñero del lower east side

you were a fucking movie star!—Miky
"Short Eyes," "Fort Apache—The Bronx"
on television—"Miami Vice"
in one season they killed you twice

they scatter your ashes
all over the lower east side
like you say in your poem
and they even play a fucking videotape
of you reading the poem
as your ashes take to the breeze

and then they have a party, a feast for you
miguelito *cumbia para bailar*

and at this party
I saw a Latina play an African drum
along with the *cumbia* record
playing while everyone danced
and there were others playing
and others chanting in time
when the time came
drumming   chanting   dancing
at the same time
and then at once everything in the room
became another avenue of time
Santo Latino rhythms
on the fringe of the fringe
bridges between worlds
between black and white—Miky!
cumbia para bailar

bob holman **1990**

the taking of flash photos & use of recording devices of any kind,
including pens, pencils, eyes & ears, is strictly encouraged.

It's 1990
& Nelson Mandela is free!

& people are looking at each other
They're going like "Wha?"
& the other people are looking back
& they're going like "Duh?"
& finally, after this deep interaction,
You hear the wild cry of:
"Excuse me, could you tell me the time?"

What time is it?
It's Wake & Shake Time
It's Death of the Decade Time
It's Turn of the Century Time

220

It's Gyrate the Millennium Time
It's the End of Time
"At the sound of the tone it will be the End of Time"
It's 1 PF—it's Post Future
It's 1 PT—it's post time
It's Post Time!

It's 1990
& Nelson Mandela is free!

History's on fast forward
Make that double-fast fast forward
That's where you run past the Future so fast you're back in the Past
Sure, it's the End of History
So how come all we can think is, "What comes next?"
One minute you're rolling in ecstasy because the Berlin Wall is tumbling
    down,
The next you think, a reunited Germany! Oh God no!
Here come the storm troopers! & I'm Jewish (Well, my father was Jewish,
    so I'm not Jewish enough for the Jews—but I'm Jewish enough for the
    Nazis!)
One minute it's survival tactics & the next it's where's the angle

It's 1990
& Nelson Mandela is free!

& everybody wants a little glasnost
We know we want it cause we see Frank Zappa smoking cigarettes with
    Vaclav Havel, who 6 months ago was in jail, an artist whose work was
    banned by the government,
    now he's the President of Czechoslovakia
So stop in for free baby burritos at the corner bar
Except suddenly it's a karaoke sushi bar specializing in piranha sushi,
    & everybody here's a star,
Because you get to stand in front of the massive TV screen showing an
    MTV-minus-one video clip & sing along with the bouncing ball—
Except the words are all in Japanese and how can you sing "Feelings"
    with feeling in Japanese?
Kanjiru! Watashiwa, kanjiru!

It's 1990
& Nelson Mandela is free!

Communism has collapsed
At last the Russians get to wear the "Happy Face" masks & stand in line
    for a Beeg Mek
The Azerbaijanis are finally free so they get to beat up on the Armenians
Yugoslavia has decided to go back to indigenous cave tribe groupings
In Italy the Communists have met & decided they're not Communists
They're gonna change their name to be more appealing to the Socialists
    and the Greens
But for the time being they're calling themselves simply The Thing
The Thing! Personally, I'm planning to vote for—The Thing
For the time being For the time being
There's nothing left anymore except for the time being
You live your whole life for the time being
While meanwhile—there is no meanwhile

It's 1990
& Nelson Mandela is free!

"Play ethics by ear"
Let me out of here—but which way is out?
I'm a part of the *food chain,* isn't that enough?
At night I snuggle up close to the warm blue glow of images provided for
    everyone by a select few
Listen, they've packaged a shopping mall so small you can only visit it
    with a Video Walkperson, a cellular phone and a Visa card
The world is changing, but we're not
We're stuck in a commercial for Life
Trying to figure out who to give the money to
When, surprise! There is no money

It's 1990
& Nelson Mandela is free!

Señor Yuppie! Phone call for Señor Yuppie!
Pardon me, have to step over these homeless people to close on my Home
    Equity Loan, sorry

"Our bodies are still tender & not full-grown & the prospect of dying
frightens us all, but history calls us & we must go"
But where did they go, the Chinese students on their bicycles riding
towards the tanks at Tiananmen Square,
It can't happen here because it's already happened here
AIDS epidemic grabs Life till we don't even see it, gone like holes in heart,
Surrounded by ghosts, meeting Death in the middle of Life
While lesbians and gay men still have to fight for the right to love
& be sure to send your poetry to the Department of Official Bullshit to get
labelled
So it just has to be—time to get a Co-op!—
buy the place you used to rent, and still get to pay the rent
It's time to be a great parent—
work extra hours to pay for the best childcare while you're away
My kid is majoring in Nikes
Don't worry! Don't be happy! Explode!
The decision of birth from her body is solely & privately that of the woman
herself

It's 1990
& Nelson Mandela is free!

And everything used to be something else
Now it's *1,000* words a minute, & Times Square is just so much more
interesting
We're hellbent on something, sort of positive in a senile way
I can't even keep up with my life
It's a secret between me & my stunt double
Honey, I'm home—nuke me
Hop to it, ban cigarettes before it's too late
It's Earth Day again, if you can find any earth left
Paranoia used to be a psychosis, now it's a national pastime
Try the new fashion: the bare-breast style of no clothes at all, & it's not
cheap, either
& poetry is the Newspaper of the Future
Except it's locked out of the media
You know things! Think them!
There's optimism at the yacht club
The salad bar is open

Excuse me, isn't it time to mow your head?
I hate you! Thank you very much, have a nice day
They don't even know what it is, but they've already got an option on it
They're buying into it! Let's Not Make A Deal!

It's 1990
& Nelson Mandela is free!

& there's a guy at the microphone & he's yelling at me
& he's not using language that makes any sense from where I come from
It all rhymes & it all starts with capital letters
& it's all intense italics underlined three times in boldface headlines
& all I can remember is the part about
It's 1990
& Nelson Mandela is free!

& around the world a sense of possibility
As women slowly ease the old gray dinosaur poobahs from their penile
    thrones
The universal remote control is being passed into your hands

Zap it! Zap it!
Zap it! Zap it! Zap it!

It's 1990
& Nelson Mandela is free!

DISCLAIMER

We begin each SLAM! with a Disclaimer:

As Dr. Willie used to say,
We are gathered here today
because we are not gathered
somewhere else today, and

we don't know what we're doing
so you do—the Purpose of SLAM!
being to fill your hungry ears
with Nutritious Sound/Meaning Constructs,
Space Shots into Consciousness
known hereafter as Poems, and
not to provide a Last Toehold
for Dying Free Enterprise Fuck 'em
for a Buck'em Capitalism'em. We disdain
competition and its ally war
and are fighting for our lives
and the spinning
of poetry's cocoon of action
in your dailiness. We refuse
to meld the contradictions but
will always walk the razor
for your love. "The best poet
always loses" is no truism of SLAM!
but is something for you
to take home with you like an image
of a giant condor leering over
a salty rock. Yes, we must destroy
ourselves in the constant
reformation that is this very moment,
and propel you to write the poems
as the poets read them, urge you
to rate the judges as they trudge
to their solitary and lonely numbers,
and bid you dance or die between sets.

6 SHORT POEMS

Modern Lovers
In order to save the relationship
We will never see each other again

Night Fears
Everyone is in love
Except you

Ten Things I Do Every Day
Suicide

My Shirt
I like to put it on
My arms get long that way

Love Poems
I love poems

Goo Ahead
Goo ahead

ROCK'N'ROLL MYTHOLOGY

gotta ROCK'N'ROLL MYTHOLOGY
gotta total apocalypse pathology
got the most PostHysterical Poetry
& if it ain't comin' at you then it's breezed on by

got the heavy-duty political intent
got the worm farm free-form diamond noodle content
I got breezy ways & boppin' rays
when the word explodes the mother lode is where I'm at

& it's light here but you cannot see
doesn't matter anyway since you cannot breathe

you see the words mean, they're putting on the squeeze
that could strangle you—hey, what's that mean

say what he say
say what he say
he said he say
he said he said
say what he said
go on & say he said
what'd he say he said
that's what he said
that's what he said to say
he said to say

open up the book w/ yr finger hook
& scan it w/ yr television eyes
(televisionize televisionize televisionize televisionize)
you can stick it w/ yr eyes
stick out yr tongue & memorize
it's just you reading
the book is breathing
time's new dimension settles in

you are dancing on the edge of a thin thin dime
cause you are marching to the phone booth w/ a refugee line
you are baking in the kitchen when the walls cave
you are crawling through the desert w/ a loony rave
you are crossing all the x's for the love you save

hey who
hey who he
hey you
hey who you talkin' about, me?
hey listen to me, hey listen to me, hey listen to me, hey
listen to me
hey listen to me, hey listen to me, hey listen to me, hey
listen to me
I got to say what I say
to say what I see, I say

I don't see what you say
coming straight out of me
hey I'm coming straight out of you
why don't you try on that shoe
try it on for size
might give you a rise

cause everything I said it, I said it cause I read it
& everything I said it, I said it cause I read it
& everything I said it, I said it cause I read it
& everything I said it, I said it cause I read it

gotta debunk all of those trashy ideals
gotta reintegrate all the ideas you steal
"I understand" means I stand under yr heel . . .

woowie, hey man, you gotta light
because really I think yr getting just a little bit too
    heavy.
well I realize that. why don't you give me a break—& a
    half.
I could break yr arm. wouldn't do you any harm.
it's in the book, see. just take a look-see.
means what it says. says what it means.
"it's" only it. *see* what I *mean.*
I mean to say. there's nothing to *it.*
the book's overdue. so go renew it.

sing a song w/ a rock'n'roll band
play the guitar w/ a feather in yr hand
but the feather would rather fly than be plugged in
& the poetry just has to be freed from the pen

gotta gumbo anarchistic sensibility
& I do not exclude those who reject me
sail the manic Titanic awash in the wine-dark sea
where the language is the water & the rocks are poetry

gotta riptide w/ all hands going down
into hot pants where the love runs aground

gotta whamma jamma lamma w/ the low-down meltdown core
gotta relax the wax, Max, to de-rug the floor
gotta rocket in my pocket that can sock it more & more

& the central calmness of my Being is predicated quite simply
in the act of Seeing both within & without in a remarkable fashion
to which one must remark as a part of that act

gotta ROCK'N'ROLL MYTHOLOGY
gotta total apocalypse pathology
got the most PostHysterical Poetry
& if it ain't coming at you then it's breezed on by

got the heavy-duty political intent
got the worm farm free-form diamond noodle content
I got breezy ways & boppin' rays
& when—hey, is this the end?
where it begins
ooo what a cheap shot
what a piece of cake shot

well. I suppose y'd rather leave it w/ a little downward trail
o, a demitasse of denouement to daily detail
not a bad idea in the kitchen making almond cakes & pies
what a pleasant surprise
go ahead & take a taste
one tiny slice
how nice

patricia spears jones
SPANISH LESSON

la negra term of endearment
el blanco   dream of riches

one woman   *una mujer*
one man   *un hombre*

       tongues that begin to taste alike
tense geography
la bomba es la danza divina de los Africanos

white shoes ice the city dance floors sharp
that old pencil-thin moustache dream is dead
because *salsa es caliente y suave* and the men
want brass to blast away the crumbling buildings
the dope   the young dead carried away with candles
glowing

las chicas dulces trabajan   the garment district
cursing when necessary the others damned
in the push and pull

forgive the old pirate his coffers of rum—the *Ingles*
got more than they bargained for—the city pulsating
from borough to borough *con ritmos necesarios*

las mujeres lindas bochinchean on 14th street
about the one with his tongue hanging out
while Hector Lavoe lured the ladies
with a reel of promises made sweeter by his
Yo, no se
Yo, no se

Outlaw African breezes perfume the shining dance floors
speaking a language never sanctioned in the New World
libations poured from old pirates' stock
please the ancestors.   Here in North America where
Carmen Miranda and her mulatto progeny sashayed they stuff
across Hollywood camera eye
like comets christening the tropics

Si, como no?

SLY AND THE FAMILY STONE UNDER THE BIG TIT, ATLANTA, 1973

We waited and waited. Stoned for Sly. Southern sons and daughters
of the Rainbow Tribe. Under Georgia Tech's Big Tit.
Sucking in the marijuana, blowing out the heat.

Former debs with shag cuts and torn jeans; their good old boy
friends who used to hunt and fish, now glitter rocked, ready
with red painted nails and the latest Mott the Hoople tape
on their dashboards. Rebel boys back from Nam who used
to party with the brothers on the DMZ—that is, when they
were not beating the shit out of each other before the
VC struck up yet another victorious attack.

Sly's the perfect foil for this crowd.
"Sex Machine" and "Don't Call Me Nigger, Whitey" are
our anthems of choice. "I want to take you higher" just seems like
dessert. And of course, Sly is late.
Real late. Sly may not even be in the vicinity.
Like the airport.

Then the houselights actually dim.
The band comes out ragged. Like every musician from Provençal to
    Paducah,
they have to play, but their bodies droop. Their songs droop.
And Sly appears indeed to be stoned. By this time the audience
could care less. The show would've gone on. We could sing this shit.
We could take the stage and trash it. We could suck beers and colas
till the aluminum disappeared.

This is the end of the mighty rainbow. The brothers in huge Afros,
amulets and attitude stalk the round of the Big Tit, checking, checking
everybody out. And blonde boys with open paisley shirts parade their chest
    hair
and tight pants like so many peacocks, while we girls, just catch the
magnificent promenade.

Between the air outside and the air in here,
there are worlds galore. And we want it all.

The Rainbow Tribe picks up the mess of miscegenation, our cluttered
　　history and walks outside.
Into the Georgia night. Fucked up and full of spleen. Ripped off, someone
　　yells.
But we all had a good time. Really. Waiting for the California soul sound
to wash over us like an ocean wave, like something we've dreamed about,
　　but could not hear. Like a song of peace.

Sly Stone under the Big Tit, so pretty in that messy-colored California way.
Making music happen while the lights in his eyes dimmed.

And we too, wanted to make something work that couldn't.
The sex machine switched off.
The highs were plummeting.
An avalanche of choices awaiting all of us.

But all we wanted was to party. To mess around with the mess around.
To shift ourselves out of the Georgia sun-stroked days
and turn into each other's arms as Family,
and loving always loving the way we thought the world should be.

r. cephas jones
GOD, MINGUS AND MYSELF
for Charles Mingus

Mingus the prophet with a bass

Working fingers on her
(the only woman he really loved)
like a master shiatsu
When Mingus plays

I hear an extension of life itself
the whole outdoor scene
the sky
moon
sun
universe

Bursting with sounds
like the voices of the elements
clashing together
changing the velocity of the winds

Labeled genius
crazy at Bellevue
(the third day)
in the mental ward
he wrote a song entitled

                  "All the Things You Could Be by Now
                  if Sigmund Freud's Wife Was Your Mother"

Beyond jazz musician
a composer
a great composer
strangled
by *this thing*
called jazz
talent wasted
in the name of jazz

                  "Tote that downbeat, win that pole, hope I
                  get a mention, before I'm too old"

When I heard
Mingus play
the sounds
were forever
etched
in the rhythm
of my life

When Mingus plays
the spirit
always
sits in on the set
cats putting
major 7ths w/ minor 7ths
playing a fourth
away from the key
droppin bar lines
. . . and stuff like that

When I hear Mingus
I hear God
Buddha
Muhammed
Christ
I know
there's a higher power
in the circle
surrounding each beat
notes are played
anywhere in that circle
giving a feeling of space
notes falling
anywhere in the circle
the original feeling
for the beat
isn't changed
When I hear Mingus
When I hear Mingus . . . God
When I hear Mingus

I realize that my powers
to commune with you
aren't any less today
than in Christ's time or before
                    "Seek and Ye Shall Find"
If you don't
seek Mingus

and you will be close
'cause

When Mingus plays
I can conceive
the ocean
which feeds
the lake
the clouds
which feed
the ocean

My potential
for understanding
truth
the competence
which comes from
truth
is unlimited

Play Mingus . . .
Play Mingus . . .

And I'll stand
as a monument
of human accomplishment
rather than
the remains
of human destruction
Play Mingus . . .
Play Mingus . . .
Mingus play . . .

Let your sounds
forever shatter
the cement
that has
for years
enclosed

the lost
cultural traditions
rituals
family life
inferiority of a people

Play Mingus . . .
Play . . .
Play your prophetic visions
Play me some moral integrity
Slap me some intellectual acuity
Bow me some technological know-how
that I may explore the universe

*play*mingus*playplay*mingus*mysticmingus*divine
fingers*mingus*minguspretty*fingers*mingus*playplay*
*mingus*play*play*me*god*mingus*myself*godplay
*mysticdivine*playmystic*pretty*mingusgod*play*my
self*mingus*myself*divine*mingus*mystic*fingers*god*
mingusmingus*me*pretty*fingersplay*divine*play*
*play*mingus*me*mingus*myself*playmeplay*pretty*
prettyplay*pretty*fingers*god*mingusplayme*mingus*
divine*mystic*mingusgod*mingus*playmysticfingers
*god*fingers*mingusplaypretty*god*myself*mingus
meplaymingus*play*mingus*playgod*play
divine*mystic*fingers*god*fingers*play*mingusplay*
mingusmingusplaymeplayplayplayplaymingus

Mingus
Play
God
For Me

eliot katz # DINOSAUR LOVE

On the Museum of Natural History's 4th floor
I greeted my old friend:
"Hey, T. Rex! Long time, no see!"
My buddy flashed his killer teeth:
"Over two years, E. Katz,
I missed you."

Surprised, I asked, "You missed me?
I didn't know dinosaurs had emotions.
Rexy, did you know love?"

Rexy sighed: "I knew love
    not as humans can
but as humans do:
    love of self
    and love of finding something weaker
        to pounce upon.
E. Katz, can your species be saved
    by love's possibilities?"

"Rexy," I answered, "you haven't lost
your ability
to ask the tough question.
Let me ask you something we humans
have been curious about for centuries.
How did you die?"

"I don't know.
One day I looked around
and I wasn't there."

WHAT'S THAT CLICKING ON OUR TELEPHONE LINE?

Say what? Can't hear you under all that clicking!

Who, what, how, where is that noise coming from?

Could New Jersey Bell be that angry with me for forgetting to cross
    my *t*'s?

Could it be the bowl of homemade chicken soup I spilled last week
    eating its way into the copper wires?

The ping pong balls I slammed finally getting their revenge?

An old friend with newest microwave technology mad I forgot
    a birthday card?

"It's the FBI, stupid! The CIA, stupid! COINTELPRO never really
    ended!" a friend yells from the other end of the line.

Could anyone view a peaceful activist poet from New Brunswick
    an honest threat?

It's much more likely my partner organizing events in the new
    student movement and her number on too many blue-inked
    brochures . . .

Another friend yells: "They've got new digital laser technology! It
    doesn't click anymore, just picks up key words and the coffee on
    your breath!"

Maybe it's paranoia spreading through nervous system to my left
    ear?

Oh no! Now it's jumped out the receiver! It's headed for my throat!
    Christine, help me! It's choking me! Hang it up! Hang it up!
    There . . . now . . . thanks . . . that's better . . .

Could it be Dr. King sending messages to activists across America
    that it'll take more than a holiday to make up for his bedroom being
    bugged?

The spirit of Karen Silkwood trying to tell us where the power
    company and FBI hid the documents?

Infiltrated daycares, soup kitchens, health clinics, artists in 1990
    wondering in Morse code where the First Amendment is
    hiding?

Children in Thomas Paine's treehouse with hammers and nails
    trying to build on America's most democratic foundations?

238

Could it be someone running a test of my conflict-avoidance
    mechanisms? "If this had been a real emergency, you would
    have been told to stay tuned to the nuclear radioactive static on
    your melting TV set . . ."
The liquor companies mad I haven't watered their wallets in years?
Maybe UFO creatures finally got the message I'd like to call a
    meeting?
Maybe whales have learned to sing into the telephone lines?
Could it be the fur coats? The oil spills? The tritium? Atmospheric
    test fallout? Earth shaking from tests underground? Benzene in
    the Perrier? Solar energy cells clicking for attention?
Hey boss! You know my number . . . no need to click!
Sure, I remember that ridiculous night at the bar! No need clicking
    to remind me!
Could it be old relationships that didn't work while I still needed
    to grow up, now breaking in to say "I told you so"?
A common psych-intervention technique to actually remind me
    there's still a long way to self-actualize?
It sounds like thundering reindeer! My childhood chemistry set!
    The car battery I recharged right before crashing the car! The
    seventh grader in front of me grinding his teeth!
How am I doing on the sound blotch test?
Could it be the students murdered at Kent State? Jackson State?
Could it be Fred Hampton? The Wobblies? Haymarket Square?
    Birmingham 1963? Chicago 1968?
SDS? SNCC? CPUSA? The Black Panther Party? Redstockings?
    American Indian Movement? Amiri Baraka's Spirit House?
    Allen Ginsberg's "Howl"? Plowshares? The Maryknoll
    Sisters? New Jewish Agenda?
Could it be Malcolm X fighting armed designer white sheets sewn
    by paid informants?
Abbie Hoffman on the run after frame-up #165?
Antennaheads tracking Angela Davis across radar U.S. highways
    and bloodstained U.S. byways?
Movement women and men of every color being splintered into a
    million different glass factions by forged letters typed on a D.C.
    bureau machine?
Could it be an agent's loud boots chasing shadows at CISPES
    regional office?

Has the ultimate computer virus gone haywire?

Could it be the weight of a hundred thousand pages gathered on civil
liberties lawyer Frank Wilkinson?

Echoes of the attempted assassination of Peter Bohmer organizing to
protest the '72 Republican Convention?

The keys clicking on the typewriters of *off our backs,* a feminist
journal labeled "armed & dangerous—extremists" by FBI
in 1973?

Did someone discover I once read Brian Glick's *War at Home:
Covert Action Against U.S. Activists and What We Can Do
About It?*

Could it be Joe McCarthy's ghost sizzling in the afterlife?

J. Edgar Hoover's brain poked in the lowest dead circle?

William Casey's brain sorry it ran out at an inopportune moment?

Could it be the bugged jail cells of New Haven, Connecticut?

Ten thousand dead critics clicking that my poems are too political?

Could it be the memories I'm not yet ready to remember?

The timeclock keeping track of Earth's surviving seconds?

Dorothy clicking her heels, Toto there is no Kansas anymore?

Could it be the deathclick of an aging empire and the inspiration
for a new democracy?

Could it be I've forgotten to take the potato out of my ear?

roland legiardi-laura
TRICKSTER RABBIT

I am your trickster rabbit
I accept this role in society
      with gracious humility
I will wreak havoc forever on you all
I will shit on the table of my host
      while singing grateful praise of the meal
I will bleed the hand that bites me

I am trickster rabbit
      the crusader of rags

I will rewrite all the messages on your fortune
                     cookies
instructing you to dial ecstasy for the
                     dialectic
I am the furry little clawed foot
     you keep in your back pocket
     the one that cuts deep into your butt
     every time you sit down too fast
I am your Uncle Steve and Crazy Eddie
     if you undersell me I'll break
     that panasonic coda-phone over
          your head
I am trickster rabbit,
                 I'll hop down your
throat and suck your lungs dry . . .
             you'll spit and cough and yell
                     Uncle.
I am your neighbor who plays trumpet and
             tap dances and yodels
and when you complain yells art in your
                  face.
I am the silent deadly digital watch
     that tells you the date, time, lunar phase
        and astrological sign.
     My tick is your tick
        tickless cold dead feather rubbing up against the
     soft spot on the inside of your left nostril.
I am your therapist and lover
             curing you once and for all of your
             fears of riding up in elevators at the
             Hyatt Regency
I am your dance teacher
     explaining the secrets of the pelvis
     your disks all slipped
        you lie prostrate before me
        while I demonstrate the
boogaloo, the twist, the shimmy and the most mysterious
mouse.
I am your Clint Eastwood you are my
     Sunshine, my only sunshine.

I come to you disguised as rabbit stew,
        Lapin Roti,
all ears, pink furry cutesy ears
        my carrot in hand.
        I ask you to tell me all
without hesitation. "What's up, Doc!!!"
    I am your conductor on the L
        Canarsie line who tells you
that because of construction, that's right
        new construction the train you are
            on will pass its regularly scheduled
            stop on Bedford Avenue and a changeover
            has been arranged for you at Montauk Point
I am your cab driver
            your museum curator
            your arts council auditor
I am judgment day in a plastic no break no mess
            bottle.
I am lead guitar for the Clash
            I am page 74 of The German Ideology
            and babies are my business
                my only business
I go to sleep with you naked
            and wake up wrapped in the
                biggest pampers you ever saw
I am Trickster Rabbit, Ricochet Rabbit,
        Crusader Rabbit and Bugs Bunny.
I am a rotten Easter egg on the White House
        lawn
painted day glo brown
I'm hung like a guinea pig and
            I like to watch.
When you're walking home late, about
            to enter Tompkins Square Park
            I am the street lamp that
                flickers—
'Whitey you a sucker, your ass is mine
            gimme your wallet.'
I am your wallet with your YMHA

membership card   your plastic Eye and
                Ear Infirmary card
and a faded picture of Roy and Trigger
            the wonderhorse
        I am your green, sweaty crumbling
            wallet with twenty-two
dollars, a cancelled check and two ticket
        stubs to the Kitchen.
I am your trembling hand that wants to
            take the mugger's knife away from him
            do a back flip, land on his shoulders
            and whisper gently into his ear
"Home James or I'll slice the smile right outta
                your face."
I'm your panic button that says 'no'
I'm your logic button that says 'wooah'
I'm your belly button that says 'ho ho ho'
            I am your trickster rabbit's foot
            pressed between your wallet
            and your ass
            I am the font of wisdom
the hole that passes gas
You know now I have power
                over you
I am your report card
            your telephone bill
            the meter maid
            the Good Humor man
I am a goddamn fudgesicle in July
I am your change of address card
I am the seven arms of Shiva
the six hammers of Thor
the hot lips of Hera
the fox lock on your door.
I am a bag of Pepperidge Farm cookies
and a quart of milk,
Dylan's born-again christianity
and a dress made of blue silk.
I am heart of rabbit

and my pump will never stop
I am heart of rabbit
hop hop hop hop
   hop hop hop
      hop.

MANAGUA MIDNIGHT

We walk back to our sweaty cots
you, soaked, carry with you your empty bottle
        of Flor de Caña
with a lime stuffed in your cheek like a tumor.
It's late
and there's no political significance left
to this shabby little
shit hole of a country
the only thing important here you say
is the hole.
You think the hole is important
as we walk you almost fall
into an open sewer duct before us
a twenty-foot drop in the middle of a street
at the bottom a cracked grill soaks in rust
and slime
like a rotten waffle
waiting for more human syrup.
Then there are the holes made by bullets
shot years ago into walls,
the holes in the tops of mountains
letting out a hot white smoke that burns the eyes.
Then there are the holes in children's shirts
so frayed
they cannot bear the tug of new thread.
Then there are the holes you saw

in the bodies of dead soldiers
shot clean through
so that you can see light on the
          other side bloodless holes
and there are the holes that people dig
so they can have something to throw themselves into
when the bombs begin to fall
and the holes left in newspapers
that we fill in here up north
with our own black hole of words
ink upon ink upon ink
until the letters blur and smudge
and the pages become so thick with words
they stick to each other
gooey lumps of dark meaning.
And there are the holes
that were once streets
where the earthquake swallowed a building
the holes in the lakes where the boat sank
the holes in the earth where guns are buried
the holes dug to make a second transoceanic canal
and the holes made to plant coffee trees
and the holes where land mines and mortar shells exploded
the holes where people shit and piss
the holes where people go to drink water
and the hole down the barrel of a gun.
No there is no political significance
in this shabby little shit hole of a country.
Only holes, as we sit out the night under
a rum-soaked
brown moon.
And you stare at me with your one remaining eye.

nancy mercado MILLA

Mi abuela, Puerto Rico

Milla lived eons ago
When sandals pounded dirt roads
Blazing hot under palm tree lined skies.
Milla's long dark hair flowed side to side,
Glistened in the noon light.
Mahogany skinned, she shopped;
Platanos, yucas, a bark of soap.
Milla worked,
Striking clothes against wooden boards,
Gathering wood for evening meals,
Feeding chickens, hogs, dogs,
And roasters at dawn.
Milla traveled only once
To Chicago.
A color-faded photograph serves as document.
Smiles and thousands of hugs
For the grandchildren on a park bench.
Milla's a century old
And still remembers every one of us
Even those left over in the U.S.
She still carries a stick
Certain of her authority
Over four generations.
Milla outlived two world wars,
Saw the first television,
The first electric bulb in her town,
Hitler, segregation,
The Vietnam War,
And Gorbachev.
Milla can speak of
The turn of the century land reforms,
Of the blinded enthusiasm
For a man called Marín
And the mass migration of the 1950's.

Milla can speak of her beloved husband,
Sugar cane cutter for life.
She can speak of the love of a people,
Of the pain of separation.
Milla can speak of the Caribbean Ocean,
The history of the sun and sand
And the mystery of the stars.
Milla maintains an eternal candle lit
Just for me.
Milla will live for all time.

JUANITA

Mi tia, Puerto Rico

Juanita between sugar canes
Peeking through a wonderful face,
Splendid eyes,
Beautifully shaped nose & lips
To speak melodies with.
Beaming bronze skin,
Perfection of an earthly figure
Strolling through the plaza square.

Juanita
Breathing life into the dead,
Medium of light that makes us all so happy.
Materializing miracles from impossibilities,
Providing food from soil,
Creating homes from ashes,
Teaching tolerance by living.

Juanita
The eye against harm,
Keeper of the key
Kneading dough for fried patties,

Tending to crippled children,
To the salt of the earth
Beneath a warm sea breeze in the evening.

Juanita
Mending broken souls all her worldly days,
Providing smiles at every end,
Lending breasts for pillows to the brokenhearted.

Juanita
Hummingbirds at her feet.

jose montoya
THE UNIFORM OF THE DAY

          Strong and bold
They came—alone, in teams,
          Droves—early on
To sociologize us an' to
          Weaken us

          One day
There they wuz—in the Barrio
          Studying th' points, us—
Y nosotros estudiando el punto
          Scrutinizing as well
This army of scholars wearing
          Corduroy and clipboards
          And audacity huffing and puffing
          Crooked briar pipes
An' ours of deer horn, stone
Or clay and wood even—
Good pipes, good smoke I miss.
          And I miss th' girls

That loved boys, women
Men, and went on
Some even to graduate school.

. . . and my colega who has become
Invisible on campus who I miss
From old action days now I see
On Saturday mornings strolling
There lonely in th' uniform.
      Corduroy jacket with elbow patches
      Clutching a pipe, brow
      Furrowed deep, suffering—
      Yet, digging his latest
      Findings, enjoying his
      Research, walking his
      Cocker spaniel.

. . . why is that sound so succulent?
Spaniel—Spaniard—Hispanic, Hispaniel?
      Well, every uniform should have
      A dog—I myself walk the Derelict Dog

An 'en there's my own trapos—
My uniform de la calle—boogies
(Baggies) khakis o gabardine o
Sharkskins, gauchos en el
Summer, workshirts for th' cold
Blue, cotton or Pendleton
And if colder my blue Sir Guy jacket,
Calcos del fil
Or Rockport biscuits
For diabetic feet y mi tapa
Stetson Beaver stingy brim
Or watch cap!
      Now if that ain't a uniform!

And how absurd that
Uniform must look on
Campus!

As out of place as
Corduroy and briar
Pipes in th' Barrio

. . . but that's what the contract
Called for, muy conformes
        In uniform.

EL SOL Y 'L ROVATO LOCO

So there I was
Soaring like poets are wont
To soar
Above and beyond th' trees
And the palms
Going ZOOM
Straight al Sol.

        (Que suave ser poeta, jefita!)

When on impact
El Sunjefe Solchief
Exploded—Virtualmente,
Aclarando todo, claro!
Y en la revolcada
I caught glimpses down below
And saw giant
Erector-set-vatos-rovatos
Walk dance energy
Over hills and vales
And mountains
And then I felt
An enormous sorrow
For those children down there.

(Que joda ser poeta, 'ama!)

But the palms
And the pine trees
And the children down below
They just looked up
Past th' metal warriors
Only to see
Battle-ready gunships
Helicoptering south!
South! right under
Mine bruised
And the Solchief's own
Noses!

gavin moses   P O I S O N

first heard of the infection
in jr. high school back in
ardmore, pennsylvania joey b said he
read somewhere in central africa there
wuz a sickness men got that cld not be cured
years later, in nyc papers read the infection
wuz from green african jungle monkeys
wuz told our govt wuz testing
new germ warfare on people of color
as monkeys
then, heard only white men got the infection
that it came from haiti from white men who slept with ducks
sheep and island boys
then some Black people in my building started coughing
incessantly, started going to prayer services with me
on wednesday nights, would come over and tell me their
his-stories, once outta fear, i boiled a cup after one with
the infection drank from it, then threw it away. wuz afraid
the infection would bleed through its pores like poison.

BOOMERANG

Walking down 9th ave.
depressed bout a love
gone one hour past despair,
a six-foot-three nappy-headed
prostitute, in broken-down brown heels
approaches, "Need a date?"
No, but thanks, I said, waiting
for the light to flash its
emerald eye.
"Where are you going?"
Home.
"Can I come?"
Well—
What you need, she said, *is to*
be good to you and treat yourself.
She meant to her. I understood it
to mean spend more time on me.
Love you, I retorted. Catching her
reflection offguard in my eyes
she smiled like a kid comin' out the
circus holdin' a balloon in one hand,
cotton candy in the other, thinkin' bout
eatin' some ice cream. The light winked.
She turned the corner on cue. We both needed
to hear what we said to each other. What we said
to each other, we needed someone to say to us.

MOONDANCE

E-lec-tric candles flickering in the eyes
of this concrete pumpkin-patch metropolis,
dark as mo-lasses tonight.

giant jack o'lanterns
giving up the ghost, one-by-one;
from the seaport to Shea
every window has a different drama,
every dreamer holds a separate view.

walking around with their heads down
Walking Around with their Heads DOWN,
folks coming back from going nowhere
(full of people all into nothing)
walking around with their heads down;

cold as Aunt Marie's living room now.
A spray of moonlight does a ripply jig
on the Hudson. don't know how to get off
this planet without pain. Harlem preacher

shouted, "If you quit in the middle of the
journey, God can't take you through."
Shoot, you can light a candle and still be in the dark.

Yep, black as mo-lasses tonight,
mischief lines these tar-paved streets;
keep hearing Ruth Brown singing "Mama, He
Treats Your Daughter Mean." Being a woman
is being in prison, Lisa said,—cause you
can't go anywhere at night alone—and

Donna's 7-year-old daughter doesn't think of
lovers embracing when she sees the moon's full-
bloated belly, she imagines all the men in
Philadelphia are beating their wives.

Phew, river stinks worse than a week-old turtle
bowl, I'm sleeping through this one, the street
can hold its own. Then there's tomorrow.

The sun will be stronger than 100-proof whiskey,
luminous poxed-pearl postured in nocturnal pale-ness,
you can have this hallowed eve. Ain't nothing in the
street—but the street.

louis reyes rivera   MARIANITA

wrapped
inside the print of cotton flowers
those rose hips, they
       dip & lift
       rise & drop
       lilt & sway
& i, jose antonio
caught
in the fragrance of her rolling web
watch
her toes toss the dust
down the mountain road

     "MARIANITA?"
             i want to call
   "esta hecha!"
             i want to say
but i, jose antonio vargas
drool through the lisp
in the water of my mouth
     as i wait
constricted in the shadows of the sun

    who is the sinner
    quien es el pecador
    the root & the cause:
        ES MI ALMA QUE GRITA CON AMOR!

my loins bewildered
olive leaves tremble from the kiss
as her hips greet
each
branch
on their way to la marqueta en la
plaza de mi pueblo en mi corazón

my loins
taken in
jut / jerk / trek
soft / silk / neck
shift the plate of wood
on your green black/green black
strands of grease & hair
                    "Sigue, nena! Oye! Como vas!"
balance bananas, Marianita
the way you
swing sway   twist turn
pull & . . . shudder me

                Guineos verdes son for sale, today!
y yo, jose antonio vargas de gonzalez y colon
no se hacerlo bien
                "Marianita?"
can i caress the winding road
to your ripe brown bosom
sift the slopes past the curves
into your young green heart
                "Por donde vas, Marianita?"
she does not hear
pero my flower is your stroll
you bathe in the river of my blood
tingle the winds that sing
against the leaves
but i remain
lurched
in the shadow of your glance

your rays. mi cielo
they both cry out:
          "CONJURE US A MAN, MARIANITA
               WHO LOVES HIMSELF"

pero como te vas a meterte asi
con las manos tan suerta
sin saber: quien soy yo

I. Yo.   seed of an invader wasted by greed
         fruit from a comely womb snatched in another land
I. Yo.   hombre who sweats from the shade of the bowl
         on your face holding bananas with a cool dry
         breeeeeze touched by your touch
pero yyyyyyy, quien soy yo
pero yyyyyyyyy, who am i
pero yyyyy, how can i
pero yyyyyyyyyyyy

                 ¡Marianita!

PORTRAIT: DOGS AT THE WELL

David's dogs were at the well again.

Well, it was actually a fountain
in the middle of a small town square
watersprays
upward bound
clean paved streets
one car seen
& a crop of strays
lazily surrendering to heat.

Well, actually this scene takes place in Maine
where even when it's hot it's cool
like a breeze welcomed in pursuit of sunrays
beating gainst the ground.

Except for these five dogs
balled around the fountain wall
no one would complain . . . just watch
as that man who cares for strays
leads them strolling to the water of the fountain

& sits beside the edge of concrete slope
feeling the spray of water on his back.

Five dogs of different breeds no one else had wanted
curled up or stretched out loud
lying at his feet;
his eyes ahead & staring off
& wondering what next
as issue & complaint
before the walls & wells & halls
of Portland's city council
forcing condominiums to rise around
his beat up shack shackled at the edge of town.

But you can't take my home
you can't shack me out
I don't pay rent
& don't earn work
& these five dogs
are all the friends I have.

& behind them all—
behind the well or fountain
behind the dog reaching up to drink
behind the others laid around
behind the man sitting on the brink
there was this other standing tall,
a blue suit badge staring hard
like marines on guard
left elbow arched
hand on hip
like a woman on the edge
of a fussing cuss
right arm dangling near a gun
& waiting . . . just waiting for a smirk—
yeah.
The dogs were at the well
like anarchy circulating blood
& stretching discord's leafless pamphlets

without a care.
Ka-plow
like thunder sound
David staring at the clouds of raindrops
clearing both the air & plaza
in the center of a small town square
where the well was actually a fountain
near a sign that often bled:

> No dogs
> No loitering allowed!

Actually, there was only one dog there.
The others were merely elements of life
passing through. . . .

luis j. rodriguez MEETING THE ANIMAL IN WASHINGTON SQUARE PARK

The acrobats were out in Washington Square Park,
flaying arms and colors: The jokers and break
dancers, the singers and mimes. I pulled out
of a reading at New York City College
and watched a crowd gather around a young man jumping
over 10 garbage cans from a skateboard.
Then out of the side of my eye I saw someone
who didn't seem to belong here, like I didn't
belong. It was a big man, six feet and more,
with tattoos on his arms, back, stomach and neck.
On his abdomen were the words in huge Old English
lettering: Hazard. I knew this guy, I knew that place.
I looked closer. It had to be him. It was—Animal.
From East LA. World heavyweight contender,

the only Chicano from LA ever ranked
in the top ten of the division. The one who
went toe-to-toe with Leon Spinks and even
made Muhammad Ali look the other way.
Animal! I yelled. "Who the fuck are you?" he asked,
a quart of beer in his grasp, eyes squinting.
My name's Louie—from East LA. He brightened. "East LA!
Here in Washington Square Park? Man, we everywhere!"
The proverbial what part of East LA came next.
But I gave him a shock. From La Gerahty, I said.
That's the mortal enemies of the Big Hazard
gang of the Ramona Gardens Housing Projects.
"I should kill you," Animal replied. If we were in
LA, I suppose you would—but we in New York City, man.
"I should kill you anyway."
Instead he thrust out his hand with the beer and offered
me a drink. We talked: What happened since he stopped fighting.
The time I saw him at the Cleland House boxing arena
looking over some up and coming fighters. How
he had been to prison, joined a prison gang.
"Soy soldado azul—a blue soldier." How he
ended up homeless in New York City, with a couple
of kids somewhere. And there he was, with a mortal
enemy from East LA, talking away.
I told him how I was now a poet, doing a reading
at City College, and he didn't wince or look
absurd at me. Seemed natural. Sure. A poet
from East LA. That's the way it should be. Poet
and boxer. Drinking beer. Among the homeless,
the tourists and acrobats. Mortal enemies.
When I told him I had to leave, he said "go then,"
but soon shook my hand, East LA style, and walked off.
"Maybe, someday, you'll do a poem about me, eh?"
Sure, Animal, that sounds great.
Someday, I'll do a poem about you.

HUNGRY

My wife left me, taking the two kids
and everything
but the stereo, TV and a few dishes.
Later in this squalid hour,
I began an affair
with my wife's best friend.
But she already had three kids and no man
and talked about love and marriage
and I didn't know how to get out of it,
being also an alcoholic.
Soon I couldn't pay the rent
so I kept getting notices in death tones,
insinuating broken bones or whatever.
My friend Franco helped me sneak
out of the place.
Franco and me arrived in the middle of the night,
and loaded what I had left onto a pickup truck.
I would come back
on other late nights to get the mail.
And the woman, who was alone with three kids
and looking for a husband,
kept leaving notes,
and I kept throwing them away.
But the hunger had just begun.
My only property of value was a 1954
red Chevy in mint condition.
It had the original skirts, whitewalls
and chrome hood ornament.
What a prize!
I never wanted to part with it,
even as layoff slips and parking tickets
accumulated on the dashboard,
even when I found myself living with Mom and Dad
and the '54 Chevy got stashed out in back.
But the hunger and the drinking

and looking for love in all the wrong faces
blurred into a sort of blindness.
I stared out the back window,
at that red Chevy,
and thought how it resembled a large steak
with egg yolks for headlights.
No, no, I couldn't do it;
I couldn't turn my back on it now.
The days withered away
and again I looked out that window,
with Mom yelling behind me
about getting a job,
and I could taste that last scotch,
that last carnitas burrito,
and perhaps take in the stale scent
of a one-room apartment somewhere.
Then the hunger became a fever.
The fever a pain in my head.
And as soon as some dude with 200 bucks came along,
I sold it. God almighty,
I sold my red Chevy!
For 200 bucks!
For nothing, man.
Oh, I thought it would help
stop my wife's face
in every reflection;
her friend's staring out of my coffee cup.
That it would help hold me
for more than a week,
and end the curses
ringing in my ear.
I sold it! My red Chevy.
Prized possession.
200 bucks.
Gone forever.
Days later, the 200 bucks spent,
I was still hungry.

sapphire   IN MY FATHER'S HOUSE

1.

together alone one night we were watching t.v.
& my father shot to his feet as *The Star-Spangled Banner*
hailed the network's last gleaming.
he stood at attention saluting the red & white striped
tongue gyrating on the t.v. screen.
"Daddy," I said, "you don't have to do that."
"I know I don't have to but I want to," he said.

my mother slipped on her sweater & disappeared.
we rolled loose to corners of the room.
buttoned in cold; bones of children knitting shadows in the dark,
dreaming of pullovers, cardigans, cashmere & mohair.
"She never wanted children," he explained.

he told me his father put his foot on his neck
& beat him until his nose bled.
he left home when he was 14,
an Aries full of blind light
trying to wrap barbed wire around the wind.

my father bent a piece of rubber hose
into a black ellipse, then taped the ends together
to make a handle. he beat me with this.

I was grown, in my own apartment,
when the cat sprang up on my record player
claws gouging Bob Marley's *Burning & Lootin'*.
I snatched that cat off the record player
slammed it to the floor,
beat skin, teeth, skull with my fists,
tied its legs together & yanked its tail back
exposing the anus, tiny fist curled pink.
I picked up a burning cigarette from the ashtray

262

& started to stick it up that cat's asshole—
something stopped me.

spliced between the blind night of a forgotten scream
it would be ten years before I remembered
my father breaking open my asshole.
the memory would walk up behind me like bad news,
as unbelievable as Mayor Goode dropping a bomb on Osage Avenue,
as unbelievable as doctors betting on how much oxygen it would take
to blind a baby in an incubator then turning up the oxygen to see.
it would come like the nurse in the Tuskegee syphilis night,
basket full of magic light, lies & placebos.
it would come counter-clockwise like bent swastikas.
it came just when I was learning to stand, to speak.
it grabbed me by my knees & dragged me down the years
stopping where I disappeared 35 years ago.

    2.
we had a tree,
an avocado tree.
first my father painted it
then he killed it.
even before he decided
to cut the postage stamp size
swimming pool
into the lawn,
he downed the tree.
I was gone then,
gone long & gone far.
but denial & amnesia
made me send father's day & birthday cards.
in one card I asked,
as I rarely did,
for something:
some avocadoes.
I said send me
some avocadoes
from the tree, Daddy.

I got $20 in the mail
& instructions to go
buy some avocadoes.
he didn't tell me
what he had done
to the tree.

3.
I say you raped me
you say it's a damn lie

you remember being a boy
running after rabbits in Texas
fast as the grass
tall as the sun

crazy slut of a life leaves you with 4 kids & no wife,
3 gone bad
1 just like you:
an achiever
a star
a homeowner
a heterosexual
an athlete
who buys a Mercedes
for his wife & a Porsche
for himself.
a son shining
finally like you.
you fill the rooms
with him,
blue ribbons
& trophies fall
off the wall,
but strange whispers crawl
off the pages of the
local colored tabloid
to *The New York Times:*
they say

this youngest boy rapes,
humiliates women.
he is tried,
but acquitted—
you know how
women lie.

4.

at 14 I cooked, cleaned
no one asked how school was going,
what I needed or dreamed.
I had to have dinner ready at 5:30 p.m.
biscuits cornbread ribs chicken meatloaf
I was cooking dinner one night
& my father offered to help me
as he sometimes did,
relieving me of some small task.
that night he offered to set the table.
the food was hot, ready to eat,
my little brother had just come in
from football practice,
I went to sit down at the table
& stopped shocked.
my father had only set a place
for himself & my little brother.
"I thought you had already eaten," he offered.
I made no move to get another plate,
neither did he.
he served his son
the food I had prepared.
they ate,
I disappeared,
like the truth
like the tree.

5.

I crawl from under
childhood's

dark table,
black tree
bleeding
spiralling to apogee,
broke doll yawning:
ma ma   ma ma
childhood consumed.
black moon
rising,
eating up
the sky,
a survivor—
heading home,
to my own house.

WILD THING

And I'm running,
running wild,
running free,
like soldiers down
the beach,
like someone
just threw me
the ball.
My thighs pump
thru the air
like tires
rolling down
the highway
big & round
eating up the ground
of America
even tho I never been any

further than 42nd Street.
Below that is as
unfamiliar as
my father's face,
foreign as the smell of
white girls' pussy,
white girls on the bus
white girls on TV.
My whole world is
black & brown & closed
till I open it
with a rock,
christen it with
blood.
BOP BOP
the music
pops thru me
like electric shocks,
my sweat is a river
running thru my liver
green with hate.
My veins bulge out
like tomorrow,
my dick is
the Empire State Building.
I eat your fear
like a chimpanzee
on its 6th bunch of green bananas
ow!
ow whee ow!
My sneakers glide off
the cement like
white dreams
looking out at the world
thru a cage of cabbage
& my mother's fat,
hollering don't do this
& don't do that.
I scream against the restraint

of her big ass sitting on my face
drowning my dreams in sameness.
I'm scared to go
it hurts me to stay.
She sits cross-legged in front of the TV
telling me no
feeding me
clothing me
bathing me in her ugliness
high high in the sky
18th floor of the projects
her welfare check buys me $85 sneakers
but can't buy me a father.
She makes cornbread from Jiffy box mix
buys me a new coat
$400, leather like everybody else's.
I wear the best man!
14 karat gold chain
I take off before I go wildin'.
Fuck you nigger!
Nobody touches my gold!
My name is Leroy
L-E-R-O-Y
bold gold
I got the goods
that make the ladies
young & old
sign your name across my heart
I want you to be my baby
Rapper D
Rapper G
Rapper I
me me *me*!
my name is lightning
across the sky.
So what I can't read
you spozed to teach me
you the teacher
I'm the ape

black ape
in white sneakers
hah hah
I rape
rape
rape
I do the wild thing
I do the wild thing.
My teacher asks me
what would I do
if I had 6 months
to live.
I tell her I'd fuck her,
sell dope & do the wild thing.
My thighs are locomotives
hurling me thru the
underbrush of Central Park,
the jungle.
I either wanna be a cop
or the biggest dope dealer in Harlem
when I grow up.
I feel good!
It's a man's world,
I am the black man's sound.
Get off my face whining bitch!
No, I didn't go to school today
& I ain't goin' tomorrow!
I like how the sky looks
when I'm running,
my clothes are new & shiny,
I'm fast as a wolf
I need a rabbit,
the sky is falling
calling my name
Leroy Leroy.
I look up
blood bust
in my throat,
I remember when

Christ sucked my dick
behind the pulpit.
I was 6 years old,
he made me promise
not to tell
no one.
I eat cornbread & collard greens.
I only wear Adidas,
I'm my own man,
they can wear New Balance or Nike
if they want,
I wear Adidas.
I'm L.D.
lover
mover
man with the money
all the girls know me.
I'm classified as mentally retarded
but I'm not,
least I don't think I am.
Classes for the
mentally retarded
eat up my brain
like last week's greens
rotting in plastic containers.
My mother never throws
away anything.
All those years
I sat
I sat in classes
for the mentally retarded
so she could get
the extra money welfare gives
for retarded kids.
So she could get
some money
some motherfuckin' money!
That bitch
that bitch

I could kill her.
All those years
I sat next to kids
who shitted on themselves,
dreaming amid
rooms of dull eyes
that one day
my rhymes would
break open the sky
& my name would be
written across the marquee
at the Apollo in bold gold,
me bigger than Run DMC
Rapper G
Rapper O
Rapper *Me*
"Let's go!" I scream.
My dick is a locomotive
my sister eats like a 50¢ hot dog.
I scream, "I *said* let's go!"
It's 40 of us
a black wall of sin.
The god of our fathers
descends down & blesses us,
I say thank you Jesus.
Now let's do the
wild thing.
I pop off the cement
like toast outta toaster
hot hard crumbling
running
running
the park is green
combat operation
lost soul
looking for Lt. Calley
Jim Jones,
anybody who could direct
this spurt of semen

rising to the sky.
Soldiers
flying thru the rhythm
"Aw man!
nigger *please*
nigger
nigger
nigger,
I call myself
nigger."
My soul sinks
to its knees &
howls under the moon
rising full,
"Let's get a female jogger!" I shout
into the twilight
looking at the middle-class thighs
pumping past me,
cadres of bitches
who deserve to die
for thinking they're better
than me.
You ain better than
nobody bitch.
The rock begs my hand
to hold it.
It says, "Come on man!"
T.W., Pit Bull, J.D. & me
grab the bitch.
Ugly big nose white bitch
but she's beautiful cause she's white
she's beautiful cause she's skinny
she's beautiful cause she's gonna die
cause her daddy's gonna cry
Bitch!
I bring the rock down
on her head
sounds dull & flat
like the time I busted

the kitten's head.
The blood is real & red
my dick rises.
I tear off her bra
feel her perfect pink breasts
like Brooke Shields
like the bitches in Playboy
Shit! I come all over myself!
I bring the rock down
the sound has rhythm
hip hop ain't gonna stop
till your face sees
what I see every day
walls of blood
walls of blood
she's wriggling like
a pig in the mud
I never seen a pig
or a cow 'cept on TV.
Her nipples are like
hard strawberries
my mouth tastes
like pesticide.
I fart.
Yusef slams her
across the face with a pipe.
My dick won't get
hard no more.
I bring the rock down
removing what she
looks like forever
ugly bitch
ugly bitch
I get up
blood on my hands
semen in my jeans,
the sky is black
the trees are green
I feel good baby

I just did
the *wild thing*!

michael scholnick   TO A CERTAIN MR. RICHARD ALBERT, MY LANDLORD

You're a man looks afraid to sleep
May you never rest in gladness
May you never enjoy a spring scent,
Life's colors, a sky inexplicably real!
May you never enjoy life!
May your food of the marketplace taint
Or spoiled in preparation be

In humped obeisance 'fore hooves of the Golden Calf of ruin,
May your capacity to understand emotions
Dwindle to a flea's and convulse your nerves' bounty
May you never take a second to breathe deeply

And talk about repairs!
Do something about that wife!
Buy the right gift, make her smile
She hasn't my dog's politeness
May you and the missus both stink awfully bad,
Like defiled rooms, as you age forgetting to wash
Watch out, on your crooked road of lies!
Cruel, no place hereafter
Your menacing of the effulgent void, pipsqueak,
Makes shabby your every gesture

Die without water for abusive thirst!
Where's the flame to treat your possession?

Spurned by martyrs, licking your ears demons' torments,
Fall to hell via uninspected elevator shaft,
Wearing your piece of shit raincoat

FOR IRWIN HEILNER

Experience is disappointing,
that's why life's absurd.
I learned this watching you shave
lecturing about Beethoven
and prison reform
Polite man bathrobed
standing in your livingroom
I was company
". . . and all we can do," you said,
finger scanning skin neck cheeks
feeling baby red smooth skin,
"Is punish, punish, punish."
Now finding a hair then clipping
delicately
with a conductor's wrist

Wisdom flows in your speech
of an art to consciousness
heavier than Beethoven's fist
Amazing how he tamed such wildness
ordering blue soldiers in blue chariots
to march around the white Chinese teacup of his mind
How zapped with power he lifted his wrath
above the birds and clouds
above Napoleon's imagination
And smashed antiquity
dropping Quartets 14 15 & 16
on God's porcelain tongue

For you a musician
An eccentric librarian
whose deepest thoughts
dwell dusty and unpublished
The eternal is fierce and now
Who can deny your chilly chords?
For you scores of inspiration
Manuals cartons of sage sense
A humble universe
The science of your soul
in an unknown basement
on Dawson Avenue
in Clifton, New Jersey

GOOD GRACES

I have no questions, Kiss me
Beggar's loving qualities
& branches, snow-pursued, Kiss me

Air of great, saber-toothed waves, Kiss me
Kiss me, instill something hilarious

Your step a nocturnal detail
Pregnant wind, remote & sketched
Centipede upon a balustrade of bedimmed sequence
Darkness of the woods' closure

Kiss me, I'm a gardener
No pills, Kiss me
I know I never doubted you
Teach me to drive

Light breaks through the blinds
The bird chirps inventing pleasure
I half-smiled at the bridge, Kiss me

Programs Tickets Kiss me
Six dancers Two beats
See you soon, Good-night, Kiss me
Mixed reviews & hoola-hoops, Kiss me

Last call, Kiss me
Let's cut here, Kiss me
Sounds interesting, Kiss me
Alternative to coffee, Kiss me
One wish granted, Kiss me

Nervous rendezvous & seamy aftermath
Utterly heartless, amusement
Ignorance analogized
Diaphanous commonplace

You are scrubbed & absurd
In the wings of melancholy paroxysms, Kiss me
At a party with security guards, Kiss me

patricia smith   SKINHEAD

They call me "skinhead," and I got my *own* beauty.
It is knife-scrawled across my back in sore, jagged letters,
it's in the way my eyes snap away from the obvious.
I sit in my dim matchbox
on the edge of a bed tousled with my ragged smell,
slide razors across my hair,
count how many ways
I can bring blood closer to the surface of my skin.
These are the duties of the righteous,
the ways of the anointed.

The face that moves in my mirror is huge and pockmarked,
scraped pink and brilliant, apple-cheeked,

I am filled with my own spit.
Two years ago, a machine that slices leather
sucked in my hand and held it,
whacking off three fingers at the root.
I didn't feel nothing till I looked down
and saw one of them on the floor
next to my boot heel,
and I ain't worked since then.

I sit here
and watch niggers take over my TV set,
kings walking up and down the sidewalks in my head,
walking like their fat black mamas *named* them freedom.
My shoulders tell me that ain't right.
So I move out into the sun
where my beauty makes them lower their heads,
or into the night
with a lead pipe up my sleeve,
a razor tucked in my boot.
I was born to make things right.

It's easy now
to move my big body into shadows,
to move from a place where there was nothing
into the stark circle of a streetlight,
the pipe raised up high over my head.
It's a kick to watch their eyes get big,
round and gleaming like cartoon jungle boys,
right in that second when they know
the pipe's gonna come down, and I got this thing
I like to say, listen to this, I like to say
"Hey nigger, Abe Lincoln's been dead a long time."

I get hard listening to their skin burst.
I was born to make things right.

Then this newspaper guy comes around,
seems I was a little sloppy kicking some fag's ass
and he opens up his hole and screams about it.

So this reporter finds me curled up in my bed,
the TV flashes licking my face clean.
Same ol' shit.
Ain't got no job, the coloreds and spics got 'em all.
Why ain't I working? Look at my hand, asshole.
No, I ain't part of no organized group,
I'm just a white boy who loves his race,
fighting for a pure country.
Sometimes it's just me. Sometimes three. Sometimes 30.
AIDS will take care of the faggots,
then it's gon' be white on black in the streets.
Then there'll be three million.
I tell him that.

So he writes it up
and I come off looking like some kind of freak,
like I'm Hitler himself. I ain't that lucky,
but I got my own beauty.
It is in my steel-toed boots,
in the hard corners of my shaved head.

I look in the mirror and hold up my mangled hand,
only the baby finger left, sticking straight up,
but fuck you all anyway.
I'm riding the top rung of the perfect race,
my face scraped pink and brilliant.
I'm your baby America.
Your boy.
Drunk on my own spit, I am goddamned fuckin' beautiful.

And I was born

and raised

right here.

SWEET DADDY

for my father, Otis Douglas Smith

62. You would have been 62.
I would have given you a Roosevelt Road
kinda time, an all-night jam in a
twine time joint, where you could have
taken over the mike
and crooned a couple.

The place be all blue light
and JB air
and big-legged women
giggling at the way
you spit tobacco into the sound system,
showing up some dime-store howler
with his pink car
pulled right up to the door outside.

You would have been 62.
And the smoke would have bounced
right off the top of your head,
like good preachin'.
I can see you now,
twirling those thin hips,
growling 'bout *if it wasn't for bad luck*
you wouldn't have no luck at all.
I said,
wasn't for bad luck,
no luck at all.

Nobody ever accused you
of walking the paradise line.
You could suck Luckies
and line your mind with *rubbing* alcohol
if that's what the night called for,

but Lord, you could cry foul
why B.B. growled Lucille from the jukebox,
you could dance like killing roaches
and kiss those downsouth ladies
on fatback mouths. *Ooooweee,* they'd say,
that sweet man sho' knows how deep my well goes.
And I bet you did, Daddy,
I bet you did.

But hey, here's to just another number.
To a man who wrote poems on the back
of cocktail napkins and brought them home
to his daughter who'd written her rhymes
under the cover of blankets.
Here's to a strain on the caseload.
Here's to the fat bullet
that left its warm chamber
to find you.
Here's to the miracles
that spilled from your head
and melted into the air
like jazz.

The carpet had to be destroyed.
And your collected works
on aging, yellowed twists of napkin
can't bring you back.
B.B. wail and blue Lucille
can't bring you back.
A daughter who grew to write screams
can't bring you back.

But a room—
just like this one—
which suddenly seems to fill
with the dread odors of whiskey and smoke,
can bring you here
as close as my breathing.

But the moment is hollow.
It stinks.
It stinks sweet.

sekou sundiata   MANDELA IN HARLEM. (JUNE, 1991)

Mandela, after 27 years, running behind schedule.
And the drums in front of the bodega
hip hop and asé. These names we got
picked from a book to spell us past perfect.
Hair all locked, and the Africa we fashion
in the shape of a map? that map
has shaped us too.
Maybe we don't know who
and where exactly
the cord was cut, but it was.
We jigsaw in the sun
hot without stopping. Our colors on us
like a flag for each madness we suck and bleed
each pure joy we kente into Carnival, and carry
from one time to the next like a true love.
The ancestors, drunk on the taste we pour for the boys upstate,
got us running and jumping and shaking our heads.
And Legba directing traffic near the methadone clinic,
the Monkey signifying tricks for the tricks.
You been gone so long Mandela
the Miracles been done broke up, and the Temptations
play now for remember.
Is that what it cost you
to know the killers
better than they know themselves?
Is that why the traitors get the gasoline
and the necklace of fire?
See, there he is, we point you out for the children,

but all they see is us
pointing through the crowd to a place they have to reach up to.
See see and see, the look on our faces the only vision
that finally counts.
And the thieves, out of work on that day.
And the whores, can't wait to see a real man.
And the leaders, all negro in the camera
terrible as the terrible history they pose for.
They got the mayor, the big house and the chief of police.
What's next, coup d'etat?
Arms swollen, tubes tied, virus snaking through our blood and cum,
look at us in our free: our powerful enemy.
Scholarship and the science of cool
laid up in the shade, taking in the news.
What we know about signs
fits us like a dream.

KING

Maybe because winter comes twice each year
and by the second time the first time was back in January
and that was a year ago.
There must be a place where this duality adds up,
some destination some destiny.
In this country, they wear black all the time.
It's not the absence of color they want
enough abstraction to pick and choose off the rack
and still be cool and cool be code
to keep whatever light they get from the North
from December, from any window that looks out.
The wisdom of black is to go with anything unopposed.
It don't really matter that they days are getting longer
but people act like it's getting darker.
In a few weeks, we go up to the Audubon by heart.

And in the field of that heart, of soldier away
these last days.
The year could begin with a birthday candle for you,
and a prayer for Malcolm.
And then breaking through
the black of winter into spring: flower red,
a rupture with the cold,
and then, May green.
Just then, you get the prayer and he gets the candle.
Not everybody who talks about you talks to you.
To have a dream is to be dreamed.
I got that from the bullet in your head.
In the language of what we got coming to us
we call this place, this place.
To shift and carry the weight,
we call ourselves African American now,
still laughing deepest at what ain't funny,
like how spirit still don't play:
Up be looking like down: on television today
that man spit in your face
and you asked your God to bless him.

PHILOSOPHY OF THE KOOL

a blues for poets

I been swimming since water,
learning to sing like the songs.
The oldest one I know goes like this:
Some people came from the trees,
I remember coming out of the undertow: the ocean
of seas: the electricity the explosions
billions of us crashing with the waves,
then blown away into memory.
You can still hear us in the piece of a beat
or in that music made from scratch.

The first words still had roots,
like a James Brown syllable.
It was a single cell one minute, a slam dunk the next.
Speed was our need.

I remember salt and air, water slime and mud,
upright and thumb, fire and iron.
And most of all, the poetry we had then.
It was open verse, later called Africa.
I remember human life beginning female.
Gamete that I was when I knew it, zygote
that I was when I recalled it.
The earth was yet negative space, a canvas
stretched from hymen to foreskin to drumskin.
And sleep told us in those days,
to stay awake: the blackness begins
the blackness ends.
Whoever said there was a light at the end
never lived at the end, never had to run
up ahead to see what it's going to be: womb
to tomb to womb.

Whoso knowso, I mean I seen
Buddha and Krishna on the D train.
And you wouldn't know the river gods, the prophets
or the turn of the century
if you couldn't read the latest fashion
like proverbs on tee shirts:
the best things in life are toll free
I don't like questions I don't like answers, I just like to dance
I don't have to drive, I'm already driven
What you got is what you love
Good things come to those who wait, better things come to those who don't
Some people look down and find money, some people look down and lose their souls?
Shit happens and it floats

I recall the first ships
that appeared like shadows on the horizon.
And we ran out to greet them with our sweet palm wine and guaguanco

thinking their books and harmolodics could tell us something
about love and beauty.
But it was more than a notion
in the middle of that frigid Atlantic: the vomit
the sharks the babies with umbilical cords around their necks
the earthless rhythm of the water pitching to and fro.
I witnessed the birth of rock n roll.
My mama name Lucy, her real name Lucille.
Without the blues, we go under.

cheryl boyce taylor　　**FENCES**

Concrete walls
ribboned in barbed wire
fences

out from under the wings
of midnight
comes a sufferer with hungry
eyes and seething skin

de white oman holin she purse
tight　tight　　wheee papa
but he eh wan dat　yu kno

he wan restitution
from she grandfather
3 generations removed

he wan she balls
an she dignity
he wan　she sorry
to geh she pardon
fer de padlock
still on she mind

he could mash up she face
and feed she   she pocketbook
she holin it   tight   tight
running when she see he

she down in he country
putting up   high   high
barbed wire fence
with broken bottles atop
round "she" property
and a sign that   reads
"Trespassers will be
perse—   prosecut-
perprosecuted . . ."

sweaty cops patrol
private beaches
riot gear swing from coconut palms
twoface night sticks
tapping fences
seeking neighbors
seeking lovers   trespassers

    In tranquil Trinidad
the water still offers blood
if you listen past the wind chimes
you will hear the bamboo shrieking

"No Natives Allowed."

YEARNING

A long white space
with blue dots and orange lines
a wide winter space

for hummingbird sounds
steel pan pounds
a space turned out
with yearning

ah say ah yearning
ah say   ah have   ah yearning
ah yeeeeeeearning   yearning
for nite tepid breeze
big fat moon dat eh fraid yu
big moon shining
like meh neighbor Merle face

oh god ah yearning
for mango dodooo
sticky and sweeeeet
for melongen   curry cabbage
and blue dasheen

ah yearning
to see de green jaundiced eyes
of Ratty mangy dog smiling
after he eat up de saltfish bone
de chiney man throw for he

ah yearning for—
"gurl come out de canal
ah go tell yu mudder
yu cursing"

ah yearning for—
"oman whey meh kiss-meh-ass food
whey pappa it sounding
like yu vex"

"oh god ease meh up
nah darling
yu can't see ah nursing
de baby"

"bu wha de ass wrong wid dis oman"
"use de stove we broda"

ah yearning
for meh ole goat Sheela
de textile gate up Victory Street
where ah let she drop she shit balls
in de white people yard
one at a time

ah yearning
for stand-pipe water
an belly full breadfruit
chennet to make meh tongue tight
an mauby so ah could pee bitter

ah yearning
yearning for she geh me hot
an ah cuss she ass
ah call she mudder ah prostitute
my mouth eh ha no cover
me eh fraid nobody yu know

ah yearning to drag tongue
up Fredrick Street
mass oh mass in meh ass

ah yearning for rum shop
christmas parang
and obeah to get de man ah want
ah lil blue bag to swell de foot
ah he chile mudder belly

ah yearning for roti and
roast corn by Curepe junction
a nice cold Carib
to send it down

ah yearning
for voices ringing shrill

from B-flat to high-C
bamsee rolling
one hand on left hip
de other flying
leaping in meh face

o gosh ah yearning
yearning   yeeeeeeeeearning
hungry for meh people.

emily xyz

STRONTIUM: It sits in your bones, it sits in my bones/and it will still be
there long after we are gone, strontium/I wonder whose idea it was/Was it
the government? Was it the Christian Scientists? Sometimes I wonder
about them, strontium/Don't worry on getting drafted, don't worry on
world war three/Everything that you're afraid of/is inside you already.

SLOT MACHINE
(for 2 voices)

CASH	
	CASH
Quarters	
	Quarters, quarters
Gonna do the laundry	
he says	
	he says
	Takin the car
he says	he says
Gets on the highway	
lighted like a landing strip	
	lighted like a landing strip

lighted like a landing strip
the slate of darkness scribbled on with
a neon pen
somebodys carton car
flyin thru analog Ann Landers land

flyin thru infrastructure
flyin thru statistical abstracts of the

United States past encryption past the

bank machine past past lives into the

beating heart of the last days of the
twentieth century he comes to a
slot machine.
CASH

CASH

CASH CASH

Who knows where his heart is
His heart was ripped out and

buried in a mattress stuffed with cash
he guesses

he guesses/every couple of weeks he

takes his metal detector out to
the national park
hikes up to the big chasm that separates
us and them

which the founding mothers and fathers
did not envision
which nobody thought would happen

lighted like a landing strip

somebodys cartoon car
flyin thru dark dark digital
    backyards
flyin thru bank's glass door
flyin thru bankrupt economies
    and emptified
ghetto streets made morbid by
    gut reaction
of kids backed by gat not by
    gold not by
god

slot machine. CASH
cash machine
CASH

CASH

CASH

His heart is in a bus station
    locker
His heart his remains he says he says
he questions he questions things
    but no
answers ever seem to come he
    knows
religion is not the solution
every couple of minutes
postal worker massacre
slaughtering law firms court
        rooms
where does it end
how does it happen
how does it happen

wonder how it happened
wonder how it happened

how'd the rich get that rich
how'd the poor get that poor
how did everybody get so murderous

how did everybody get so ready to kill

over the stupidest shit
he thinks it must come down to CASH

must be everything comes down to CASH

in this country anyway
in this country anyway
to avoid misery

Pulls into the parking lot
lots of money in his pocket
gets a drink
drinks it
drinks it
drinks it
and the quarters
go in
the slot
machine
gets a drink
drinks it
drinks it
drinks it
and the quarters
go in
the slot
machine
and the quarters

wonder how it happened
wonder how it happened

how'd the rich get that rich
how'd the poor get that poor
how did everybody get so
     murderous

how did everybody get so ready
     to kill

over the stupidest shit

he thinks it must come down to
     CASH

must be everything comes down
     to CASH
CASH CASH
everything comes down
to this:
CASH

gets a drink
drinks it
drinks it
drinks it
and the quarters
go in
the slot
machine
gets a drink
drinks it
drinks it
drinks it
and the quarters
go in
the slot
machine

Gets a drink
drinks it
drinks it
drinks it .
and the quarters
go in
the slot
machine
CASH

cherry cherry blank
lemon orange lemon
orange orange lemon
lemon lemon orange
lemon orange lemon
lemon orange lemon
orange cherry lemon
orange orange lemon
lemon lemon orange
blank blank cherry
cherry cherry lemon
blank blank cherry
blank cherry lemon
cherry blank lemon
cherry blank lemon
cherry blank cherry
cherry blank blank
cherry lemon lemon
cherry lemon lemon
cherry lemon lemon
orange lemon lemon
lemon cherry orange
lemon cherry orange

Gets a drink
drinks it
drinks it
drinks it
and the quarters
go in
the slot
machine

orange cherry lemon
orange cherry lemon
cherry lemon lemon
cherry lemon lemon
cherry lemon lemon
cherry lemon lemon
orange cherry blank
orange cherry blank
orange cherry orange
orange cherry lemon
orange cherry blank
orange cherry blank
orange cherry cherry
orange cherry lemon
lemon blank cherry
orange lemon blank
lemon blank cherry
orange lemon blank
cherry orange lemon
cherry orange lemon
cherry orange lemon
cherry orange lemon
cherry orange lemon
cherry orange lemon
cherry orange lemon
cherry orange lemon
cherry orange lemon
cherry orange lemon
cherry orange lemon

lemon cherry orange	cherry orange lemon
lemon cherry orange	cherry orange lemon
lemon cherry orange	cherry orange lemon
lemon cherry orange	cherry orange lemon
cherry cherry cherry	cherry cherry cherry
CASH	CASH
he took the day off work	
so he could be with his friends	
Sammy and Davis	Sammy and Davis
and ride around Telluride	and ride around Telluride
and ride around Vegas	and ride around Vegas
He says he wants to live	He says he wants to live
a life free of boredom	
a life free of pain	
says this the U.S.	says this the U.S.
and there's money everywhere	and there's money everywhere
in the desert hills	
in the darkest bar	
in the deepest casket	
in the poorest excuse	
in the flat expression	in the desert hills
in the fabrication	in the darkest bar
in the sliding land	in the deepest casket
in the Sands Hotel	in the poorest excuse
I'm goin the store/	I'm goin the store/he says
takin the car	takin the car
ignoring the index of	
economic indicators	
and the statistics	and the statistics
that tell me I'm poor	that tell me I'm poor
I'm goin the store	I'm goin the store
I'm goin the store	I'm goin the store
I'm goin the store	I'm goin the store
	isn that what money's for?

III.
FOUNDING
POEMS

miguel algarín   HIV

1) Revelation: to tell in strength. "The telling," when to tell, leads to a discovery between the teller and the listener. Acquiring knowledge; the teller holds his/her information as a tool for health, movement towards truth.
2) Salvation: to converse as a movement towards recuperating, a holding on not to die.
3) Speech: to acquire "language" for talking about a plague in the self.
4) Sharing secrets: who to tell? Is there someone? The search for what to tell.
5) Mature Masculinity: welcome the responsibility to do the work of building verbs, adjectives and nouns for mortality and its subsequent eternal breaking of concrete.

   Revelation
Revel at ion,
rebel at I on a course
to regret erections,
to whip the cream in my scrotum
till it hardens into unsweetened,
unsafe revved elations

of milk turned sour
by the human body,
of propagation of destruction:
the epiphany: I am unsafe,
you who want me,
know that I who want you,
harbor the bitter balm of defeat.

    Salvation
If I were to show you
how to continue holding on,
I would not kiss you,
I would not mix the fluids
of my body with you,
for your salvation
can not bear the live weight
of your sharing liquids with me.

    Language
To tell,
to talk,
to tongue into sounds
how I would cleanse you with urine,
how my tasting tongue would wash your body,
how my saliva and sperm would bloat you,
to touch you in our lovemaking
and not tell you
would amount to murder,
to talk about how to language this
so that you would still languish
in my unsafe arms and die,
seems beyond me,
I would almost rather lie
but my tongue muscle moves involuntarily
to tell of the danger in me.

Of Health
To use my full and willing
body to reveal and speak
the strength that I impart
without fear,
without killing,
without taking away what I would give,
to use my man's tongue
to share,
to give,
to lend,
to exact nothing,
to receive all things,
to expand my macho
and let the whole world
into the safety of my mature masculinity.

Quarantine
Sometimes I fear touching your plump ear lobes,
I might contaminate you.
Sometimes I refuse odors that would
drive my hands to open your thick thighs,
sometimes closing my ears to your
voice wrenches my stomach
and I vomit to calm wanting,
can it be that I am the bearer of plagues?
Am I poison to desire?
Do I have to deny yearning for firm full flesh
so that I'll not kill what I love?
No juices can flow 'tween you and me,
only dry sands
will suck me in.

SHEETS

She brought me back,
I thought I had seen the last,
the end of love's orgasm,
she held on to the tar thread
my moist love impulse
had become that rainy March Monday,
when for the first-neon-light moment
I was told of killer dark-red-cells
circumnavigating my life line,
she held tight,
no nonsense here she said,
love saves the day,
so let us make do,
  let us invent
magic touches in tubercular time,
she held her body proud,
not bound by coquettish charm,
she held her love upright,
till I one morning woke
into her "I won't let you hide"
hugs and turns and legs upright,
perpendicular to the bed,
yes, she brought me back
to the sheet of breath
that connects sperm and egg,
that blends guilt and love
into rushing for towels
to wipe the demon of desire
from her thighs, from her breasts,
from her,
demons away from her,
thighs not milked by me,
life not threatened,
wipe, wipe, wipe,
wipe the sperm,

get it off the sheets,
off her,
off our love,
off, off, off,
off with the plague,
what? An orgasm?
how dare I?

SUNDAY, AUGUST 11, 1974

    Sunday afternoon and it is one-thirty and all the churchgoing latinos
have crossed themselves and are now going home to share in the peace of
the day, pan y mantequilla, una taza de café and many sweet recollections of
el rinconcito en Juncos, donde Carmencita, María y Malén jugaban y pelea-
ban.

    Sunday afternoon and it is one-thirty and all the churchgoing latinos
fuse each other with love and the women dress so clean and pure and the
children walk so straight and pure and the fathers look so proud and pure
and everything so right and pure and even as I wake up to my nephew's
voice coming through the window, there is pleasure in awakening. My
mother and father and Grafton and Johnny come in, there is light in
their eyes,
there is pleasure in living,
there is no shame in being
full of love,
there is no shame in being
nude while my mother's
eyes look in at me,
looking at my nude body,
body that she made mixing her blood
with my father's,
and there's no rushing for clothes
just sweet openness in being
loved by my family.

Sunday afternoon and it is
one-thirty and all the church-
going latinos have crossed themselves
and my body swings free.

BODY BEE CALLING: FROM THE 21ST CENTURY

XIII

A void
Avoid
A void is something to avoid,
it's hard to be at zero point
at the still point reflecting the whole
in that there isn't anything in nothing
just like a circle is all ways not flat
but rounder than a belly nine months
into that other eternal circle
around the biological/chemical time clock
measured accurately by Swiss-made
round-face father Timex,
avoid a void at the still point
where no thing becomes some thing
in that it is out of nothing that something comes,
avoid a void with a circumference,
it's a circle around the zero point
where a straight line that never goes round
begins a voyage that avoids a void
and heads towards a swell.

FATHER AT ZERO-POINT-PLACE

Part I
My mother's pleading voice, not resigned,
sang a crying song wishing for a rebirth,
my uncle, weeping for the first time,
in my memory, sobbed about,
"His eyes are open he's still looking at me,
you better get over here, I don't know what
to do we've lost it."
I transformed each telephone word
into concrete objects:
      I was there looking at father's soft skin,
      touching his gentle lips,
      caressing his still warm hands and fingers,
      craving for a breath to escape him,
      tricking myself into feeling his air
      pressing, still, in my cheek,
      running my hands over his body,
      looking for the warm spots,
      his belly's hot
      his armpits still lukewarm,
      his thighs, grown so thin, beginning to be cold,
      my hands grab at his feet,
      not yet icy cold,
      I run my hands into his groin,
      and there I find body heat, I find
      his scrotum still simmers with an
      amber temperature, his penis still
      holds a glow, his buttocks
      are now room temperature,
there is still a chance for a revival,
his eyes involuntarily open,
is there here a miracle?
will he stand up and walk
among the sinners and the ill?
will he continue to walk the earth beatified

spreading saintliness
just as he had during my youth?
a kinder man lived only in books,
father's feather-weight touch
opened all of us to a fault,
because nowhere else were we ever loved
so gently and so fairly
he was a judge with mercy and kindliness
in his heart
and understanding and balance were his law,
he knew that at the heart of law was generosity
and that mercy made human contracts work,
here was a Daniel, a Solomon,
a worthy homespun philosopher of family justice,
yes, there is still a chance for a revival,
the rebirth that takes place in the mind.

   Part II
I've already found my Deep-Nine photograph,
but mother spins an endless reel
she cannot stop to cradle a single frame,
she keeps on running the tape,
the tape of her fifty-seven years with him,
the tape of their never having slept a single night apart,
the reel to real joy of eternally
rejuvenating happiness in married partnership,
the video of never having been lonely,
or alone or without her man,
or without his warming her slippers
so that they wouldn't be cold to her feet,
or his cooking her special diet to cure her ulcer,
or his buttoning her blouse,
or pulling up her zipper,
or his patience with her mental break-ups,
or the way in which he crossed his legs
when company arrived,
but the reel that drives mother hauntingly wild
is the empty bed, life without him,

even the seventy-five pound,
more fragile than frail body
that his wasted frame had become,
even that was her man,
still there, still needing pillows,
still needing his teeth brushed,
his feces cleaned and removed,
needing his enemas, needing his spit suctioned,
needing his liquid food,
cleaning his intestinal tube
through which travelled medication and nourishment,
yes, that's the real reel,
the non-occupied space,
the zero-point-place,
the nobody in space and place,
that's the terror Uncle Al
experienced this morning,
that's the tremor that rocked mother,
they both awoke hoping a dream had passed
and that the zero-point nobody-in-place-space,
had evaporated and that father's
more fragile than frail body
would still be there.

   Part III
Mother and Uncle Al
arose hoping that the police
had not been there,
that the death certificate
had not been signed,
hoping that the body
had not been picked up
by the La Paz Funeral Parlor embalmer,
who made a southbound turn
onto the northbound traffic on Queens Boulevard
with my father's cadaver
neatly tucked into a body bag
in the rear of his station wagon,

which I was following,
furiously blowing my horn,
waving my hands,
screaming, whistling,
frantically blinking my lights,
fearing a collision
that would catapult father's corpse
unceremoniously into the chill, rainy night air,
a flying body bag and me,
my old man
doing triple somersaults
in the midst of his encroaching rigor mortis,
finally, the embalmer, dazed by the oncoming headlights,
crossed over the median divider,
stopped at the red light,
looked over at me, shrugged, and said,
"Hey, he's at zero-point-place
and nothing else can get at him,
only the great blaze
shines on him now,
he's at home plate and safe."
Then the light turned green
and my father and the embalmer
drove off into the pure white light of forever.

richard august   MARIAM

Tanzanian woman
residing in Rego Park
prays at her Queens mosque
every evening after work
buys dishtowels for its kitchen
and toys for the festival prizes
sends international money orders
to her husband's parents

in Dar es Salaam
"I am an orphan, you see,
brought up by a stepmother"
and laments the high cost of postage
so that's why she's always
asking me about my mother
saying I'm mean

MASON V. FUREY

(June 18, 1951–October 29, 1990)

"I am going to die in this room."
He pulled the blanket over his head
and wept. I was scared.
"No you won't," I said lamely.

       ***

today
a year ago
8:30 a.m.
"Richard, I'm ready."
Coney Island Hospital
Emergency Room
lost among beds
returned home
expecting him to be there
didn't realize
the seriousness . . .
Did he ever
come home?
No, he never did
come home

       ***

red glow
draws me to the window
setting sun suspended
across the Narrows
above Linden, New Jersey
where he is buried
a reminder
I had forgotten
Hello, Mason

INTERPRETING DREAMS

I dreamed I was dead
I lay on a lawn chair
in a yard in the country
it was night, quiet and dark
except for a lit-up window
on the second floor
which I stared at
I wanted to go up to that room
to listen to music
I awoke remembering the silence
that's how I knew I was dead
then I heard a story
read over the radio saying
dreams about death mean
there's new life coming
I felt better

jorge brandon
LA MASACRE DE PONCE

Venian desde las montañas,
por las veredas, por las veredas bajando,
y de los hondos caminos en Ponce se vaciaron.
Batallón de voluntades,
ejercito de cruzadas,
en alto va el pabellon
retorcido como un látigo,
en alto va la bandera Puertorriqueña
que gloriosa y alta bandeaba
en su asta azotada por el viento.

Guardias de honor van haciendo Elias Beauchamp,
los tres valientes Velazquez y el no menos Juan Gallardo.
Para aplaudir a los heroes
se abre la gloria a su paso.
En un instante de vertigo,
un disparo de revolver
mordió el polvo de su marcha
con ira y plomo de llano.

El sol lloró claridades
y el cielo se bajo tanto
que hasta una niña de siete años de edad
llamada Georgina arrancó,
arrastró los angeles con su mano,
y en este andar mañanero
por confines del espacio,
Cristo el maestro divino
los apreto en un abrazo
y les dió de campamento
una faja entre dos astros.

A Ponce, ramos de honor, y todos juramentan,
hagamos de Puerto Rico
un pueblo libre de esclavos.

EL ASTRO DE CAROLINA

para Roberto Clemente

Al astro de Carolina,
en espiritú presente,
a tí Roberto Clemente,
vaya la gracia divina.
Llevo clavada una espina
dentro de mi corazon,
y aquí en esta triste ocasión,
a pesar de mis pesares,
yo te ofrezco mis cantares
con mucha resignación.

Hoy te llora el pueblo entero
y en espiritu te aclama,
porque subiste a la fama
como atleta y caballero.
Fuiste muy noble y sincero,
bueno con la humanidad,
te quisimos de verdad,
compatriota distinguido,
y hoy que en el mar te has perdido,
fuiste a la immortalidad.

Al pueblo de Nicaragua
te esforzaste en ayudar,
y con empeño llegar a la ciudad de Managua.
Hoy sepultado en las aguas
del Mar Atlantico reposas.
Mas no importa,
allí las diosas mitológicas te besan,
mientras que en el mundo,
hoy rezan por ti las almas piadosas.

Roberto! Carolinense!
prestigioso ciudadano,

moriste dando la mano
al pueblo Nicaraguense,
es seguro que en Puerto Rico
hoy se hable y se piense
acerca de la ciudad deportiva,
la que tu con ansias vivas
te esforzaste en conseguir,
pues habra de construir,
alma y corazon arriba.

américo casiano, jr.   SALICRUP

at the cellar of your imagination   hatchet hand about to chop
rooster's neck   coiling cognition   pheasant's crest

phallic profile   it leans long until adam's apple's huge breast
picturing a womb   its lips hair a woman   body oval
tits joining rooster's wing   again hard curving lines
again the phallic head   the prick like nose of el pichón

abstraction   buddha   the hanging tit   eyes   composition
the tight angles running perpendicular to an african mask
eyes shadow the tiger   growl   it is the soul of your conscience

thought thighs your brother about to mine a cannon
cocaine   pussy   leg suit   a shirt and tie

claws floor other organic growth   the boyish butterflies flutter
they are the real free creatures   hen gobbling water   pechuga
skeleton   all is ass and hinting old san juan

anal hair   another face   legs   foot   a vulture's beak
between the legs of this awkward hen a seed stems about to flower

beyond your imagination   bridges slope manhattan
sheet metal rusts and corrodes the river
pillars wade   reflections   a neon city

the east river curves   bridge splits   the avenue turns into
figures   the court jester juggles his balls
the impossible one smokes pot   the bricks plain   like building
downed by arson   the shrub browns as urine waters its roots
traffic stalls   it blurs the morning   hellgate pier
the bleating river   creation   it's the green grime edging harlem
the fungi seeping the old schools   raping our children
candy stores rack-up their shelves   billiards eight-ball hispanics
christmas   hailing snow   a bedsheet on the ground.

TONIGHT BY VENDOR'S BOOTH

drums make legs jump   hair glow like night
in Cabo Rojo   tumba plays
mosquitos buzz among mango leaves
wind crossing the fruitless tree

twilight creeps through my father's eyes
tart like the quenepas on the old tree
they have sprinkled salt on his hair
added half a keg to his waste

mellowing
i have pilgrimaged here
to moon with him
along quiet road   spirit sulky
along the shore

lucky cienfuegos
POEM TO A WOOD SCULPTURE

As he works on his wood sculpture
His tools cry with sweat and joy
As his soul and tongue sing—
I have never played
I have never bowed
For my spirit and I,
We are both outlaws
I'm a carve—I'm a carve a
small tiny motorcycle
With a wheel bigger than
my wife Wheel
A tricycle—a toy
A little boy would love to have
I'm gonna carve you . . .
I'm gonna kiss you with my lips
I'm gonna breathe
And with my hands, I'll give you life
I'm a give you detail
No, I have never bowed
Neither have I bent
So let me carve
A wood cycle
Which a little boy
Will someday treasure.

IN THE POCKET AND SPEND IT RIGHT

People—people
Chinese philosophers
Philosophers of mystical magics
With talk of
Tossing pennies away
For good luck
Talking of throwing coins
In dark corners
To bring about magic
To glow
Pennies thrown
For good luck
Believe that not, my friend
Put it in your pocket
And spend it right.

PISS SIDE STREETS

Weaving, bobbing, conniving
piss staining lonely night street
gutless buildings hanging loose
tiger rose and wild irish wine
turning winos ugly framing
designing their tiredness
drawings of human flesh
lying and people just glide
with a design and frequent smile
yeah, bad doing studs peeking
through dark shadow alleys
polishing their desiring dreams

with empty butcher knife eyes.
pushes the back of the mind
the empty desiring dream forward.
the knife red stripes crying eyes
and all that remains
a graffiti design on a piss
side street.

victor hernandez cruz   AN ESSAY ON
WILLIAM CARLOS WILLIAMS

I love the quality of the
spoken thought
As it happens immediately
uttered into the air
Not held inside and rolled
around for some properly
schemed moment
Not sent to circulate a cane
field
Or on a stroll that would include
the desert and Mecca
Spoken while it happens
Direct and pure
As the art of salutation
of mountain campesinos come to
the plaza
The grasp of the handshake upon
encounter and departure
A gesture unveiling the occult
behind the wooden boards of
your old house
Remarks show no hesitation
to be expressed

The tongue itself carries
the mind
Pure and sure
Sudden and direct
like the appearance
of a green mountain
Overlooking a town.

THREE SONGS FROM THE 50S

Song 1
Julito used to shine the soul
of his shoes before he left for
the Palladium to take the wax
off the floor while Tito Rodriguez
flew around the walls like a
parakeet choking maracas
It was around this time that
Julito threw away his cape
because the Umbrella Man and the
Dragons put the heat on all the
Ricans who used to fly around
in Dracula capes swinging canes
or carrying umbrellas
Even if there was no rain
on the horizon
That same epoca my mother
got the urge to paint the
living room pink and buy a
new mirror with flamingos
elegantly on the right hand
corner because the one we had
was broken from the time that
Carlos tried to put some respect

Into Julito and knock the
party out of him.

    Song 2
All the old Chevies that the
gringos from upstate New York
wore out
Were sailing around the neighborhood
with dices and San Martin de Porres
el negrito who turned catholic
Hanging in the front windows.

    Song 3
There was still no central heating
in the tenements
We thought that the cold was
the oldest thing on the planet earth
We used to think about my Uncle Listo
Who never left his hometown
We'd picture him sitting around
cooling himself with a fan
In that imaginary place
called Puerto Rico.

ART—THIS

Lucy Comancho is an artist
Art this
She makes all the stars in Hollywould
seem like flashlights which have
been left turned on for a week
She had a *frenesi*

A friend in C
A friendinme
with paintings and blowing things
up into color which came from nowhere
No one knows where she got these things
Her mother says too much thinking
She painted the walls in her house
She painted the hallways and stairs
the stoops the garbage can tops the
squares in the sidewalk the tar on the
street the plastic bags from the cleaners
the brown grocery bags the inside of milk
containers   She herself had to be contained
from painting your face the closest layer
of the sky elements everything she gave
brush to rush to paint your *nalgas* if you
gave her room She never thought of canvas
where they sell it absent from her view
Sometimes she was called Picassa feminizing
Picasso
She painted Josefina as I was writing
that Josefina is the feminine of José
Josés who are also known to go under the
nicknames of Cheos or Pepes and so
Josefina got tagged on her the name Pepa
which is female for Pepe and she dug that
Pepa for if you look close the other name
José *y fina* means José and thin or sounds
like *oficina* like Joseoffice also it had
something in it of José if *fina* José is
finis finished   no this for someone being
composed by an artis
To top it off Pepa also means *pit*
you see what is inside of fruits This
is all in Spanish and something is being
lost in the translation just like you lose
your natural color when you leave a tropical
country and come to a city where the sun
feels like it's constipated Ask Lucy Comancho

She knows about all this
art this
artis.

HAIKUKOOS

City News 1
Wallet in pocket
Money stuffed like burrito
Look!   gone man slices wind

City News 2
Into self-service
Elevator he goes smooth
Bang!   now stuck he hums

Legislator Sheet
Government talk shit
Then file it in office jobs
Everyone flushed

Andalusian Thought
Skirt of silk music
Woman sits back in darkness
Wait!   Is she naked?

City News 3
All morning he heard
Screwdriver making hall sounds
Mailbox!   now he thinks

Movement of Molasses
Men argue honor
While twenty blocks away their
Women train horsies

Textile
She wear the pants red-
dish and tight what is under-
neath nature hills fly

Iota
A roach from Colom-
bia has enough legs and
walks the ocean back

sandra maria esteves
PUERTO RICAN DISCOVERY #20: ODE TO *PAPIROS DE BABEL* EN EL ATENEO PUERTORRIQUEÑO
for Pedro López-Adorno

Charged with energy around Arabian mosaic
Shadows of war heroes inhabit a back room
Betances, Bracetti, Lloren Torres
Julia, Don Albizu, Lolita . . .
The ceiling-high windows have been removed
The old texts are locked behind glass
Vacationing descendants examine crystal formations
Vacated seats seek conscious alignment
Students strike for their right to learn
Nuyorican words fly free in Bahia

Silent elders keep watch from a forgotten balcony
La Cruz de Malta still blooms along the garden's edge
The neighborhood undergoes renovation
The gatekeeper waits by the door.

PUERTO RICAN DISCOVERY #17:
TREASURES OF THIEVES

In the South Wing of the Museum of Natural History
Native American spirits of disrupted ancestors
moan ancient chants
over precious relics, empowered talismans
bought and stolen, betrayed outright
acquired and acquisitioned
in a reversed magic of an earlier holocaust

The Metropolitan's newly added hall of glass
preserves the ancient tomb of a misplaced Mesopotamian
a staged backdrop in cocktail lounge motif
for fundraising collectors
exchanging anecdotes at the piano bar

His kingly coffin hidden elsewhere
a parallel eviction
in a secluded corner across the way
from previously incarnated Queen Myra
Her burial regalia dissected around her
numbered and catalogued
for auction into uncertain futures

Yet, under the microscope bloodlines reveal
daggers wiped clean
disinfected offerings to the mind's eye
conjuring battles

details of cultural autopsies
psychic landmarks
for descendants who witness
this arrogant display of bloodthirsty victors
erasing accuracy from history
claiming glory in the salt

While the elegant remains of elders
stare back from frozen exhibits
of primitive lifestyles in tune with their God
in natural scientific balance
to Earthmother song.

PUERTO RICAN DISCOVERY #23: PORTRAIT IN RAISING SELF-ESTEEM

Flirtatious dreamers
we judge ourselves all wrong

Backward guilt
feet-first jumpstarts into birth
innocent to realize
rain days can be good
blessings from heaven
disguised

We watch for signs
Survival manna
Slow to discover learning lessons
on an oceanic route
full of rocky struts
fathomless caves

voluptuous hills
sea water from the unexpected

The colors in our eyes are misleading
Trapped in partisan confrontations
about the cost of rice
the oil franchise
a video game rat race
for electronic cheese
Every car and plastic bag, a failure
Signatures we tag around
Cheap ads cheating
our children, ourselves

There are no joysticks to the inner life
despite wrappings easily discarded

We are infants compared to the universe
a wise great-grandmother
who can harvest the stars around the moon

She cannot be bought
No pricetags are attached
The inner life has no boundaries
No jail cells—not a one
No fixed points of reference to confine a soul
No eye-catching boxes
to pollute everyday sidewalks

The names of all things are sacred
like thoughts breathing clean air
More than loving
living means giving
Like homegrown food
from the eternal harvest within

But for real.

TWO POEMS FOR DAVID ALLAN

   1.

In the pouring rain
walking down the street
he did not know me
My Brother, I said
What is wrong?

Soaking wet
drifting thru the block
without a coat or umbrella
shirt buttons flying open
coughing bad
could not remember my name
My Brother, My Brother
It's me

Drenched to his shoes
with holes and no socks
a child lost
a man with no memories
I let go of the laundry
held his hands
called his name
kissed his face

Only then
did he remember.

   2.

I did not know
how AIDS kills memories
until I saw him
lost in the rain

My Brother, I asked
Where are you going?
His answers long forgotten
even his name escaped him
A body with no identity
wandering by habit or instinct
searching, pleading, crying
needing help

I did not know
how AIDS can strip a life
fighting to remember
all that is to blame
on an undetermined journey
deluged in darkness

Feeling so very much alone.

lois griffith CHICA

In front of Marian Bracetti Welfare Project
Hollywood agents are not looking for stars.
Chica
pepita of your mother's
worries a youngblood's eyes.
The virgin question written on your tight whites
recalls illusions of romance gone stale
recalls speaking crude words
having to do with the price of fresh meat.
Chica
pepita of your mother's worries—
Démelo
commands a smashed pack of Newports from your back pocket
and your radio sound box

you let him hold it
being tough enough to give it up
give it out
hiding no part for yourself
jacked up in a hallway
on a doorknob in a hallway
on the sticks aced on the wallway.
Give it up
not having anything to say
or words to call inside
the giving up
to change the beat in the heat.
Chica
pepita of your mother's worries
there is no stopping of desire's dreams
that take the skies waiting for the deep of night.
Chica
pepita of your mother's worries
you'll get lost at the shooting gallery
or make love a playground on the stairwell
bringing back the bread and milk
your mother worries
what took you so long
so lately coming in the heat of the giving up
in the beat of the deep of night.

DITTY AND JITTY

Hard Sister Ditty Bop
can't turn in her pants
so tight
so straight and lean
that's reflecting a look on her face that's mean—
ooo-ah-ooo

There are those who'd like to make her
who'd like to take her
off in a dream in the arms of night
but hard Sister Ditty Bop is out and hot to trot
waiting for her best friend Jitty Bop
coming along now seen from afar
this Queen of Spades
in her knife-sharp creased
double-edged straight-legged blades.
—Que pasa Ditty?
—Ain't nothing much happening Jitty.
—Girl, let's take a stroll.
—Well, I'm down for some rock and roll.

Is this city ready for the switch
of one more blue-eyed Ditty
and the heady perfume
of one more brown-skinned Jitty?
Hard Sister Ditty Bop
and her best friend Queen of Spades Jitty Bop
write their names in the streets
cop a disco box off a slow sucker
new on the scene
unaware of how keen
you have to be on the beat
with your dancing feet
if you want to hang
and not get banged up
in a cycle of moving fast
pre-guessing the next turn
never forgetting what you have learned
and tucked away in the hip
of your straight-legged jean machines.

No denying the streets are mean.
No denying we carry the baggage from where we have been.
Ditty and Jitty make etchings in time
the world they inhabit
rewards the slick way

they hustle-bop on the face of a dime
the bitter and brutal now in current fashion
reject soft attitudes for those with more passion.
But no one knows better than
hard Sister Ditty Bop
with her blue-eyed stare
and Queen of Spades Jitty Bop
with her midriff bared—
the double-edged blades
are just an illusion they cultivate
the double-edged blades
are just an illusion they cultivate
to satiate a need for acclaim
in a universe that takes no notice of street names.

BY THE HAIR

People ask you:
—What did you do to your hair?—
You are colored
only non-colored people ask such questions
if you're colored you know
what coloreds do to their hair
in the beauty parlors
the unisex salons
the houses of style—
this is a custom particular to the colored.
If you're colored
the coloreds in the colored part of town know you
even if they don't know your name
they know your head
they know the colored you that's nigger and nappy
and kinky and wooly and dark
even when you no habla ingles

parce que tu parles français.
This habit you have of doing your hair
you learned it from your mother—
not that she thought being colored
was something less—
only, she thought knowing colored was not good enough
not straight enough
not manageable enough
not acceptable enough
to face a world that fears your difference
the darkness of you—
this is the custom of the country you live in
these are the ways of the coloreds in the country you live in
and people ask:
—What did you do to your hair?—
Why are scar tattoos on the cheek
marks of beauty
and the anorexic blond
the property of the white hunter?

DANZÓN: THE NIGHT BEFORE THE WAR 1/15/1991

for Julio & Miguel & Roy & Marge & Rosalie

The french doors open on a balmy winter night
threats of war in the Middle East
stages set
world stages
the globe on the end table totters
shaken by the hem of a skirt
the vibration of feet on the wood floor
the globe falls
becomes separated from its axis
and the music goes on

floating in the open spaces
a sea of music we bob and weave
in a current from the past.
The music is Havana 1952
a soft tropic winter
a balmy winter night.
Copacabana feathers and sequins
and the great oceanliners in the harbor
lights reflected on the seas
the music of the danzón floating in the air
the slow cha-cha couples on the balconies
palms rustle the night fabric of dreamers dreaming a new order
on a world spinning on a wood floor
rolling out beyond the french doors
to the battlefields and the blood on the sand
on the streets the surprise of terror.
And maybe because there is no sun or moon
and the dark sky is caught in the mystery of eclipse
we are free for a moment to be loose in the rhythm of our
    footfalls
to the lilt of melody
to the quiver of the string tuned to the body of a
    guitar—
our bodies loose in the air with the music
and the world stuck in a corner
pieces coming apart
pieces scattered on an end table.

The coward's way is to get drunk and forget
to sleep through the night
to let a blanket of clouds detach us from yesterday—
but the music continues
makes the past present
tunes our breath to survive
and we recognize the faded muffle of a march in the beat
the confetti line of the violin
that catches on the railing of our night ship.
We rock on the swells of trouble
holding hands against armies that will have their way with us

and the gray vixen behind the voice
sings about old friends reminding us
"No ash will burn, no ash will burn."

UNTITLED

for Pedro Pietri

We sat
spilling mucus from our brains onto the floor
the floor got slippery
we put words on our feet
and skated on the puddles
banged into walls
fractured the mirrors on our eyes
splinters of our vision fell up into the sky
reflected the sun that fingered its way through the blinds.
A broken night lay around us.

BACALAITOS AND FIREWORKS

for Arlene Gottfried

Loisaida
you are the keeper of fireworks
I left your glitter nights behind
I thought to be free of your fire-brand of hunger
but you clamped the sharp teeth of memory onto my tail.
The tale of my past shadows me
shows me I will never be free of you
even in the now sunlit gray of your forgetful streets
those same streets that kept watch

with my red spiked heels on the stoop
waiting for the eye of midnight to cut the darkness
knowing all the while that death is just a shot away—
the candle heat that liquefies
the time I shoot in my veins—
you hold my time
you and the streets.

In front of Iglesia del Dios de Siete Días
prayers jump out of the tambourines
I was a young bride of ten in my crinoline
and layers of tulle swinging around my hips
I walked past the junkies roasting a pig on the sidewalk
past the rats scurrying from the song of my white patent innocence
I paraded with an army of black virgins like me
believing at my first communion I drank the blood of God
believing the priests who said that wine
was only for homeless bums crawling for chump change on your corners
believing in your power
holding the priests and the winos together
believing my black virgin eyes that told me the world was no bigger
than the picture on my grandmother's TV screen.
I would go to my grandmother on Sundays
after drinking the blood of God
I would go to her apartment dodging the pleading hands on your corners
I would sit on her plastic slipcovered living room chairs
making valentines for a drumbeater
the young congero across the way
he haunted your streets sending kisses in the melody of his rhythms
he knew the music of my prayers.
I never knew his real name until
I saw it printed on the ribbons that tied his funeral flowers—
there were red ribbons and white flowers at his funeral—
and you kept all those colors—
the dead man in his casket
not even looking like himself
like the boy I had loved—
you reminded me and I bit my tail
tried to cut you off

and to run from grief I filled my belly with wild seeds
let myself become swollen till I burst from my bride's dress.
I had no language for anger except confession.
I stood for hours leaning against light posts
I stood and birthed my dreams on you
waiting for lights to go on over my head
unaware that you saw who I was.
And to run from my shadow
I threw on my red blouse
the one with the cuchi-cuchi ruffles around the shoulders—
you kept that blouse too
the gaudy red of it unfaded.
In your closet of fireworks you kept the intimate real of me
jumping to stain the sky with my breath.

tato laviera SOLEDAD

people talk about loneliness

is only sexual companionship
that's soon forgotten

people talk about solitude

beneath its seven layers
nobody can talk about solitude

and soledad

well, there is no english
translation

MY GRADUATION SPEECH

i think in spanish
i write in english

i want to go back to puerto rico,
but i wonder if my kink could live
in ponce, mayagüez and carolina

tengo las venas aculturadas
escribo en spanglish
abraham in español
abraham in english
tato in spanish
"taro" in english
tonto in both languages

how are you?
¿cómo estás?
i don't know if i'm coming
or si me fui ya

si me dicen barranquitas, yo reply,
"¿con qué se come eso?"
si me dicen caviar, i digo,
"a new pair of converse sneakers."

ahí supe que estoy jodío
ahí supe que estamos jodíos

english or spanish
spanish or english
spanenglish
now, dig this:

hablo lo inglés matao
hablo lo español matao
no sé leer ninguno bien

so it is, spanglish to matao
what i digo

                ¡ay, virgen, yo no sé hablar!

SKY PEOPLE (LA GENTE DEL CIELO)

Eye-scratching mountain view
Puerto Rico counting houses
upon houses, hill after hill,
in valleys and in peaks,
to observe: la gente del cielo,
fingering on clouds,
climbing further and further,
to preserve taíno folklore,
gente del cielo,
toiling the land,
artcrafting musical symbols,
giving birth to more angelitos del cielo,
whose open-spaced hands captured moon waltz:
solemn serenity serenading life,
la gente del cielo,
who prayed in nature's candlelight,
galaxies responding with milky way guiñaítas
winked in tropical earth smile,
as God gleefully conceded,
what we had perceived all along,
that Puerto Rico is 100 by 35 by 1000
mountains multiplied by the square root
of many cultures breathing: ONE.

TITO MADERA SMITH

for Dr. Juan Flores

he claims he can translate palés matos'
black poetry faster than i can talk,
and that if i get too smart,
he will double translate pig latin
english right out of webster's
dictionary, do you know him?

he claims he can walk into east harlem
apartment where langston hughes gives
spanglish classes for newly arrived
immigrants seeking a bolitero-numbers
career and part-time vendors of cuchi-
fritters sunday afternoon in central
park, do you know him?

he claims to have a stronghold of the
only santería secret baptist sect in
west harlem, do you know him?

he claims he can talk spanish styled in
sunday dress eating crabmeat-jueyes
brought over on the morning eastern
plane deep-fried by la negra costoso
joyfully singing puerto rican folklore:
"maría luisa no seas brava,
llévame contigo pa la cama," or
"oiga capitán delgado, hey captain delgaro,
mande a revisar la grama, please inspect
the grass, que dicen que un aeroplano,
they say that an airplane throws marijuana
seeds."

do you know him? yes you do,
i know you know him, that's right,

madera smith, tito madera smith:
he blacks and prieto talks at the same time,
splitting his mother's santurce talk,
twisting his father's south carolina soul,
adding new york scented blackest harlem
brown-eyes diddy bops, tú sabes mami,
that i can ski like a bomba soul salsa
mambo turns to aretha franklin stevie
wonder nicknamed patato guaguancó steps,
do you know him?

he puerto rican talks to las mamitas
outside the pentecostal church, and
he gets away with it, fast-paced i
understand-you-my-man, with clave
sticks coming out of his pockets hooked
to his stereophonic 15-speaker indispensable
disco sounds blasting away at cold reality
struggling to say estás buena baby
as he walks out of tune and out of
step with alleluia cascabells,
puma sneakers,
pants rolled up,
shirt cut in middle chest,
santería chains,
madamo pantallas,
into the spanish social club,
to challenge elders in dominoes,
like the king of el diario's
budweiser tournament
drinking cerveza-beer
like a champ,
do you know him?
well, i sure don't,
and if i did, i'd
refer him to 1960
social scientists
for assimilation
acculturation

digging
autopsy
into
their
heart
attacks,
oh,
oh,
there
he
comes,
you can call him tito,
or you can call him madera,
or you can call him smitty,
or you can call him mr. t.,
or you can call him nuyorican,
or you can call him black,
or you can call him latino,
or you can call him mr. smith,
his sharp eyes of awareness,
greeting us in aristocratic harmony:
"you can call me many things, but
you gotta call me something."

pedro pietri   YOU JUMP FIRST

you jump first
one wino says to the other
do not disappoint your friends
they have been waiting down there
in below zero temperature
for the past 365 days to see you
practice what you preached
do not wait until it gets dark
the lights do not work around

this neighborhood of old-time religion
strangled by police sirens
hurry up before the reverend
who shows you where the roof was at
changes your mind with
another bottle of gypsy rose
& deports you back to night school
so you can learn how to count
& jump off higher buildings

PROLOGUE FOR ODE TO
ROAD RUNNER

A downtown train
A downtown train
A downtown train
A downtown train
A down
  down
  down
  down
town train down train town
A train downtown
A train downtown
A train downtown
A downtown train
A down
  down
  down
  down
down train
down train
down train
train down

train down
train down
A downtown train
A train downtown
A train town down

Part Two
train A town down
down A train town
A downtown train
A train downtown
A downtown train
   down
   train
   down
   town
   down
   train
A downtown train
A train town down

UPTOWN TRAIN

I predict that at exactly 10 to 10 it will be 10 to 10 again
then at exactly 10 after 10 it will be 10 after 10 once again
until the hands of time change the subject at which time I will
make another accurate prediction for the science friction public
I predict that if you are caught in a sudden violent rainstorm
& you don't have an umbrella available you will get soaken wet
I predict that if you forget to brush your teeth for one week
your breath will smell worse than all the sewers of the universe
I predict that if you wake up late in the morning you won't get
to work on time & be deducted & instructed to be punctual or else
find yourself another fulltime job to pay for a decent funeral
I predict that the more you demonstrate the less you masturbate
your demands will be met after you forget what your demands are
I predict that after friday night it will be saturday morning
I predict that if you don't put gasoline into the engine of your
car you will have a difficult time getting out of your garage
I predict that if you stop wetting the bed you will become senile
I predict that if you blow your nose snots will come out of them
I predict that if you can't sing you can't sing if you can't act you can't act
if you can't dance you can't dance & if you can't lose weight you can't
lose weight & you must love or hate yourself
I predict that if you have nothing to say you have nothing to say
I predict that if you go away & don't return & leave behind no
forwarding address your mail will be returned to the post office &
discarded to oblivion if not claimed by anyone within thirty days

TELEPHONE BOOTH NUMBER 102

you and your bottle
and your smoke
and your coke
are cordially invited
to attend a party
if you cannot make it
send your bottle
and your smoke
and your coke
to keep the party going
until you are able
to party with us

TELEPHONE BOOTH NUMBER 227

come over
to my apartment
this evening,
the television set
does not work,
we can watch some
thing interesting
before it is repaired

TELEPHONE BOOTH NUMBER 507

I will jump out the window
if that's what it takes
to satisfy you sexually,
but only if you live in the
basement

TELEPHONE BOOTH NUMBER 905½

woke up this morning
feeling excellent
picked up the telephone
dialed the number of
my equal opportunity employer
to inform him I will not
be into work today
"Are you feeling sick?"
the boss asked me
"No Sir" I replied:
I am feeling too good
to report to work today,
if I feel sick tomorrow
I will come in early

WET HAND ON DRY DREAMS

for Julio Dalmau

I look at the sea
The sea doesn't look back at me,
I stare at the walls
The walls disappoint me also,
I scream at the wind
The wind minds its own business,
What a relief that was
On a rainy Monday dry morning

I sit down and wonder
If the chair I'm sitting on
Is wondering also?

There is no sea
Inside this apartment—
I am staring into a mirror
With perfect impaired vision
Of forever lost memory,
Flashbacks of unseen landscape
Where the journey to nowhere begins:

The floor doesn't move an inch
As I remain where I am
Contemplating my latest decision
To think about nothing else
For as long as it takes
To feel I have been here before
Inside this room I never left—

Is at this precise moment
A suitcase I lost a long time ago
Whispers to the clouds above
This conversation I'm having,
That I have to leave town
Or risk never again being unoriginal!

A sunken ship surfaced
Inside shut eyes of glass mirror
Holding my thoughts hostage—
Passengers who proudly perished
In Easter Suits that outgrew them
Wave at mourners they cannot see,

This apartment isn't a beach!
The sea has no business in here,
There are no seagulls in sight
Not even on the insipid wallpaper,
Someone dialed a right number
And got the wrong person paranoid

And now what goes up stays UP
And we all have a drinking problem
Because the origins of gravity
Is still a normal fucken mystery,
Anyone who makes any sense
Ends up on the manic toilet seat
Of the divorce court of the mind
Suing their sanity for malpractice!

No one is holding you here
Against your will in this room
Where the door never opens
And the windows never stay shut,
You can leave if you aren't lonely
Others won't be arriving soon
I don't advise you to be present
And witness yourself absent
When no one else arrives,

It's never too late to change
Your mind about not being here
And hide by not moving an inch
And convince yourself & others
That a mountain can be climbed
If you stare at it long enough
Without a worry up your sleeves!

Right about this time
Rumors are we all are doomed
So why bother to leave the room?

Chico, you have no choice
But to start feeling significant
About wasting precious time
Now that the end is redundant—

Something else has to happen
For nothing to continue happening!
Whether your roots approve or not
This empty room also goes to Puerto Rico!

There's an airport in your mind,
We can take off whenever you please,
You will still be able to order
Something scrambled about your eggs
And analyze the salt shaker
Should pepper come out instead!

A kiss is still nothing but a kiss,
Human beings have been sticking
Their tongues into each other's mouths
Since the very beginning of time,
You don't have to feel bad at all
About not answering the knocking
You thought you heard at the door,

We have come a long way
To have nowhere else to go,
And realize that to steal
Doesn't mean to be a thief,
It takes much more courage
To stay seasick long enough
To become truly anti-social

This is the bottom line
The bottom line all the time:
The lamp will stare at you

When you least expect it to,
As you cross a mental river
Praying to forget how to swim
Before reaching the other side

To meet an eternal blind date
At the gates of the great desert,
In transparent long black veil
The size of her womanly shadow,

She will applaud as you enter
And immediately lose your sense
Of direction for then & forever,
Following her who walks around
Blindfolded all day and night
To remind her bright admirers:
Only death can make her come!

Nothing will be accomplished
As far as pleasure is concerned,
She never said she loved you
She only warned us to stay awake
Long before we decided to be born
To grow up to become orphans—

It was then you looked at the sea
Expecting to see yourself drowning
And just saw the palms of my hands
Wondering why were you so depressed?
Thinking that the end of time
Had decided to doubt your existence!

That was when you lost control
And started calling yourself up
At all ungodly hours of the night
And dared not answer the telephone
For fear of hearing something
That might solve your problems,

You really wanted to get some sleep
But it wasn't time to leave yet,
There were no doors to imagine open,
The coast will never be clear!
You have to keep talking to yourself,

And that can be very exciting
As long as we keep climbing walls
And not let anyone know about it
Not even yourself or that mirror
Your thoughts keep getting lost in,

If you don't leave your house
Your house will leave you
And you will have nowhere to go
Next time you have nowhere to go,
The future will have no future
But you still have to get out of bed!

Like it or not you are the host
Of an uninvited ghost who drops by
In low-cut blouse and tight skirt,
Her purpose is to convince you
To fit right shoe on the wrong foot

And finally decide to go outside
And immediately start feeling
We are being followed once again
And run back into the apartment
To avoid finding out who's behind
The conspiracy to keep us alive?

She was as light and as dark
As the night will ever become,
No end in sight inside her eyes—
We pretended not to notice
She reposed in a romantic coffin
And had taken full advantage
Of the right to remain silent

You and I were just 5 years old
Experiencing our first hardon
In funeral parlor turned peep show
For a memorable fleeting moment
Of being overwhelmed by doubts
Inducing multiple cemetery orgasms
In dreams that take forever to end
If you happen to be wide awake,

Looking for clues to leave
The apartment without having
To open the door to get out
Or jump out the window screaming,
To discover there's no end in sight,
And sweat instead of staying cool!

Life didn't have to be so hard
All we had to do to see the sea
Was take the train to the plane
Not stare at four blank walls
Because someone refused to dance
A slow record with our horny pride,

The sea could have really been
The sea and not tears from eyes
Too busy looking to see anything!

We could have both opened
The bi-lingo refrigerator door
And taken out a bottle of red wine
And poured wine into a lonely glass
As the sun is about to forget
What day of the week it has been,

And together decide it was
No longer necessary to worry
About anything "especially nothing"
And pay no attention to the glass

Of wine on the table for hours
Before deciding not to drink it,

Until the time finally comes
To do nothing else but listen
To the sound of water dripping
From water faucet in nursing home
We imagine someone else captive,
Because we will never grow old
As long as you continue to be
A teenager in love for all eternity!

miguel piñero

LA BODEGA SOLO DREAMS

dreamt i was a poet
&
writin' silver sailin' songs
words
strong & powerful crashin' thru
walls of steel & concrete
erected in minds weak
&
those asleep
replacin' a hobby of paper candy
wrappin', collectin'
potent to 'pregnate sterile young
thoughts

i dreamt i was this poeta
words glitterin' brite & bold
strikin' a new rush for gold
in las bodegas

where our poets' words & songs
are sung
but
sunlite stealin' thru venetian
blinds
eyes hatin', workin' off time
clock
sweatin'
&
swearin'
&
slavin'
for the final dime
runnin' a maze
a token ride
perspiration insultin' poets'
pride
words stoppin' on red
goin' on green
poets' dreams
endin' in a factoria as one
in a million
unseen

buyin' bodega sold dreams . . .

THE BOOK OF GENESIS ACCORDING TO ST. MIGUELITO

Before the beginning
God created God
In the beginning
God created the ghettos & slums
and God saw this was good.
So God said,
"Let there be more ghettos & slums"
and there were more ghettos & slums.
But God saw this was plain
so
to decorate it
God created lead-based paint
and then
God commanded the rivers of garbage & filth
to flow gracefully through the ghettos.
On the third day
because on the second day God was out of town
On the third day
God's nose was running
& his jones was coming down and God
in his all knowing wisdom
knew he was sick
he needed a fix
so God
created the backyards of the ghettos
& the alleys of the slums
in heroin & cocaine
and
with his divine wisdom & grace
God created hepatitis
who begat lockjaw
who begat malaria
who begat degradation
who begat
    GENOCIDE

and God knew this was good
in fact God knew things couldn't git better
but he decided to try anyway
On the fourth day
God was riding around Harlem in a gypsy cab
when he created the people
and he created these beings in ethnic proportion
but he saw the people lonely & hungry
and from his eminent rectum
he created a companion for these people
and he called this companion
capitalism
who begat racism
who begat exploitation
who begat male chauvinism
who begat machismo
who begat imperialism
who begat colonialism
who begat wall street
who begat foreign wars
and God knew
and God saw
and God felt this was extra good
and God said
VAYAAAAAAA
On the fifth day
the people kneeled
the people prayed
the people begged
and this manifested itself in a petition
a letter to the editor
to know why? WHY? WHY? qué pasa babyyyyy?????
and God said,
"My fellow subjects
let me make one thing perfectly clear
by saying this about that:
No . . . . COMMENT!"
but on the sixth day God spoke to the people
he said . . . "PEOPLE!!!

the ghettos & the slums
& all the other great things I've created
will have dominion over thee"
and then
he commanded the ghettos & slums
and all the other great things he created
to multiply
and they multiplied
On the seventh day God was tired
so he called in sick
collected his overtime pay
a paid vacation included
But before God got on that t.w.a.
for the sunny beaches of Puerto Rico
He noticed his main man Satan
planting the learning trees of consciousness
around his ghetto edens
so God called a news conference
on a state of the heavens address
on a coast to coast national t.v. hookup
and God told the people
to be
COOL
and the people were cool
and the people kept cool
and the people are cool
and the people stay cool
and God said
Vaya . . .

NEW YORK CITY HARD TIMES BLUES

NYC Blues
Big time hard-on on me blues

New York City hard sunday morning blues
yeah
Junkie waking up
bones ache trying to shake
New York City sunday morning blues
the sun was vomiting itself up over
the carbon monoxide detroit perfume
strolling down the black asphalt dance floor
where all the disco sweat drenched Mr. Mario's
summer suit still mambo-tango hustled
to the tunes of fiberglass songs
New York City sunday morning means
liquor store closed
bars don't open 'til noon
and my connection wasn't upping
a 25 cent balloon
yeah
yeah reality wasn't giving me no play
telling me it was going to be sunday
24 hours the whole day
it was like the reincarnation of the night
before when my ashtray became
the cemetery of all my lost memories
when a stumble bum blues band
kept me up all night playing me cheap
F.M.
dreams
of hard time
sad time
bad time
hell we all know times are
hard
sad
bad
all over
well I thought of the pope
welfare hopes
then I thought of the pope again
Om . . .

it didn't hear my incantation
there has to be an explanation
wasn't it true
when you
Om . . .
you are one
Om . . .
make me warm
Om . . .
is part of god
Om . . .
make the cold wind stop
Om . . .
perhaps if I
Om . . .
stronger
Om . . .
louder
Om . . .
LONGER
OMMMMMMMMMMMMMMMMMMMMM
it don't work
Om . . .
I feel like a jerk
I'll try once more just to make sure
OMMMMM
maybe if I pleaded on my knees
to J.C.
he'd take heed of my needs
and melt the icicles
from the tears in my eyes
but it was still cold
I'm told if you sing
"I'm gonna lay down my sword and shield
    down by the river side . . . down by the river side"
I get no signal
maybe if I do it bilingual
"en la cruz, en la cruz yo primero vi la luz"
oh come on chuito

have a heart
take apart the winter winds from me
please . . . J.C. . . .
OM . . .
en la cruz
down by the river side
10 hail marys I offer
and 5 our fathers
but the cold was no further
than before
I should know it's very rare when
a prayer
gets the boiler fixed
OMMMMM
yeah
New York City december sunday morning
was whippin' my ass in a coldblooded fashion
treatin' me like a stepchild
putting a serious hurting on me
watching me bleed
thru my sleeves
as I tried to get high
shooting up caffeine without saccharin
that some beat artist sold me down
on eldridge st.
yeah
but that's the ghetto creed
that the strong must feed
yeah
brotherman
everything was happening faster than the
speed of sound
my whole seemed like it was going down
I wonder who ever wrote that tune
about being back on top in june
nigger forgot about september and december
now that's a month to remember
when each cold day becomes like a brick wall
and you're the bouncing ball

yeah I kept seeing my fate being sealed
by the silk smooth hands of the eternal bill
collector
who keeps rattling my doorknob
pressing my avon ding dong bell . . .
my pockets were crying the blues
telling me that I ain't fed them a dollar in years
and was it clear that they couldn't hold
any more unpaid debts . . . traffic tickets . . . or promissory notes
and hey that was when I wished I was back in
L.A.
laid back
L.A.
kick back
L.A.
smog town
hollywood . . . driving down to malibu
hollywood U.S.A. . . . hey hey U.S.A. hollywood
seedy-looking film producers smile at you
over a burrito with taco bell breath
explain the plots to fellini movies
they aint ever seen
hollywood . . . down to malibu
at two a.m. if you get tired
of cal worthington shit-eating grin
you walk out on him hit santa monica blvd.
and watch the manicured thumbs caress the
homosexual airs of rolled-up jeans and silver buckles
as westwood camaro rides very slow very low
down western ave.
where neon lights scream
the latest kick in adult entertainment
masturbation
enters your thoughts
when pornographic stars with colgate smiles
whisper
inane
mundane
snides of flicking your bic

or I'm nancy fly with me national
well I'm going nowhere got nowhere to go
going nowhere fast
got me a couple of dollars a few dimes
and plenty of time
go into some bar on alvarado
and temple listen to some mariachi music
or stroll into some dive joint off sunset
sit in some naugahyde booth
with some dishwater blond
with sagging breasts
wearing a see-thru blouse
and listen to all her 1930 starlet dreams
as she smokes all my cigarettes
sure what have I got back at that
refugee from a leprosy colony hotel
but a one station A.M. radio
feeding my neurological cells
with those south street philadelphia blues
she wants to cruise thru griffin park
no thank you
I'd rather listen to linda ronstadt instead
and the bartender tell dirty jokes
and his customers recite 12% alcoholic aluminum
recycled viet nam horror stories
reading the signs of our times
the obituary of a dying society
the folktales of yesteryear's gonorrhea
history
hollywood going down to malibu
malibu . . . pretty people and fonzi T-shirts
flex their muscles spreading spiritual bad breath
and joe namath perfume
yeah
but i'm in New York City
crying the junkie blues
welfare afro hairdos sprout out
of frye boots
yeah punk rockers hitting on you

for subway fare three times
soon the mohair slick lines
at penn station are getting impatient
wanna get home
to alone
make the scene with a magazine
or with a plastic doll
cause the missus got another headache
gaze at the farrah fawcett poster
that adorns his horny teenage son's walls
yeah these days always
have a way of showing up
like rubber checks
I wish I could cop a bottle of muscatel
stroll thru the bowery with a pocket
full of wino dreams
but sunday morning in New York City
for the junkie there ain't no pity
we just walk the streets with loaded dice
and hear people say there goes miky
miky piñero
they call him the junkie christ . . .

THE RECORDS OF TIME

Two hundred fifty million years ago, long before the recorded history
of man, someone sat down and recorded it; And this man's name was
Time, and so it was only right that he should call his writings
"records" and add his name to history. Time, a young and ambitious
energy, lived in the summer hills of the Antarctic. He lived near a wise
old gentleman named His Story and his wife Truth, and their two sons
Hypocrisy and Reality. Truth was a very blunt woman who always
tried her best to please all her family and friends, and being such a
pleasing woman, she always ended up on the bottom of the list and

was chosen by His Story to be in the kitchen doing dirty dishes. At places she would try to get away from the kitchen and take Reality for a day at the amusement center. Though she loved her family equally, she had a certain affection for Reality, because everyone in the community was afraid of him (for reasons known only to Unknown, a distant uncle) and she always tried her most to be with him to comfort his loneliness. But that was only once in three lifecycles that she would enjoy taking Reality in hand and walk on the beaches of the North Lifeantic ocean and the earth would shake with pleasure, as well as pain for both of them—Pain was there only because Earth had some wild notion that there's a pain in pleasure and so on. Once Truth and Reality were about to leave the house to buy a new set of garments of the spring. His Story caught them at the door with faithful Hypocrisy at his right side (they were more like brothers under the skin than like Father and son). They began to accuse them of not loving them enough, and to give foundation to their argument, they enlisted the aid of the poker-playing buddies, Shame, Guilt, and Complexes. Reality ran out the door, and Truth stayed behind after much verbal abuse. She succumbed to their will and hid the dirty laundry. That night, feeling very relieved of a heavy burden, His Story and Hypocrisy spent the night at Coward's Bar & Grill where they celebrated their chained freedom, drinking lies and making passionate love to the whore Cheat. This is where His Story met Time. With the fumes of lies in their heads, Time and His Story became pretty good companions. They all sat around listening to Hypocrisy tell tales. Greed and Opportunity, two men who shared the work of the lower forty's, had stepped in through the door and, picking up on the good vibes surrounding the table of His Story, bought a round of lies for the group and stood drugged at the words of Hypocrisy, a heavy rapper—in fact his nickname was Quibber with the Jibbers. Opportunity hit upon an idea on how to become immortal and ran it to Greed, who told His Story and Hypocrisy, and Time was jotting it all down for his records. Simultaneously they saw Reality passing by the front of Coward's window display and fought among each other for the richness of it all. His Story, having the most intelligence and just plain good old game, told them that he had the secret of immortality and that there was only room for one more in the zone of immortality. Being a fair man, he declared that whoever came to his house with the largest number of followers would share the bed with the secret of immortality, his wife Truth. Greed, Opportunity, and Hypocrisy jumped out of their chairs and raced out the door in a mad dash for followers, circling the globe a million ways in charades. Hypocrisy crawled, Greed took to the winds, Opportunity sailed the seas, while His Story laughed at the tears his wife Truth would shed, and time—well Time, he just stood still. . . .

bimbo rivas **A JOB**

A Job
to feed the time I spend adrift
in search for substance in the street
Awake at three a.m.
not knowing where or when the end
will come to my disdain
A Job
A simple job
A place to meet the day head on
with force and vigor
with fervor bigger than a winning independence slate
A Job
A Job my brain to put to work
My brain that tells me I'm OK
My brain that can produce the necessary rhythm
to set my idle body straight
My brain that yearns for a sincere break
I don't expect the world to stop for me
To stop its mission for my sake
I only ask for a clearer path
to put my brains and hands to work
to prove my worth
A Job
A Job my God
A Job that's better than the street
its hustle

and its pests
A Job
A Job that also fills my heart
not just my belly as does the city welfare
check
A Job with all the benefits
correlated with the sweat and time
invested by myself
A Job that don't step on my pride
A Job that don't shorten my life on earth
that will inspire me to help my bosses
their part of the proceeds collect
I need a JOB to keep my peace with God
A Job to make me stop wishing for an early grave
A Job
A Job
I NEED A JOB TODAY
Folks that got a job
a job that does its job
can see some sense in this relate
folks that lost their faith
that rot away with pain
DAY AFTER DAY
Strike at each other
hoping to find
in greater pain
a sedative
it's all too relative
my friends
A man without a JOB
is lost in the labyrinth of
HELL.

LOISAIDA

Lower East Side
I Love You
you're my lady fair
no matter where I am
I think of you!
The mountains and the
valleys cannot compare,
my love to you
Loisaida, I love you!

I dig the way you talk
I dig the way you look
me vacila tu cantar
y yo me las juego
fria pa'que viva
para siempre,
En mi mente, mi amada,
yo te llamo Loisaida.

Cuando estoy lejos de ti
se me acaba mi esperanza
En tus calles yo me
Siento muy feliz y
Saludable
Loisaida, yo te quiero!

Increíble
una mezcla, la perfecta
una gente bien decente
de todas rasas
que estiman
que te adoran

que no saben explicar
lo que le pasa

cuando ausente de
tus calles peligrosas
si te aman
A ti, mi hermosa Loisaida.

O what a 'hood . . .
even with your drug-infected
pocket parks, playgrounds
where our young bloods
hang around
waiting, hoping that
one day when they too
get well and smile again
your love is all
they need to come around.
Loisaida, I love you.

PARADOX AND SLEEP

In the silence of night
when dreams take over
and would-be lovers whisper curses at each other's follies,
and old men sit by dusty windows
waiting for the light of day
to spray their tired bones with loving warmth;
it seems that hordes of images from sleeping heads
invade the stillness of the night
and strike a humming sound
that by careful, quiet meditating souls is heard.

That silence sounds like gentle waves in a lagoon
and interrupted yet by dreams of being awake.
In such a state, the old men nod
and lovers pain forget.

The songs of days are put away
to deal for themselves a one-eyed jack of spades;
while centuries of time to come
await their time to make its impact felt.

And I, assured that my ears are right,
with silly, bashful fright
of being taken for a ride to time immortal before my time,
relate to you some feelings and some visions
of quietness I've heard.

I felt a bearded homosexual paint her face a crimson red
and make her beard and hair turn metallic with a simple
thought request.
I fished a fence from a sand dune
and broke a coca-cola bottle
with a single drop of sweat.

I rode a speechless speck of dust to a kiddie park in Harlem.
And I marveled at the size of candy wrappers blowing past
my head.

A flea in heat mistook me for a flea that bothers fleas;
and almost swatted me to eternal sleep.
I did not fight.
I ran away.
I'm not ashamed.
Was not awake—
I did survive to fight another day.

I thought I was a crosstown bus
whose carburetor sprang a leak
and felt ashamed when all my passengers
refused to flee at the alarm.
It wasn't me who was in charge of me
I became a ragged death-wish slave
remembering the days of Roman conquests
and the rats in Nazi jails.

I dreamt of ending purgatory stays
by giving food stamps to all the souls in hell . . .
I was afraid . . .
I became the "A" of a "SALVAGE AREA" sign
and I had a fit of jealousy
cause I couldn't be the "S."
I saw a dried-up Christmas Tree
buy a pair of Spanish Boots
for a friend called Jingle Bells.

I saw a pregnant woman's baby stretch inside her swollen belly.
I heard the baby wishing, praying
that the mother guessed that the fetus was a girl.
That unborn baby had a dream
about surviving the rugged trip to birth.

A pine tree made a bet with me
about the unborn's quest
I took the baby all the way
and I was happy as a lark
as I heard some folks say
"It's not so strange, that thing called birth,"
the pine tree said.
"It happens every day," a better bet is death.
Just then, I dreamt awake that I became an oil molecule
and felt a sadness through my legs.
I was a thought condemned forever to forget all about sex.
The molecule collided with an electron charged up
and made me come awake.
As an oil molecule my legs got wet
the sadness went away—all without sex.
Oh! The things I heard!
If I should tell you in detail are stranger yet.
The images that fly the night when human beings do dream
to satisfy their need for temporary death
solidify themselves in painter's brush
and poet's pen
and will haunt the cobwebs of the minds of men forever or
until all demands for living life are met.

ntozake shange PEOPLE OF WATTS

where we come from, sometimes, beauty
floats around us like clouds
the way leaves rustle in the breeze
and cornbread   and barbecue swing out the backdoor
and tease all our senses as the sun goes down.

dreams and memories rest by fences
Texas accents rev up like our engines
customized sparkling   powerful as the arms
that hold us tightly black n   fragrant
reminding us   that once we slept and loved
to the scents of magnolia and frangipani
once   when we looked toward the skies
we could see something as lovely as our children's
smiles   white n glistenin'   clear of fear or shame
young girls in braids as precious as gold
find out that sex   is not just bein'   touched
but in the swing of their hips the light fallin cross
a softbrown cheek or the movement of a mere finger
to a   lip many lips inviting   kisses southern
and hip as any one lanky brother in the heat
of a laid back sunday rich as a big mama   still
in love with the idea of love   how we play at lovin'
even riskin' all common sense cause we are as fantastical
as any chimera or magical flowers where breasts entice
and disguise the racing pounding of our hearts
as the music that we are
hard core blues   low bass voices crooning
straight outta Compton   melodies so pretty
they nasty   cruising the Harbor Freeway
blowin' kisses to strangers who won't be for long
singing ourselves to ourselves Mamie Khalid Sharita
Bessie Jock Tookie MaiMai   Cosmic Man Mr. Man
Keemah and all the rest seriously courtin'
rappin'   a English we make up as we go along

turnin' nouns into verbs   braids into crowns
and always fetchin' dreams from a horizon
strewn with bones and flesh of those of us
who didn't make it   whose smiles and deep
dark eyes   help us to continue to see
there's so much life here.

PORQUE NO ESTAS CONMIGO

my song for Hector Lavoe

if hector lavoe is not jackie wilson
who sings you to sleep at night ?
in whose arms did you sleep well or not ?   tell me
cuz i've raced thru streets and dreams kept
undercover
by interpol
and the state police
folks swear never existed   why i've been held in a
coro as far as the *archipelago* and *toda la gente conose*
el señor hector lavoe
mira
tú puedes ir conmigo
hasta managua &
the earthquake was no more a surprise
than you

con tu voz
que viene de los dioses
and the swivel of the hips de *su flaca*
as you dance or
when she sucks the hearts
out of the eggs of
tortugas

anglos die to see float
while all the time we dance around them split up
change partners
and fall madly in love

all this time *compañero*
when they come for you
becuz an inhospitable world

es incomprensible

don't you know
that jackie wilson took up
the flack that su flaca couldn't handle
escúchame
criollo
hay personas en detroit
on your side & they don't care
how the syllables fall
or the linguistic niche
they create for market identifications
what we are dealing with here is
an inexcusable disruption of a way of life
thousands upon thousands
whose every move
is determined by the sound of your voice,
does it matter
you seek out women other men wish they'd had the nerve
to want for their own ? does it matter you don't
always show up
or you attend and your
voice could not make it ? no, negro, no en mi vida
porque
nobody put a tec-9 to your head
tied you up like philip wilson
or prostrated themselves
como machito
si nada es real

nuestra vida es permanente

si ellos vienen con todas las armas, n'importa porque
nosotros somos an army of marathon dancers
lovers
seekers
and collectors

we have never met an enemy we can't outlive

querido, i can assure you myself
that nobody's gonna take you away,
mangle
deform
the sound of you
in our lives
no guns
no napalm
no drogas
no martial law
and U.N. condoned invasions

of our actualities can take you from me

oh sparrow oh ismael,
oh the closest i ever got to beni moré in my lifetime,
do you really believe
that i would let you cease to be

carnal

i asked jackie wilson
and he said "we can't do widout him
he's just like me."

BLOOD RHYTHMS—BLOOD
CURRENTS—BLACK BLUE N STYLIN'

*(French sugar-beet farmers, overwhelmed by mulatto competitors, plastered Europe's cities with
advertisements proclaiming: "Our sugar is not soiled with black blood." A popular Afro-Cuban
saying is: "Sugar is made with blood," while in the South of the United States, cane growers
processed natural sugar "to get the nigger out.")*

Fragrant breezes in the South
melt to melodies round small fires
mount tree limbs
with bodies black
and swayin' black n croonin'
songs of sunsets
comin' from the fields bawdy
brazen
hard to put yr finger on
like the blues
like the strum of guitars on dark damp

southern nights
hard to put your finger on
like screams in the black bloody southern soil
sweet black blood echoin' thru the evenin' service
grindin' by the roadhouse door
sweet black blood
movin' with slow breath

outta breath
young negroes run to pick up a bale of cotton
run to flee southern knights
crosses *bare blazin'* signals black bloods
gone runnin'
for Chicago
for the hollow
for the C.C. Rider
for the new day *sweet*

blocked melodies ache in young girls' throats
rip thru their lips like the road to freedom was lit
all lit up with the grace of God and
Sears Tower
the Ford plane and Pontiac's vision
all lit up *sleek* fires
sheddin' the haunts of poll taxes and test questions *like*
where is America
cost a *finger*
a ear
a heart
a teardrop fallin' from the saggin' front porch
to the project stairway
from the water fountain to the chain gang

the *night train* carried *smuggled* goods *news*
of struttin' signifyin' fellas with gold teeth
neath *they feet and brawny sway* for blocks and blocks
far as the eye cd see from Biloxi to Birmingham
the *contraband* of freedom *seeped* thru the swamps
the air hung heavy
with the cries of "ain't gonna let nobody turn me round"
and *young* boys in nice-cut suits
who was awready standin' with they heads up
awready prancin' with finesse and grand stature
like men wit eyes
don't never look down
men wit eyes burstin' wit glory
from the red sedans
and the *seats in schools*
to the right to set wherever they want
and when the sounds of the harmonica was slowed
by snarlin' dogs and hoses
when the *washboards* and *bottleneck players*
was skedattlin' *out the bullets way*
up came a roarin'
force a light blue controlled fire in un-mussed lamé
pleated silk and faces
bearin' no scars
to say *"we ain't been touched"*

we the *sweet black fires of dreams*
& of unobfuscated beauty

like the trails of freedom
the Good Lord himself lit up
we gonna *take this*
new city neon light
sound
volumes for millions to hear
to love themselves
enough to turn back the pulse of a whippin' history
make it carry the modern black melody from L.A.
to downtown Newark City
freedom buses
freedom riders
freedom is the way we walk that walk
talk that talk
gotta take that *charred black body out the ground*
switch on the current to a new sound
to a new way of walkin' a new way of talkin'
blues

electrified
blues
boltin-the-lynchin-tree-
n-tremblin-n-chirren-
blues
defyin' the sound of gravity

for a people singin'
about the sashay of blood rhythms set free.

piri thomas
BORN ANEW AT EACH A.M.

The street's got kicks man,
like a bargain shelf,
In fact, cool-breeze, it's got
love just like anyplace else.

It's got high-powered salesmen
who push *mucho* junk,
And hustlers who can swallow
you up in a chunk.

It's got sewers that swallow
all the street pours down its throat
It's got hope wearing
an old overcoat.

It's got lights that shine up
the dark and make the scene like new
It sells what you don't need
and never lets you forget what you blew.

It's got our beautiful children
living in all kinds of hell
hoping to survive and making it well
Swinging together in misty darkness
with much love to share
Smiling a Christ-like forgiveness,
that only a ghetto cross can bear.

The streets got life, man,
like a young tender sun,
And gentleness like
long awaited dreams to come.

For children are roses with nary a thorn,
forced to feel the racist's scorn,
Our children are beauty
with the right to be born.

Born anew at each a.m.
like a child out of twilight,
flying toward sunlight,
Born anew at each a.m.

PROLOGUE. *SEVEN LONG TIMES*

Like I'm standing here and nuttin's happening. Diggit, man, what's in this here world for me? Except I gotta give, give, give. I'm tired of being a half-past nuttin'. I've come into this stone world of streets, with all its living, laughing, crying, and dying. A world full of backyards, rooftops, and street sets, all kinds of people and acts, of hustles, rackets, and eyedropper drugs. A world of those who is and those who ain't. A world of name-calling, like "nigger sticks" and "mucho spics."

I'm looking at me and no matter how I set my face, rock hard or soft sullen, I still feel the me inside rumbling low and crazy-like, like I'm mad at something and don't know what it is. Damn it, it's the craps of living every day and not diggin' what's in tomorrow. What's the good of living in a present that's got no future, no nuttin', unless I make something. I fell into this life without no say and I'll be a mother-jumper if I live it without having nuttin' to say.

I know this world is on a hustle stick and everybody's out to make a buck. This I can dig, 'cause it's the same here on the street. I gotta hustle too, and the only way to make it is on a hard kick. I dig that—copping is the main bit and having is the main rep. You see, I'm really trying to understand and see where you're at.

How many times have I stood on my street corner, looking out at your blippy world full of pros? At all you people who made it and got to be great, a real bunch of killer-dillers. I know about you. I've gone to the big school too. I've dug how to live too.

Are you willing to learn about me and what makes me click? Well, let me run it to you nice and easy.

Have you ever sensed the coming danger as on a bop you go? A rumbling of bravery, of puro corazon, and gusto to the nth degree? Have you ever punched a guy in the mouth with a ripped-off garbage can handle, or spit blood from jammed-up lips? Have you ever felt the pain from a kick in the balls? Have you ever chased in victory a gang fight supreme or run in tasteless defeat with all the heart you can muster? Have you felt the bond of belonging when with your boys you went down?

Tell me, did you ever make out in dark hallways with wet kisses and fumbling hands? Did you ever smother a frightened girl's rejections and force a love from her? Did you fill your dreams with the magic of what you wanted to be, only to curse the bitchin' mornings for dragging you back on the scene? Did you ever smoke the blast of reefers and lose your freakin' mind? Did you ever worry about anything at all—like a feeling of not belonging? Did you ever lover-dubber past this way?

Did you ever stand on street corners and look the other way from the world of muchos ricos and think, "I ain't got a damn"?

Did you ever count the pieces of garbage that flowed down dirty gutters, or dig the backyards that in their glory were a garbage dump's dream? Did you ever stand on rooftops and watch nighttime cover the bad below? Did you ever put your hand round your throat and feel your pulse beat say, "I do belong and there's not gonna be nobody can tell me I'm wrong?"

Say, did you ever mess with the hard stuff—cocaine, heroin? Have you ever filled your nose with the wild kick coke brought or pushed a needle full of the other poison and felt the sharp-dull burning as it ate away your brain? Did you ever feel the down-gone-high as the drug took effect? And feel all your yearnings become sleepy memories and reality become illusion—and you are what you wanted to be?

Did you ever stand, small and a little quiet-like, and dig your mom's and pop's fight for lack of money to push off the abundance of wants? Did you ever stand with outstretched hands and cop a plea from life and watch your mom's pride on bended knees ask a welfare investigator for the needed welfare check, while you stood there, getting from nothing and resenting it just the same? Did you ever feel the thunder of being thrown out for lack of money to pay the rent, or walk in scared darkness—the light bill unpaid— or cook on canned heat for a bunch of hungry kids—no gas—unpaid?

Did you ever sneak into the movies and dig a crazy set where everybody's made it on that wide wild screen? They ride on long, down shorts, like T-Birds, Continentals, Caddies. Such viva smoothies, with the vines—the clothes—like you never ever saw. And, oh, man, did you ever then go out of that world to sit on hard stoops and feel such cool hate and ask yourself, "Why, man? Why does this gotta be for me?"

Have you ever known the coldness of getting busted . . . the scared, hollow feeling of loneliness as you're flung into a prison cell?

Have you ever heard voices inside screaming, "Don't bitch about being busted, turkey—you done broke the law and that's wrong," and had that truth eased off by another voice saying, "Don't fret, little brother. How could you ever have done it right when everything out there in them streets was so goddamned wrong?"

So carry the burden with mucho corazon and try like hell to make the shadows of the prison bars go away by closing your eyes to the weight of time.

Hard days, long nights. Without a name, a number instead. Your love of color blighted by a sea of monotonous blues and grays. Warmth replaced by cold steel bars. Tiny bleak cells surrounded by chilly concrete, mountain-high prison walls. Within is lost the innocence of a smile . . . The tears that flow are unsalted and the laughter is unreal. The days that eventually turn into long years are each terrible in themselves:

Hey world!!
You don't want to hear me. I'll make you hear me.
You don't want to see me. I'll make you see me.

Punto!!

IV.
THE
OPEN ROOM

elena alexander SLANT

Fantasy caroms
off pain,
ball in
side pocket
of all we
wish for,
deny wanting.

We will lose
that game.

Picket announcing
doom while
denouncing is
tying himself in
comfortable nots
and naysays, psychic

bondage, love
all the lovelier
for pain unforgiven,
wounds given, received
equivalent of Our
God the Father, stigmata
of father the
god, our mother
the goddess who
spoils in the swamp
of unmet needs, desire
like rotting vegetation
throwing off
its fervid stench.

If we are
to admire decay
let us at
least play
in forests and
thickets where
smells of
death are pungently
scented and made
for our flesh
and bone.

david allen # THE REVOLUTION WAS POSTPONED BECAUSE OF RAIN

The underlying
immediate
political
socio-economic
and trigger mechanism causes
were all in place when
some nee-gro or the other got hungry
had to stop at the McDonalds
had to get on the line
with the new trainee cashier
"uhh, where's the button for the fries?"
so we missed the bus

Then the leader couldn't find his keys
didn't want some poor ass moving
his brand new 20" and VCR
out his living room on the shoulders.
It was too late when the locksmith came

Then our demo expert Willie Blew got arrested
came out with his head hanging under his hoody
"Didn't know they started doing that
for jumping the turnstiles," he said.
"How many times must we tell you—
don't get caught."
we voted against shootin' him on the spot

In the winter we were all depressed
so we leaned our guns against the sofas
and listened instead to Tim Tim Tiree
singing about his dysfunctions:
Sometimes I wonder if ah'll ever be free
free of the sins of my brutish daddee
Like the cheating, the stealing, the drinking, and the beating . . .

The weatherman said the 17th would be sunshine
and it wouldn't be too hot—
Tim Tim Tiree doesn't like sweatin'
but that night the weatherman came on crying
saying he didn't control the weather
that God was real
that he's lucky He, God, didn't strike him, the weatherman, with lightning
for taking the credit sometimes
and that he, the weatherman, was in no way responsible
for the hurricane coming
and that we, the viewers, should
pray Jesus into our hearts
before it was too late

Superbowl Sunday was out
all the women wanted
to see the game
and the men were pissed
at their insensitivity

The 20th was supposed to be a definite
we looked for some Bastille to storm
didn't find any
settled on the armory instead
before they moved the homeless in
"We'll bum-rush it anyway," i said
"It smells like a collection
of a thousand farts in there," they said
So we waited for the approval of the city
contract to build a Bastille
which set the revolution back five years.

Peace wanted to start the revolution on Tuesday
She was in a pissed-off mood
her tax return didn't come in time for the rent
But they showed the *We Are the World* video
on cable that evening
and we all held hands
and cried to stop from laughing

and our anger subsided
Looking back, it could've been a plot
but there are more substantive plots to expose
than the We Are the World conspiracy

Now we wait for the rain to stop
All forces on the alert
some in Brooklyn basements
packed in between booming speakers
listening to Shabba Ranks and Arrested Development
bogling and doing the east coast stomp
gargling with Bacardi and Brown Cow
breaking that monotony with slow movements—
slow, hip-grinding movements
with the men breathing in the women's ears to
Earth Wind & Fire's *Reasons*
and wondering what the weather will be like
next weekend.

sheila alson   VACANT CHILD

I see a ball, a red burning ball
taking off from the ground and shooting up into the air
in a curvilinear space and coming back down
meanwhile everything there is to know has been known
meanwhile you live in a state of trying to do

meanwhile violence
meanwhile each project's our own
goes off from its inner diameter
meanwhile we dwell on the eyes of a vacant child
in the body of a man
meanwhile we dwell on the ashen skin of a man
abandoned
long ago

child of the street
vacant child, vacant eyes
child of the street in the body of a man
child of the ashen skin
child of the street in the body of a man
child with his hand held out
child with his eyes held out

body of a man in a business suit
body of a man in a three-piece suit
body of a man who owns his eyes
body of a man who does not give up his eyes to the passerby
body of a man with a limousine waiting
body of a man who is tall and his hands are to his side
body of a man that doesn't yield
body of a man covered up
body of a man wrapped in a pin-striped suit
chest of a man is all that's visible
chest of a man in a pin-striped suit
head of a man eyes of a man skin of a man who owns his face
keeps his eyes
wraps his body behind a pin-striped suit
keeps his eyes

indran amirthanayagam   THE LAST
CONDORS IN MANHATTAN

When you lose a job and you're alone
looking outside the window, and
there are birds from South America
in the pet shop on Atlantic Avenue
and in the dress shop ponchos
and hats you think, yes,
I can go south again

but if the firing took place
in what's called a massacre
you with the thin brown envelope
while your friend on the staff
for the last 10 years receives
the fat brown instructions to work
again, your anger and sadness

reduced to imagining why
your friend's been saved
while the free receive
paychecks and the unfree dream
of South American birds
and the morning
and lying down to sleep

passing away of pleasures
getting old knowing
you will die dying
turning again to the facts
of your disappearance . . .
how many newspapers
will follow you down south

pack their cameras on burros
and ride behind your donkey

past the terraced vegetables
past the long cool drags
on some ecstatic plant
to the caves on tops of mountains
that are home to the last condors.

rudolfo anaya   WALT WHITMAN
STRIDES THE LLANO OF NEW MEXICO

I met Walt, kind old father, on the llano,
    that expanse of land of eagle and cactus
Where the Mexicano met the Indio, and both
    met the tejano, along the Río Pecos, our
    River of blood, River of Billy the Kid,
    River of Fort Sumner where the Diné suffered,
    River of the Golden Carp, god of my gods.

He came striding across the open plain,
    There where the owl calls me to
        the shrine of my birth,
    There where Ultima buried my soul-cord, the
        blood, the afterbirth, my destiny.

His beard, coarse, scraggly, warm, filled with sunlight,
    like llano grass filled with grasshoppers, grillos,
    protection for lizards and jackrabbits,
    rattlesnakes, coyotes, and childhood fears.

"Buenos dias, don Walt!" I called. "I have been
    waiting for you. I knew you would one day leap
        across the Mississippi!
    Leap from Manhattas! Leap over Brooklyn Bridge!
        Leap over slavery!
    Leap over the technocrats!

Leap over atomic waste!
Leap over the violence! Madonna!
Dead end rappers!
Peter Jennings and ungodly nightly news!
Leap over your own sex! Leap to embrace la gente
de Nuevo México! Leap to miracles!"

I always knew that. I dreamed that.

I knew you would one day find the Mexicanos of my land,
the Nuevo Mexicanos who kicked ass with our
Indian ancestors, kicked ass with the tejanos,
And finally got their ass kicked by politicians!
I knew you would find us Chicanos, en la pobreza,
Always needing change for a ride or a pint,
Pero ricos en el alma! Ricos en nuestra cultura!
Ricos con sueños y memoria!

I kept the faith, don Walt, because I always knew
you could leap continents! Leap over the squalor!
Leap over pain and suffering, and the ash heap we
Make of our Earth! Leap into my arms.

Let me nestle in your bigote, don Walt, as I once
nestled in my abuelo's bigote, don Liborio,
Patriarch of the Mares clan, padre de mi mamá,
Farmer from Puerto de Luna, mestizo de España y
México, Católico y Judío, Moro y indio, francés
y mountain man, hombre de la tierra!

Let me nestle in your bigote, don Walt, like I once
nestled in the grass of the llano, on summer days,
a child lost in the wide expanse, brother to lagarto,
jackrabbit, rattlesnake, vulture and hawk.
I lay sleeping in the grama grass, feeling
the groan of the Earth beneath me, tierra sagrada!
Around me, grasshoppers chuffing, mockingbird calling,
meadowlark singing, owl warning, rabbit humping,
flies buzzing, worms turning, vulture and hawk

riding air currents, brujo spirits moving across
my back and raising the hair of my neck,
golden fish of my ponds tempting me to believe
in the gods of the earth, water, air and fire.
Oriente, poniente, norte, sur, y yo!
Dark earth groaning beneath me, sperm flowing,
sky turning orange and red, nighthawks dart, bats
flitter, the mourning call of La Llorona filling the
night wind as the *presence of the river* stirred, called my
name: "Hijo! Hiiiii-jo!"

And I fled, fled for the safety of my mother's arms.

You know the locura of childhood, don Walt—
  That's why I welcome you to the llano, my llano,
  My Nuevo México! Tierra sagrada! Tierra sangrada!

Hold me in the safety of your arms, wise poet, old poet,
  Abuelo de todos. Your fingers stir my memory.

The high school teachers didn't believe in the magic
  of the Chicano heart. They fed me palabras sin sabor
  when it was your flesh I yearned for. Your soul.
  They teased us with "Oh, Capitan, My Capitan!"
  Read silently so as to arouse no passion, no tears,
  no erections, no bubbling love for poetry.

Que desgracia! What a disgrace! To give my soul only
  one poem in four years when you were a universe!

Que desgracia! To give us only your name, when you were
  Cosmos, and our brown faces yearned for
  the safety of your bigote, your arms!

Que desgracia! That you have to leap from your grave,
  Now, in this begetting time, to kick ass with
  this country which is so slow to learn that
  we are the magic in the soul! We are the dream
  of Aztlán!

Que desgracia! That my parents didn't even know your name!
     Didn't know that in your *Leaves of Grass* there was
     salvation for the child.
     I hear my mother's lament: "They gave me no education!"
     I understand my father's stupor: "They took *mi honor, mi*
     orgullo, mi palabra."

Pobreza de mi gente! I strike back now! I bring you
     don Walt to help gird our loins!
     Este viejo es guerrillero por la gente!
     Guerrillero por los pobres! Los de abajo!

Save our children now! I shout. Put *Leaves of Grass* in their
     lunchboxes! In the tacos and tamales!
     Let them call him Abuelo! As I call him Abuelo!

Chicano poets of the revolution! Let him fly with you
     As your squadrons of words fill the air over
     Aztlán! Mujeres chicanas! Pull his bigote as you
     Would tug at a friendly abuelo! His manhood is ours!
     Together we are One!

Pobreza! Child wandering the streets of Alburqué! Broken
     by the splash of water, elm seed ghost, lost and by winds
          of spring mourned, by La Llorona of the Río Grande
     mourned, outcast, soul-seed, blasted by the wind
          of the universe, soul-wind, scorched by the
     Grandfather Sun, Lady Luna, insanity, grubs scratching
          at broken limbs, fragmented soul.

I died and was buried and years later I awoke from
     the dead and limped up the hill where your
          Leaves of Grass lay buried in library stacks.

"Chicano Child Enters University!" the papers cried.
     Miracle child! Strange child! Dark child!
          Speaks Spanish Child! Has Accent Child!
     Needs Lots of Help Child! Has No Money Child!
          Needs a Job Child! Barrio Child!
     Poor People's Child! Gente Child! Drop Out Child!

"I'll show you," I sobbed, entering the labyrinth of loneliness,
    dark shadows of library, cold white classrooms.

You saved me, don Walt, you and my familia which held
    Me up, like a crutch holding the one-leg Man,
        Like Amor holding the lover,
            Like kiss holding the flame of Love.

You spoke to me of your Manhattas, working men and women,
    miracle of democracy, freedom of the soul, the suffering
    of the Great War, the death of Lincoln, the lilacs' last
    bloom, the pantheism of the Cosmos, the miracle of Word.

Your words caressed my soul, soul meeting soul,
    You opened my mouth and forced me to speak!
    Like a cricket placed on dumb tongue,
    Like the curandera's healing herbs and
    Touch which taught me to see beauty,
    Your fingers poked and found my words!
    You drew my stories out.
    You believed in the Child of the Llano.

I fell asleep on *Leaves of Grass*, covering myself with
    your bigote, dreaming my ancestors, my healers,
    the cuentos of their past, dreams and memories.

I fell asleep in your love, and woke to my mother's
    tortillas on the comal, my father's cough, my
    familia's way to work, the vast love which was
    an ocean in a small house.

I woke to write my *Leaves of Llano Grass*, the cuentos
    of the llano, tierra sagrada! I thank the wise
    teacher who said, "Dark Child, read this book!
    You are grass and to grass you shall return."

"Gracias, don Walt! Enjoy your stay. Come again. Come
    Every day. Our niños need you, as they need
    Our own poets. Maybe you'll write a poem in Spanish,
    I'll write one in Chinese. All of poetry is One."

cynthia andrews   # AMNESIA

Springsteen screams out of
the radio like a cat on
fire for a little of that human
touch beyond that of his steel
guitar cutting beneath the fingers.

It's Saturday, a motionless after-
noon in the heat of late June
blurring my vision to
the immediate only, the chair
and Springsteen screaming
through the fans.

I am too old now to remember
even last year, a month is
a decade and days play
their games with my brain
like short sarcasms or
those brief, cold
sweat seconds after a bad
dream.

Like amnesia in a heat
spell I am lucid only when a
certain word is called like a catch
phrase or someone suddenly
clasping my wrist, and then
I recall a name or a
book, a few words may
be tied in string around my
mind, but loosely, until

I'm back in the dog-day sleep
of mid-afternoon with the
immediate again around me like
shrubbery, hard and sharp

and biting at my skin while
I sleep.

zoe anglesey
HOLDING HIM NOT AS A CHILD

Do his lovers cradle him like this guard
to prevent the intervention of tremor our sound
defend against invasions of mind not minding itself.

Do his lovers breathe over him this way
pace the lungs filling and the heart
stave off any fear from a sudden wakening.

Do his lovers wave away flies green and loved
going for the moistness of lips
end the taste for the nose and the eye's salt.

Do his lovers prefer the silence of his sleep
the peace of his being length of his lips rounded and pulsing
his head sinking as the sleep deepens.

Do his lovers know do his lovers not think
that his head and wide shoulders feel weightless
lifted and light in the fold of a woman's lap.

Do his lovers whisper do they look at him
as one might at one's child needing a nap
the child in the hammock of this man.

Do his lovers believe wild under stars the tippy moon
dangerous in the dark to his tune of Eliot and Yeats
a wedding song sung and beginning again.

Do his lovers give and give forever
long like this in a moment eternal holding him safely
and faithful while he listens to some pal like Burroughs.

Do his lovers not see the thinned hair his face
how serene the transparent skin when time suspends
the mounded chest rising alive full of swelling tide.

Do his lovers see this man taste him
like one could cradling him holding him
not as a child but as a man as a lover?

pauly arroyo   I'M A NUYORICAN

I'm a Nuyorican
I'm not the first   and I'm not the last   but I'm a Nuyorican
I'm a ghetto Nuyorican who runs wild
there's a beast in me always
but I'm tamed when I have to
I still practice my Zen
I still keep my chi with me in the city

I'm just keepin' my business so right
I'm just keepin' my soul to survive
and though I know I know what it really means
I'm tryin' to keep my visual steady
I'm still lookin' out to the stars
I'm breakin' myself into reality
I'm takin' my first step to tell you the truth
I did my 18 years and I want you to understand
I play my heart and soul 'til I die
I bounce my rhythm from the walls and through the sky
I still feel my heart and soul inside
I'm still a Nuyorican deep inside

I play in my room all the time
I try to listen to the reality
I try to say all those things and say no lies
I try to chant my love for you and stay there
I'm playin' my tune one more time
I'm tryin' to be a Nuyorican too
I'm tryin' to play my ghetto tune
I'm watchin' the storm come in to thunder
I'm playin' my tune for you
I want you to be a Nuyorican with me
I'm tryin' to play my song to you
I'm just playin' New York regular tune
I'm playin' my song for you
I'm just a Nuyorican just like you

And though we play our tunes
the ghetto still plays the sound with us
we bongo like madness   we bongo our dreams   we bongo our tunes
don't let us be stopped because we won't   we will keep tryin'
and if we are still a rhythm of sound
let our music bounce from every wall and town
and if we can play the tune once more
I play it just for you

asha bandele   IN RESPONSE TO A
BROTHER'S QUESTION ABOUT WHAT
HE SHOULD DO WHEN HIS BEST
FRIEND BEATS UP HIS WOMAN

snatch him up by the back of his neck   run him into his own fist   twice
tell him who the real enemy is   show him   make him swallow his own
teeth   do not help when they scratch the inside of his throat   tell him it
was his fault   make his eyes swell up so he looks like a freak   make him

go to work like that & come up with excuses why he looks so bad   tell
him it's the whiteman   show no sympathy when he tries to hide from the
whispers   tell him you're sorry   tell him you love him and then kick his
ass again   tell him it was his fault   question him on why he's such a
coward   interrogate his ass   make him beg forgiveness   watch him
crawl   put the word out on the street THERE'S AN ENEMY IN OUR
PRESENCE THERE'S AN ENEMY IN OUR PRESENCE it does not
think it only attacks   it makes weak-ass excuses it takes no responsibility
it picks on things smaller than itself and reads sharazad ali   it worships
miles davis

IT LIES   IT LIES   IT   DESTROYS
LIFE   IT LIES!!!

and if he finally understands   then go to him   find out where it started
search for burn marks beneath his flesh   peel back his pain   be a brother
whisper   haki madhubuti to him   whisper sonia sanchez   let him sleep
in yr arms   stand alone if you have to   this is the right thing to do
stand alone   let them talk   while you break centuries of vicious cycles
face the contradictions the sliced open bellies   the jaws wired shut the
assholes split the breasts scarred from cigarette butts and bloodied vaginas
this is what it looks like   do not turn away now   babies beat out of
wombs   spines curved   uneven legs that no longer walk   dead eyes that
do not see tomorrow   livers imprinted with size 12 shoes

      face the contradiction   that looks like u
                            that smells like u
                            that feels like u

and push out the violence   be unafraid   to be a man who confronts men
    about women   be unafraid   to be a man
                          who confronts men
                          big mean ass   nasty men
          be unafraid   to be a man
        who confronts
        himself.

carmen bardeguez-brown

OYE MAMÁ, OYE, MAMÁ
SHANGÓ, OSHÚN
Y
OBATALÁ

Redeem our Faith
Hunt our FEARS
SOLITARIA EN LA CALLE
POSTERGANDO LA MASACRE
OYE SHANGÓ
oyeme, oyeme, MADRE, OSHU UUUN
INFINITY
CONSUMED
IGNORED
DESTROYED

oye, SHANGÓ
LISTEN, LISTEN TO YOUR PEOPLE

ETERNITY OF SENSES
TRYING LUCK
FUCKING HOPE
DYING YOUNG

oye, OYEME
SOMEONE
SOME one
ONE
lone SOME
NONE
gone
sha_N GÓ

SHANGÓ
go

CHAINS
CHANGE GONE
dry DRUMS
MOM MORE
   mom

oh, ohoh, OH, OHHHHH
   OSHUN.

denise bell   **REALITY?**

when our sweat dries
     you light your cigarette
        after i meet your needs
           will i be like   the curling smoke
             you let disappear in the air

nicole blackman   **DAUGHTER**

One day I'll give birth to a tiny baby girl
and when she's born she'll scream and I'll make sure
she never stops.

I will kiss her before I lay her down
and will tell her a story so she knows
how it is and how it must be for her to survive.

I'll tell her about the power of water
the seduction of paper
the promise of gasoline
and the hope of blood.

I'll teach her to shave her eyebrows and
mark her skin.
I'll teach her that her body is
her greatest work of art.

I'll tell her to light things on fire
and keep them burning.
I'll teach her that the fire will not consume her,
that she must take it and use it.

I'll tell her to be tri-sexual, to try anything,
to sleep with, fight with, pray with anyone,
just as long as she feels something.

I'll help her do her best work when it rains.
I'll tell her to reinvent herself every 28 days.

I'll teach her to develop all of her selves,
the courageous ones,
the smart ones,
the dreaming ones,
the fast ones.
I'll teach her that she has an army inside her
that can save her life.

I'll tell her to say Fuck like other people say The
and when people are shocked
to ask them why they so fear a small quartet
of letters.

I'll make sure she always carries a pen
so she can take down the evidence.
If she has no paper, I'll teach her to
write everything down on her tongue,
write it on her thighs.

I'll help her to see that she will not find God
or salvation in a dark brick building
built by dead men.

I'll explain to her that it's better to regret the things
she has done than the things she hasn't.

I'll teach her to write her manifestos
on cocktail napkins.

I'll say she should make men lick her enterprise.
I'll teach her to talk hard.
I'll tell her that her skin is the
most beautiful dress she will ever wear.

I'll tell her that people must earn the right
to use her nickname,
that forced intimacy is an ugly thing.

I'll make her understand that she is worth more
with her clothes on.

I'll tell her that when the words finally flow too fast
and she has no use for a pen
that she must quit her job
run out of the house in her bathrobe,
leaving the door open.
I'll teach her to follow the words.

I'll tell her to stand up
and head for the door
after she makes love.
When he asks her to
stay she'll say
she's got to
go.

I'll tell her that when she first bleeds
when she is a woman,
to go up to the roof at midnight,
reach her hands up to the sky and scream.

I'll teach her to be whole, to be holy,
to be so much that she doesn't even
need me anymore.

I'll tell her to go quickly and never come back.
I will make her stronger than me.

I'll say to her never forget what they did to you
and never let them know you remember.

Never forget what they did to you
and never let them know you remember.

Never forget what they did to you
and never let them know you remember.

jennifer blowdryer FROM WHITE TRASH DEBUTANTE BALL

Meet the White Trash Debutantes, this is the season. The White Trash are having their own Debutante Balls constantly, you can only exclude people for so long and they will stop feeling excluded, it's not natural to feel humble over several generations. Derby, Connecticut has a lot of White Trash Debs, and they all come into Spider's studio to get tattooed. The Studio is perfect because it is directly connected to a bar called "Bottoms Up" where all of the slime that get 86'd from everywhere else end up, and Spider has a haphazard waiting area where different apprentices have tried to make homey touches: An ugly spray-painted couch, a couple of tattoo books, sketches thumbtacked to the walls.

I hate to say it but the women in the town look shot by the age of 21, some of them are too scrawny with haggard-looking faces, frizzy hair, and a standard outfit of jeans and a biker T-shirt. Unless you change your idea of beauty, which the men must have done because they keep right on having babies and getting "Rick" tattooed on their left tit. Some of the tattoos we do are to cover up the "Rick" with a cluster of lilacs, which is hard to do on a woman who is 7 months pregnant and mad.

shorty bón bón   **A JUNKIE'S HEAVEN**

His sacrifice was not in vain
though he died because of an abscessed
brain
a junkie dreamt
of his lament
When I die
I shall go to a land
where the cocaine is clean
and I'll smoke my pot only when it's
at the darkest of green
here all the angels are junkies
and the Christ is so hip
that for the crime of my bootlegged
wine
he'll demand two sips
yes, come to my heaven where all
the junkies walk free . . . and
remember all you potheads out
there
the smoke is on me. . . .

kymberly brown-valenzuela   KISS DEATH SOFTLY WITH BLUE LIPS

the doorman there without a door
is me   when the air swallows you up
away from the delicate nest of my heart
where the blue egg tosses & turns
in its speckled sleep

despair grazes at the edge of my hair
lying in the fields of wheat-colored grain
hideous is the swish of its tail
lined with the dead eyes of flies
its tongue lolls   suffocating flowers

once young and inattentive
to the creaking cries of floors
the slamming of unaided windows
the wind moaning in my head
now I am twined together my

age unraveling in the ball of time
the old grandfather clock
is ill at ease with the gray clouds
stirring in the stomach of my soul
& kittens eye me with suspicious whiskers

even I feel awkwardly distant
unable to lose sleep over the losses
I wake up screaming though
the silences I invent make me
what I am in love   with locomotives

in my dreams I have my heart attacks
hold my chest gasp wheeze can't breathe
have epileptic fits & convulsions
tongue lolling & rolling around on the floor
speaking in inarticulate sentences that shake

grow paralyzed by fear   or lack of it
cannot move limbs   go into shock   kiss death
softly   with blue lips
to awake again in the hollow of your arms
safe in the round breath of an eternal rest

alaan bowe   EVERY KNOTTED FIST

One: *Word Any Phrase*
every stroke of my pen   my tongue aflame
a little death
murder   rape   incest   torture
some poor fool
forced to sit through this poem
winces   somebody gave me a hug yesterday
as I bludgeon my fingers   I don't know who
& tongue   I didn't get that good a look at her
every stroke
tongue the nib &
spit   any sound any
blood   word any phrase
dapple the page   gonna hold all my
                    fuckin' grudges   any poem any
thick   in every knotted fist   poet any author
as the notes of a   any audience any
Bach fugue   community any
                                                communication any
don't mind me   interaction any
I'm just whining about stains that dried   juxtaposition any
to a flaky brown   opposition any
on my sheets long   murder
before puberty or   hurts
delusions of puberty clubbed
me senseless   if it's done right

jim brodey   LITTLE LIGHT

for Eric Dolphy

*"He was like an angel that came down to Earth, played his saxophone
incredibly, and passed too quickly."*

—*Clifford Jordan, 1966*

There's
A
Little
Light
Over
The
Con Ed
Tower, Eric, and it's you. Too bright
to be a star, total capacity
brightens a still-raining sky, & I'm
on stand-by, waiting for your horn
to come crashing down on Manhattan.

                          Tonight, in the bathtub,
Listening to your ancient sides, rolling over, scrubbing
my back with your delicate clarinet breeze, oh so blue,
the rain beating on my eyelids, big drowsy drops shaped
like coins, that lay their own tattoo on my palms as I,
too heavy to rise beyond as you do in your uniqueness
while the soot-tinted noise of too-full streets echoes
and I pick up the quietly diminishing soap & *do*
myself again.

           And, right now, it's noon in the tropics, as
a great big hand fondles the cherubs that cruise this ashen light,
one big whooshing sigh knocks a fleshy heave towards what snow
glides in on a severed tongue still singing, so beautifully
deranged, and squeezing some more difficult light
to dry my glazed flesh with

                    some of your happy brilliance.

lisa buscani
CHEKOVIAN DEPRESSION

And we'll never find happiness!
No, never!
And we'll never get to Moscow!
And Irina's crying again . . .

And there's never enough vodka!
No, never!
And little Masha's drowning!
And Irina's crying again . . .

Ah Sergei, how I loved you once.
The autumn leaves, golden in their sadness!
Olga, you were so lovely once.
The spring buds, green in their naive futility!

When! When does the pain subside?
Ivan Ivanovitch has hung himself, you know!
Little Masha's on fire now,
And Irina's crying again . . .

The summer smothers each
in its godless communist heat!
It's true about Alexei Petrovitch,
he died of a broken heart!
The winter clutches each
in its unrelenting Lenin-like grip!
never, never to ease!
Little Masha,
buried alive,
Somebody choke that bitch Irina,
and life,
life is death!
Death!
Death!
And thick-soled boots!

steve cannon   ORANGE

This is the story
I'm tryin' not to remember
This the dream
I don't want to recall
This is the song
of a ball in space

This is the poetics
of nations, religions and cultures
and the way we look to us all

This is the individual
constantly searching for freedom
in a world
Stumblin' thru anarchy and chaos
A cosmos that's
Indifferent to human actions
and the way night turns to day

This is a cacophonous symphony
of telephonetics and photos
This is the ecstasy of spirits
transparent shapes like shadow
dancing around the light

This is a dream
I don't care to recall

This is the carnage that gave us the orange
like the evening that brought us the dawn

nick carbo
THE PRETTY BOYS OF ERMITA

Lately, they've been offering
the *Mt. Pinatubo Special*.
Ten- and thirteen-year-old boys
promise that their tongues
can make a man's penis feel
seismic twitches.
Customers have come from Australia,
Scandinavia, and even America
for these tourist attractions.
They arrive from across the globe
in pre-paid packaged tours.
Their brochures advertise
nude boys frolicking
under an orange sunset,
on a white sand beach.
The first stop is a bar in Ermita
where these white men pair off
with the brown boy
of their choice. After an evening
of volcanic experiences,
the men and the boys are bused
to a "private" beach resort in the south,
for a week of sun, sex, and piña coladas.
On the back of the brochure,
a man from Sydney claims
that it was the best vacation
he's ever had.

I wonder if a middle-aged man
in Berlin, Stockholm, or New York
is looking through a set of pictures
of the pretty boys of Ermita.
I wonder if that man is holding
his white penis in his hand,

thinking of how those boys
are growing into men,
thinking if Jose, Tito,
or Eddie are still alive.

laurie carlos   BORINQUEN

Borinquen thru azure & rain storms in ruffles, closed in fingers. An
unknown listener of love and clear light playing guitar, answering ques-
tions about the origins of roaches and tears. Borinquen clean washed
linoleum raised against too much steam heat. High rise 10 to 4 rooms and
rice and rice and rice grateful for meat. Unable to find mangos in season or
blue water. Loving everything American. Working New York brooms and
Long Island gardens. Loving Ricky Nelson & Topo Gigo, Joselito on the
Sullivan show.
Calling Carmen! carmen morales rodriguez ortiz ayala arroacho perez cruz
carmen sanchez domingues piñero rivera santiago sonia clara jose manuelo
edgar ellia luz anna borinquen. Crying plenas in pentacostal basements. Just
good dancers. Villains cut in brillante. Singers leaning gorgeous in
Woolworth powder. The lord lives in us all! Borinquen marching on the
head of disaster. Declaring summer by congas and cheering loud for the
Yankees. Parking DeSotos sideways on Columbia Street repairing nylons for
the week. Borinquen a world of pink rollers bringing stripes to florals orange
to gold. Flirting loud on corners lined with garbage. Smelling summer in
the eyes of Borinquen thru azure. Eyelids lined in tragic black pencil.

elizabeth castagna   HAD IT BEEN

Line tease a
surface gently

406

fallen.
My sister in
pale yellow
as the summers
where.
Canoe flowers stood
still
near the outline
of
animals.
A sing to her dreams,
chasing the wind
against
her wind,
always tall.
Then perfumed entrances
never
seemed quite there.
She'd float
almost
through each question.
"Can I have your chance?
Just one?
Of them?"
Marks left on
me
of purple cinders
bury thoughts like
these.
I'd imagine it this way,
had they been.

marcel christian   FAIR PREJUDICE

If you're a white person
And you've never done anything to me

Or you're an associate or a friend of mine
You're not the Ku Klux Klan
You're just a regular person, a human being
A white human being

But if you're a white person
Who doesn't give a fuck about me
From breaking my knees with your Wall Street
      briefcase on the subway
To beating my ass down to the ground with a stick
Then you're a goddamn dirty white motherfucker
To me

If you're a black person
And I know you and I like you
Or if we're close, I love you
First of all because you're black
Then because you're my friend

But if you're a black person
Who's a shady motherfucker
You mugged me—you raped my sister
You killed my mother for four dollars
      she had in a raggedy pocketbook
I would dress in white and help the Ku Klux Klan
      nail your ass to a burning cross
Because you are one of the dirtiest fuckin
      niggers that ever lived
To me

I think that's Fair Prejudice
Seems fair
To me

gabrielle n. lane clarke ODE TO A BLACK CHILD (AKA MR. AMERICA)

I remember how Grandfather used to tell me how it was for him in the 50's—when he was my age. And how in the 60's he marched on Washington with Martin Luther King, Jr. Used ta' tell me—"Don't forget where you came from, hear?" Sometimes I wonder if it's the same for me now— you know—all these so-called "rights" we have now. Or—if it's just an undercover situation today? Like yesterday, alright, there's this kid in my class (who everyone knows his family has a lot of money), well, everytime he raises his hand in class, the teacher smiles and says, "Yes—Jake?" I mean, no matter how many kids, right, are flagging their hands in the air and screaming, "me, me—!," she always picks that kid . . . Oh, I don't know. I mean, sometimes I say to myself—what if, what if I raised my hand one day and Mrs. Sloan picked *me*! What would I say? Would I just answer her question or would I say . . .

Mr. America, Mr. America, are you there?
I am a child
standing outside in the cold
the blood that once flowed
through my veins
has recycled
and stopped at the tip of my toes
frozen from the frostbite
that forever pecks at my feet.

Mr. America, Mr. America,
I am a black child
let me in—
so that I, too,
may catch the flicker of light in my eyes
from the flame of your fire

For I am told
it can warm my ebony skin
and even, perhaps,
make me more "pleasant"

Mr. America, Mr. America,
BEWARE, I am the CONSCIOUSNESS
of the black child
and I have seen your grand doors
open many times

                    why—I have noticed—
all types of people
from all across the world
rushing in and out
brushing against each other
and they come
and they go
but I stand here
outside in the cold

and why is it—
when *I* knock
          Mr. America—

              no one seems
                  to be HOME??!!

todd colby   # LEMON BROWN

I'm going to stomp on some necks tonight.
I want to rip my fucking skin off
and be exposed to the stupid starlight.
I'm a walking nerve machine—
don't get too close—I'm a jumpy kind of guy
with a revolver.

I'm so full of decisions that I can't make—

I'm really getting tired of this century—

Don't push me around—DON'T push me around—

I'm starting to use my cats
as dairy animals—
I milk them right over
my cereal—
                    "Sure," you're saying,
"There's not enough milk
in a cat for a whole bowl of cereal."
        Well—
YOU'RE RIGHT—I just use a little less cereal
and when I really need a drink
I just hold the cat up to my face
and suck my drink.

I'm feeling more and more like a caged
animal in this city—
all this rage— building and building—
I don't want to explode
right on 12th Street—
it would fuck up any ideas
for that movie theater they've been
pounding away on NIGHT AND DAY—
building this damn city
higher and bigger and BETTER—
"Hell, it's for your own good"
they say, "It'll make life so much easier . . ."

In my hometown back in Iowa
some kids of 19 or 20
shot one of their friends in the back
of the head—pumped his head full
of several rounds—SLUGS—
        just a little cocaine dispute
they pulled him out of the farmhouse
into a field and shot him
in the back of the head—
12 of his friends—they were all there

JESUS CHRIST
It's getting more and more fucked up
and it's all designed to bring us crashing DOWN—
petty grievances settled with guns, knives and bottles.

I'm not scared
I got my piece loaded and cocked
Fuck around?
FUCK YOU—

Give me some more fear
Give me something else to be scared about
PLEASE.
I'm addicted to fear.

The show's over
the balloon went up
and the monkey died

IT'S ALWAYS SOMETHING
AND IT'S COMING FROM SOMEWHERE
AND I'M REALLY FUCKING
LOSING IT.

All my friends ask, "Why are you freaking out?"
"Why are you always so tense?"

And I answer,
BECAUSE IT'S A GREAT GOD
DAMN TIME TO BE WRITING
BEAUTIFUL LITTLE POEMS
IN EXPENSIVE LITTLE BOOKS
GOING ON AND ON
ABOUT BIRDS, TREES AND FLOWERS.

matt cook   SCIENCE WAS INVENTED BY A BUNCH OF GUYS WHO WERE SO UGLY THEY COULDN'T POSSIBLY BELIEVE IN GOD

HOW SMART ARE WE?
WE DESCENDED FROM APES
NOW WE DRESS LIKE THEM ON HALLOWEEN

IT IS SAID THAT A BARREL OF MONKEYS ARE FUN
MONKEYS EVOLVED INTO HUMANS WHO INVENTED BARRELS
   TO PUT MONKEYS IN
SO IT WOULD BE FUN
MONKEYS AREN'T ANY FUN ON THEIR OWN
SO MAYBE IT'S JUST BARRELS THAT ARE FUN
SHOOTING FISH IN A BARREL IS SUPPOSED TO BE EASY
THIS MAKES SIMPLE DARWINIAN SENSE
BARRELS WERE FASHIONED BY NATURAL SELECTION TO
   MAKE SHOOTING FISH EASY
MONKEY SEE MONKEY DO WAS THE FIRST EXAMPLE OF EYE-
   HAND COORDINATION
THE PIE IN THE FACE WAS NEXT
I THREW A BIRTHDAY CAKE AT *THE MAN WHO SHOT LIBERTY*
   VALANCE
HE WAS 24

NOWADAYS WE CAN'T FIGURE OUT WHY SMALLPOX IS SO
   FUNNY

TYRANNOSAURUS REX DIDN'T REALLY LOOK LIKE THAT
HE WASN'T REALLY BUILT LIKE THAT
WALKING UPRIGHT
      ON TWO LEGS WITH THOSE DINKY LITTLE ARMS
      EATING FLESH LIKE THAT
THERE'S NO WAY HE COULD HUNT LIKE THAT
HE WAS A VEGGO IF EVER THERE WAS ONE

WE FOUND A BUNCH OF BONES LYING AROUND
AND WE THINK WE KNOW HOW THEY FIT TOGETHER
RIGHT
THEY'VE ARRANGED THOSE BONES ALL SORTS OF WAYS
THEY'VE COME UP WITH ALL SORTS OF CRAZY-SHAPED
   BEASTS
THIS ONE JUST HAPPENS TO LOOK THE MOST FEROCIOUS
SOME KID PROBABLY LIKED IT THE BEST
IT SELLS DINOSAUR BOOKS

thulani davis
A MAN'S TAILOR / DAKAR

the sewing shop is very cool
the owner wears shades
and French trousers
African men with taste
for Patato, Totico & guaguanco
like the taxi driver
who could tell you
someone shot Chano Pozo
in a bar in Harlem in '48

the young men work the machines
like potters find the center
they work circles, snails
and recenter the cloth
leaves and diamonds
the mosaic floor of a mosque
concentric, hypnotic
like prayers or mantras
the stitches are very close
the lines quite straight
and quite curved

the owner starts to bargain
the client pretends he's shocked
they are having a sport
and both will do business
robes drift in a clothesline breeze
the needles buzz
while the pedals hum
salsa is rocking
and the machines are swaying

cristina desrosiers # MOUNTAIN CLIMB

Without care, people slip
Two are safer on a rope.
No peak is too high for me,
but when you slip, I fall.
You've been led here
I know the way
If you stay, don't follow me.
Follow the roots that
      begin in the center
and fill every inch of your
      stain
      blood
      body
      soul

I hear freedom is a
      commodity, a rare delicacy
like a panda   hard to capture
      and impossible to cage
while halfway out
I'll listen to your expressions
touch face, bones, pores, cilia
Feel speechless, free, afraid

with shattered eyes   and
a stomach that cannot relate
ME
Breaking down once again
my womb prepares
vulnerable
bleeding
free
trapped
free
trapped
free
trapped
you
with you in me.
Should I run?
Will you join me?
Will you climb again?
If I am naked, will you be?
If I freeze, will you warm rain?
Without care, people slip
Two are safer on a rope.
I cannot
be afraid to step,
          walk, palpitate
trust you with my fall
I must hear
you listen
Please secure me
so I may share my
cumbre
peak
Clouds below
my soul fills with a hit of
fresh air and is
all too awakened by you.

carol diehl **FOR THE MEN WHO STILL DON'T GET IT**

What if
  all women were bigger and stronger than you

And thought they were smarter

What if
  women were the ones who started wars

What if
  too many of your friends had been raped
  by women wielding giant dildos
  and no K-Y jelly

What if
  the state trooper
  who pulled you over on the New Jersey Turnpike
  was a woman

And carried a gun

What if
  the ability to menstruate
  was the prerequisite for most high-paying jobs

What if
  your attractiveness to women depended
  on the size of your penis

What if
  every time women saw you
  they'd hoot and make jerking motions with their hands

What if
  women were always making jokes

about how ugly penises are
and how bad sperm tastes

What if
    you had to explain what's wrong with your car
    to big sweaty women with greasy hands
    who stared at your crotch
    in a garage where you are surrounded
    by posters of naked men with hard-ons

What if
    men's magazines featured cover photos
    of 14-year-old boys
    with socks
    tucked into the front of their jeans
    and articles like:

    "How to Tell if Your Wife is Unfaithful"
    or
    "What Your Doctor Won't Tell You About Your Prostate"
    or
    "The Truth About Impotence"

What if
    the doctor who examined your prostate
    was a woman
    and called you "Honey"

What if
    you had to inhale your boss's stale cigar breath
    as she insisted that sleeping with her
    was part of the job

What if
    you couldn't get away because
    the company dress code required
    you wear shoes
    designed to keep you from
    running

And what if
   after all that
   women
   still wanted you
   to love them.

denise duhamel FEAR ON 11TH STREET AND AVENUE A, NEW YORK CITY

Now the papers are saying pesticides will kill us
rather than preservatives. I pass the school yard
where the Catholic girls snack. Cheez Doodles and apples.
No parent today knows what to pack in a lunch box
and the plaid little uniforms
hold each girl in: lines in the weave cross
like directions, blurry decisions.
A supervising nun sinks in her wimple. All the things she can't do,
she thinks, to save them, her face growing smaller.
She dodges their basketball.
Who said the Catholic church has you for life
if it had you when you were five? I remember my prayers at odd times
and these girls already look afraid.
But it's not just the church. It's America.
I fear the children I know will become missing children,
that I will lose everyone I need to some hideous cancer.
I fear automobiles, all kinds of relationships.
I fear that the IRS will find out the deductions I claimed this year
I made up, that an agent will find a crumpled draft of this poem
even if fear edits this line out . . . I have no privacy,
no protection, yet I am anonymous. I sometimes think
the sidewalk will swallow me up. So I know when the girls
line up to go inside and one screams to her friend
"If you step on a crack, you'll break your mother's back. . . ."

she means it. She feels all that responsibility, that guilt.
There's only one brown girl who doesn't do what she should.
She's dancing by herself to a song on her Walkman.
One of her red knee socks bunches at her ankle and slips into her sneaker.
And the shoulder strap of her jumper has unbuckled so her bib flaps.
Maybe she can save us. I clutch the school yard's chain link fence.
Please, little girl, grow up to be pope or president.

kathy ebel # ARE YOU MRS. LOPEZ' DAUGHTER?

No, I am not Mrs. Lopez' daughter
you big, fine lookin man
You didn't grab your cojones
and hike them on over to me down the platform
just stopped me on the subway stairs
West 4th Street, Washington Square Park
Quick lit face, hopeful question mark
"Scuse me, are you Mrs. Lopez' daughter?"

Her answer would be yes
Mine today is no
It's my new favorite word
Another time I might've stopped when I heard your voice
handed you a teasin lie
coulda led to coffee and pie
in a snakepit West Village cafe
then a vigil by the phone
I'll give you my smile
but I'm making my way to the movies
alone

Cause today is my own solid grey city Saturday
It's an individual thing

Good weather for makin love or housecleanin
Months ago I realized
that dating is a middle class masochistic ritual
a pre-marriage sales pitch
Since then I been straightenin up
instead of gettin busy
Meaning

I got flowers in the vase
Words flowing like milk and honey to the page
And a big empty bed that's been shook free
of every knucklehead I ever convinced
to be with me

I'm not havin that convincing game
Keepin my pit bull clit on a choke chain
stomach in tongue back

  Sometimes I think it must be
  a miracle I got
  Cause I never been on a sailboat
  but there's this pirate's knot
  inside
  waitin to be untied

In the meantime I pass you by
Ignore the twinkle of familiar in your eye
Grab them subway stairs two-by-two
Hit the sidewalk, the winter glare of a downtown day
Tight ponytail, orange lipstick
a sassy sway with which I keep time
That, and a solitary internal rhyme
That's mine, mine only

  I'm cool I'm lonely
  I'm cool I'm lonely

  I'm cool I'm lonely

anne elliott   SLEEPWALKING, TOLD
IN SLOW MOTION

tonight I am stuck in a red room called hell and the devil in the center
swings a hot heavy iron rod in a swift circle his arms are propellers and I
can't duck low enough

tonight men in lab coats lash me to a brass pendulum with rubber tubing
and every swing makes the clock above me tick down one more second and
scientists peer down at me through the glass ceiling my extremities lose air
and turn blue

tonight new york city is a mammoth boat and the ocean is rowdy white
and when my family comes to visit they get seasick where are the life
preservers where do you keep the life preservers honey somebody please
get us some life preservers

tonight I am riding on a swing out behind the old school and my friend
leans into my ass and pushes me higher with every swing and I tell her to
stop and she doesn't and I swing 360 degrees chain wraps the bar over and
over until I am wound too tight high above the dirt

tonight tsunami joe rears up under the pier at the end of my street and I'm
not as heavy as I thought I was and I get washed flipped over sand and
rocks up to the street through cars past taco stands past my doorstep and
back down with each wave back down to the freezing pacific like some
piece of thrown away styrofoam

tonight I take a downtown express train and it doesn't have any stops it
just goes faster wheels squeal against the rails and we descend to the spot
under the river where the air is cold glue and it isn't about to stop it just
goes faster and I notice that I'm the only female on this train

tonight I'm alone in the back seat of a moving car with no driver it is my
responsibility to keep from crashing I have no brakes no accelerator no
gears just one speed and I have to turn the steering wheel with bamboo
poles bound with scratchy rope to my forearms

tonight I fall down a long well eternally I fall and I just want to land I
don't care what surface is at the bottom water granite broken glass dry ice
garbage I just want to land

tonight I am jumping on a blue trampoline and each time I hit the rubber
surface I go a little higher and now the illusion of flight is gone the blue
rushes up at my body faster every time I forgot to ask how to stop what if I
miss the landing and hit the packed adobe ground instead

tonight I am a gerbil in a wheel and a giant hand turns a crank that turns
the wheel and I have no choice but to run the giant hand cranks harder and
I run harder and my feet are slipping oh god they are slipping I fall to the
wire mesh surface and centrifuge holds me flat on my belly and I flip
upside down with every turn of the wheel

tonight I'm in the freight elevator at eddy's loft I lower the platform slowly
hold tightly to the ropes but they slip scrape my future from my palms
swing in an arc away from my hands away from my body the room is
freefalling

tonight I lie awake and dream of standing
still

janice erlbaum THE DAYS OF POT AND ICE CREAM

The days of pot and ice cream
are no longer
we have no more phone
you owe people money
somebody has got to do the laundry
this is no time for checkers, dear
your ship's not coming in
so cartoons and afternoon sex aside

petty crimes used to impress me but
now I think it's time
you get a job.

When you picked me up for this particular
joyride I was sixteen, a girl
and your gold tooth shone with promise
you had it all mapped out to the moon
painted my face in the stars on the ceiling
and aching, flattered
needing a place to crash
I cast my lot in with yours
now it's just a little.

This is no high life of crime
I wait tables and clean houses
while you mope, hustle
spray paint, get high
we live in Queens
we have no money
we have no goddamn money.

Now, I don't mean to dis your illusion but
we're all artists, dear
nobody wants to work for the man
less than your little woman
but my good years are not free
I mean a girl can't live on lotto alone
hey I didn't drop out of high school
to pay your rent
so if you want me to stay
you're going to have to demean yourself
get off the convertible sofa
and get a job.

evert eden   # I WANT TO BE A WOMAN

I want to be a woman
so I can be 20th Century Fox desirable
flaunt my nipples in robes of lavender silk
and run like a wind in the wind
my legs snapping at the eyes of men like mad turtles

I want to be a woman
so I can be cruel and capricious
play guitar with a man's feelings
till he's lip to my zip and I pluck him by the root
like we the people pulling Lenin's statue from his pedestal
then I throw back my head
and laugh—hah hah hah
off you go, honey
go drop your lonesome yogurt on your knees

I want to be a woman
so I can femme myself beyond fatale
grow my nails as long as soda straws
paint them the colors of electricity
watch men talk to my tits and not to me
and think, no nooky for you, silly boy

I want to be a woman
so I can have hundreds of different penises
instead of just one
aah! all the handsome brutes I'll *give* myself to
more freely than Catherine the Great gave herself to her army
I'll throw them my hole damp like a Bible in a bikini
I'll ride them like van Gogh galloped canvas
yes! like Madonna dryhumps the nation
we'll slurp and slither and slime for days
sweating sweet sheets of satin to a swamp
till my orgasms run into each other
like traffic at a busy intersection in Rome

I want to be a woman
so I can lecture men in bed
gently, I'll say, easy
it's a wet grape which you can never peel
easy
it's a living thing with more nerves than you have in your brain

I want to be a woman so I can be ugly and shy
a face like a bug, a body like a beanbag
three fucks a year, they're always drunk
maybe a nice ugly man finds me
we have children and love them, they look like hell
we still love 'em

I want to be a woman so I can walk in fear
and never forget that he, he and he
carry a missile between their legs
heat-seeking me

I want to be a woman so I can be a lesbian
and woman-taste the smiling well
that toasts the wrinkles of the sea
from whence all life sprang like a foxtrot of grasshoppers
oh, I'll carry the name of the woman I love
on the tip of my tongue like the down of a dove
and grow dumpy together, wife and wife

I want to be a woman so I can be fertile
one egg taking on millions
when the blood comes every month
I'll poke that tampon in like a fat finger of fate
and think of children who'll break me open like a pomegranate
to make me the grower and keeper of bubble-blooded life
the mother of dragon-storming queen-esteem daughters
who'll rise from the dust and the ash and the dung
to trash every testicle from Plato to Tarzan
to smash Adam's Eden and God the Father's heaven

I want to be a woman so I can be a womb
who senses a little heart under her heart

a kick of life that knocks inside:
hi, here I am, I'm you, you're me
and buds into a smile that sucks
life from my life, smiles from my smile

I want to be a woman so I can cut the crusts
from my children's sandwiches
recall the innocence that calls
hey, mommy, this is my vagina, right?
yes, honey
that's your vagina, right?
yes, honey
I don't know how to tell you, mommy
but Daddy's got something stuck in his vagina

I want to be a woman
so I can understand why
I'm such a fucking . . . guy
                              heavymetal hardline
                              hangtough hotstud
                              take-no-prisoners
                              duck, scud!
                                 you lookin' at me? fuck you
                                 hey bitch
                                 lemme bang your sugarditch
                                 suck my rockcock
                                 brickdick
                                 meanest penis
                                 muthafucka
                                 superdong
                                 Steely Dannnnnnn . . . .
I want to be a woman
so I won't have to
be-a-man

john farris   MAGIC

that you
love me is preternatural: imagine
492, 357, 816: that's what
I dreamt the night we met:

I thought you
some number: you needed
a ride. I said, o señorita,
I want to take you for a ride.
You said, oh yeah, though
your lips never moved. You just
sat veiled, looking derecho,

mysterious lady passenger
in a stagecoach confused
you weren't headed west. I tipped my hat
three times, I blew some smoke to the primary

directions; I mumbled something
you couldn't understand. I knew
it to be inchoate.

gary glazner   TOAD VENOM

I've got a new drug.
Fritz has a new drug.
Toad venom you want to smoke some?
Hmm I think, what does it do?
It's a mild hash, coke, acid buzz.
Totally toadular.
Nee Deep, Nee Deep.

We drive out to the beach
Climb down the cliffs.
Fritz loads the pipe
It's a flaky wax-like substance.
I take a hit
I'm rolling on the ground.
Some kids on the cliff above
Yell down smoke that bud up here dude . . .
Fritz takes a hit
Now we're both rolling on the ground.
I yell back to them
It's TOAD VENOM!!

Frog high, web brain
A pond splashes in my mind
Buddha bug tongue buzz
Tune in to all the insects
Eyes closed Nee Deep Nee Deep
Hear it fly by
Snatch it Snatch it!!
Toad mind toad soul Wart LOVE!!

The toads come out
In the desert, in Arizona
In the evenings, in the summer.
They have these glands
in their necks
A defense against being bit
You got to squeeze those glands.
Get that venom really juicy really hot
Work that venom squirt
It on a pyrex dish
Let it dry overnight
Scrape it off, scrape it, scrape it.
Nee Deep, Nee Deep.
Buddha bug tongue buzz
Um toad venom.

gloria # WALK RIGHT

She believed that she had figured out how to walk right.
She discovered a walk to lessen the bouncing of her bosom.
Although she was not overly endowed.
She would   walk right,
past the "Psst psst, hey baby, you look fine!"
"Oh I like that" calls of men.
She would walk right.
She had mastered a walk to lessen the movement of her behind.
She would walk right.
After some time practicing her techniques
she could still not escape the sounds and approaches as
she tried to walk right.
"Such a pretty thing! . . .
Why don't you smile honey? . . .
Why you walking alone girl? . . ."
She realized she would have to discover another method to help her
walk right

mia hansford

when two straw half-featured purrings navigate
pink and vagued, across an empty cigarette box,
across the filling floor, and an absent dancing
hoards its dunces

will shelling fear my elbow's differentiated blood
surprise or desolate a hip, and all my instantaneous
heart lie still in that curling mirror?

diana hernandez-correa   # AH BILLIE

for Billie Holiday

She was Empress
under the lights
as she'd begin to cause the steam
to rise
from bellies' core
in dip and turn
injecting
sound thru waves—the mere sounds of her
first notes could be enough
to shake your soul out of its mundane lane
delivering you to a place of fantasy
where she reigned—Queen
a place where gardenias grew wild in black velvet underground
midnight blue and red blood hills as lime green rivers glowed
in
hollow caves that freely flowed from darkness into
light
sending electric chili chills of buzz
thru runaways—
from spine to temple connection
provoking god's consciousness within
to surface
Man, she could WAIL!

But no, they'd say
"She's just no good to self"
& in the absence of glitter
she'd nurse away the nonsense of life's
(unreliability of love)
in the dark with last song sung
she'd cradle her inner bruises
close her eyes tight long
enough to will herself away
having tucked the pain

deep down inside herself past
that medicated voice
and placing it into her Great Chest Cavity
where she could be at One with the
One that she was . . . and being
ONE she could find the strength again
to shake thru the thorns that wrapped their way
around her throat
scratching thru her inner body of sound thru water
to Sky

She'd emerge like a grand whale
and with voice spew out
an Orgasm
leaving behind all mesmerized
watching the entrails of her emotions
blow—like multi-colored ribbons
thru rain pour
AHHHHHHHHHHHHHHHH Billie!

Wish I could've been there to watch
your Tiger-flesh part the crowds
your dark cool strut in satin and your cigarette makin'
rings 'round your gardenia
that sat upon your head like a crown
having never heard a voice so pure
you tinted fate—turned it out/
(inside) to (colorless) almost nude & see-thru

Large thighs, bountiful breasts and bum
with your gin breath you'd intoxicate the room
you and your liquid brain food
making us wait for the next refrain
till the RA TA TA of drum
beats out the ugliness of what's given
oh heroine—I can hear you sing:

"When you hear a song in bloom
like a flower crying for the dew,

that was my heart serenading you . . .
a prelude to a kiss"

Now, time after time when
I need a fix (of you)
to penetrate sound over matter
& jolt me back to life
I spin the needle on the groove/of magic
disentangled from bone 'n flesh to liquid
injecting myself with your voice until it
streams my veins like plasma . . . of you
(and I'd grow still) and you'd arrive
& could feel you as you'd cock your neck
to my ear & whisper . . .
"Hush now, don't explain."

susan hornik **GOODBYE**

I fed the pumpkin muffins I baked you
to the pigeons.
They reminded me of you
They never said
Thank you.

alan kaufman **BUS**

At the gateway
to America
Greyhound strikers
shrieked:

"You won't
get out!"

Ninety bucks
to cross the
land by bus

For this, embarked,
anonymous, neither
lonely nor glad,

a young man
with family
stared at his
ticket, afraid

and an old aunt
stooped to her
bags as a skinhead
cursed her back

and a punk with a pierced nose
sighed: "This country's
fucked"

and beside me
an ex-con, patting
his hair, snapped:
"Man, I *done* my time!
I'm going home"

We boarded like
souls on Charon's bark
As the road
stroked by wheels
removed its dress,

one by one
we laid our tired

heads on breasts
of trembling
glass

But somewhere
in Pennsylvania
I woke,
my face a gun

rick kearns
LLANTO SUAVE PARA PIÑERO

We're walking against
a strong December wind
on a black night in
Alphabet City New York
Loisaida USA 3rd planet
from the sun.

Two light-skinned
idiots Moe and me
I am taking him on
my "beat" to show
him a homeless
encampment
lean-tos built in a circle.

I'm running my
righteous mouth about
trying to sell the
article and we
pass another Manhattan
tombstone abandoned
brownstone

just another boarded-up
3 story testimony to
greed and stupidity,
of a lethal kind,
and then the
boarded-up door flies open
an arc of light upon us,
we freeze.

Inside the door
is a wiry Boricua—
I know my brothers
even if they don't
always know me—and
we walk in
incredulous and grateful
for the warmth.

"Boricua soy," I said
to the brown-skinned
leprechaun—Miguel Piñero
Short Eyes poet of rage
poet of my cousins trapped
in the ice prison of false
opportunity
and he tells me
I must keep writing
I am glad to know you
younger brother, he makes
me feel like I have a reason,
and escorts us back to the
"music room"

room full of dinette tables
with almost no light
a refrigerator in the back
books and magazines in the
lighted front we are
in Neither/Nor

the perfect name
for a Puerto Rican poet
in a white man's country
no matter where he goes
and Miguel disappeared
for long moments

whenever I came to visit,
once with a bunch of
Chicano friends who were
climbing the ladder of
Gabacho success we
came to hear some
anguished jazz
barb wire asphalt sound and
Miky comes bouncing out of
a back room
naked bulb light
illuminating dangling spike
of his friend
kicking back on the hot seat.

I knew
in that moment.
I have
known
the face of teca,
the brutal master
hot bag murderer
who can help you
kill yourself
But I wanted my Mexican friends
to know this place to have it
haunt them because I
knew I had finally found
one of the underground caves
that winds below Puerto Rico,
that winds through
my dreams.

I discovered
a prehistoric
Puerto Rican cave
in Alphabet City.
I met a man
who knew something
important that he
could not explain.
I came
one step closer,
one step closer
one step

I miss you
Piñero.
I need you now
as much as I ever
did you crazy
motherfucker
I miss you
Miguel me haces falta
me haces falta.

michael c. ladd DEATH BEDS LOVE SONGS AND ANCESTORS

for Eleanor Cawthorne

Granny
Called out today
"LET THEM COME"

"They gonna take me home
I know they coming
sometime, they gonna take me home.

I don't want to stay here long
when they gonna take me home"

"FLORENCE   (my ma)
TELL THE DOCTOR I'M READY TO GO HOME"
"O.K. Mom," says Ma, "She'll be here Tuesday."
"THE FOOD IS TOO BLAND HERE.",
I had to go
cuz sometimes contacts with spirits
can shock the alive
besides
I had to catch a bus
not a train
"I love you Granny, I'll see you soon."
"MICHAEL PLEASE FINISH SCHOOL
I PRAY FOR YOU."

"I pray for you too Granny."
I had a bus to catch,

"They gonna take me home
I know they coming
sometime they gonna take me home
I don't want to stay here long
When they gonna take me home."

patricia landrum   WOMAN'S SONG

Everybody loves
the melody
But they keep
getting the
lyrics wrong

Listen to me
people
I'm singing
a
Woman's song

Everyone wants
to play
my tone in
half notes
But I'm
whole notes
Full, round
and long

Get into
my rhythms
I'm singing
a
Woman's song

shirley bradley leflore   **FOR DIZZ**
dedicated to Arthur & K. Kurtis

There is a man singin under my skin
Like a gourd/song w/a clear/voice
Singin the silk of a hummin/bird deep/throat
In the silver/blades of holy/grass

There is a man singin under my skin
Like a drum/choir/wind/jammin/my bluz/spot
Blowin the dust off my wings
Siftin   the texture of my nature   rich & mahogany
B'tween long chantin fingers

440

Pluckin out my ruptured nerve
Restringing me

There is a man singin under my skin
Like a brass/band/breast/strokin/my/winds
Movin w/a be/bop/eye/scattin/on/these/hants
Charmin/these/cotties/puttin/some/rhythm/on/these/blu/notes
Swingin/low on a sweet/chariot
Makin my spirit rise
Like a poet chewin on a sonnet
Rearranging my score

There is a man singing under my skin dancin

A dancin/man under my skin w/a
Boogie/Woogie/ear
Layin down a gypsy/string/bassline
Vampin in a brass/blend
Sun/dancin me gold like a mississippi/yam
Doin the kooka/rhaacha w/a hoochie/coo
Like a soulful bambouli

A dancin/man w/a whole sahara of tambourines
stringin a gospel/pearl
B'tween my rapture and my rupture
B'tween my hants and my harmony
Reconnectin my nerves/my/muscles/my bones w/a
Soprano tongue turnin my brassbones in/to rainbows

This man/this singin/this dancin/under/my/skin
          has/broke/n'/my/silence

            OUT/LOUD . . . .

gary lenhart # INTELLIGENT LOVE

Alongside every man
Not in prison
Stands a strong woman
At the end of his leash,
My mother believes.
"The best thing
That ever happened to you
Was finding Louise.
When you were twenty
I wouldn't have put money
On your living to forty,"
She told me recently.
I told Louise
This reminded me of Dante,
His belief that one
Was saved through love,
And how poets really do
Articulate obscurely
What, perhaps centuries later,
Becomes evident to many;
That though my poems
Might seem private
In subject, they too
Ponder the play
Between desire and luck
I hope will someday
Move someone
A step or two
In love's direction.
She said I was
Rationalizing
My passivity again.

robbie mccauley   # TWO STREET THINGS

In Pigalle
Long lines of brown men waiting, patiently waiting, hardly
talking to each other it seemed, the way the women—a glossy
yellow top, my eyes weren't working well—the way the women held
open their chests . . . breasts . . . something about breasts.

On the train from Nice, a calendar-maker asked me about racism aux
États-Unis. Not able to talk I quickly asked him au sujet du
racisme en France. He stopped short. Racisme n'existe pas en
France he said et c'était la fin de la conversation.

Back in Paris, waiting for money, I talked in spurts. Seeing the
brown men wait for the women made me think of my own loneliness.
The back alley place where the buses went right by in Pigalle was
the only place where whores would serve North African men, the men
who'd come without their women, someone said. They were, he said,
the ones who'd fought with the French against their own and lost,
and now had no respect. I felt fear. About home. Being able to
speak now only with my eyes now and no money, I started to hang
where the Lybians hung. It was the only place I felt safe.

In New York on the Bus
White trash dope fiend coming from Methadone Clinic
reciting numbers 20 30 more or less doses up doses down.
I don't know why she lowered my number. I coulda got more.
Much much more. Not 60. Maybe 40. She gave me 20. I coulda
got higher. I mean a higher dose. It's all me. I ain't selling.
Coulda got higher.

His small daughter. "What is that?"

"Daddy's medicine."

The mother wore a scowl. Held the little girl tight.
The father twisted his voice and whined.

The one that pass out the package, I don't think she like me.
I don't know why she don't like me.

The mother scowled again. I don't think you ever need to
think no more about that bitch she said.

He said no matter what, she's Black & I'm white. She's
always gon be Black. Fuck her.

The mother and father and daughter together on the bus
in New York.

richard martin
PROPER VENTILATION

A farm interrupted answered
the hat on the phone.
A cadillac with tens and twenties
stuck in creases covered with tarp and guarded.
All night long he breathes funny
and looks for the looker inside of him.
And there are two poems: one with
laundry hung inside the house; the other
with it on the line out back.
He would like to flow.
How many times can this be repeated?
Original friends drop by to smoke.
Sudsy rivulets head for the sewer.
Drop your duds and make suds
his grandmother ordered.
Sugar cookies in the jar with red top
underneath the sink.
The memories and the guy with a stick
in the dirt feel out of focus.

Unmake the thing for christ's sake.
Static.   Noise.   Departure.
A blue body (under a white sheet
beside an open window with wind
ruffling the curtains and light)
is all I remember.

greg masters   LOVE

I'm sick of love. Ok, I love love.
I haven't, though, done a very good job
of being in love or of being loved.
No doubt my parents are to blame yet
I love them. Shabby and expectant,
that's how I've been. Heartless and
cruel, self-absorbed, possessive.
A provider of nothing but charm.
Sometimes some Häagen-Dazs.
I'm a complete washout of the
French New Wave, whose movies
promised my eager generation
a lifetime in bed talking with
beautiful, intriguing partners.
I've lost my sense of humor and
what sensitivity those movies told
me was worth suffering for.
It's gone. I can't find it for looking.
All a big lie too's the shame of it.
I regret it all. A youth misspent.
Hung out with the wrong people,
clung to all the wrong obsessions,
adopted a stance to support all
these cranky excuses for belief.
And love, love was supposed to

be the center, the iron girder,
the permeable doily of a shared
and trusting exploration.
Instead, someone I loved called
me a sexist. Me, who thought women
were perfect, unquestionably.
So perfect I wanted to own one.
In the twilit night of this city's
dense enchantments and disenchantments,
perhaps I've learnt to recognize
that assuming is as brainless as
American consumerism. And this is how
I will find love. My number at work is

bobby miller
MY LIFE AS I REMEMBER IT

AT TWO YEARS OLD I WHISTLED AT THE MAILMAN
AND SET A PATTERN FOR YEARS TO COME.
AT FOUR I DANCED IN THE SUNSHINE OF OUR FRONT YARD,
AN INTERPRETIVE DANCE TO THE GODS.
THE NEIGHBORS SWORE I WAS RETARDED.
AT SIX I TOLD MY CLASSMATES THAT I WAS FROM ANOTHER
   GALAXY
LIGHT YEARS AWAY.
MRS. JACKSON, OUR FIRST GRADE TEACHER, THOUGHT IT
   WAS NECESSARY
TO ALERT MY PARENTS.
BY TEN MR. GRADY THE ART TEACHER WAS ALARMED BY
   THE COLORS
I CHOSE TO PAINT WITH, RED, BLACK AND PURPLE.
IN JUNIOR HIGH I WAS CONSIDERED WEIRD AND NEAT
   AT THE SAME

TIME BECAUSE I DRESSED FUNNY AND MY PARENTS HAD
    TATTOOS
AND HARLEYS.
MY NINTH GRADE REPORT CARD WAS ALL Ds AND Fs EXCEPT
FOR ART AND MUSIC CLASS.
ALL WRITTEN REPORTS FROM THE FACULTY STATED,
"TALKS TOO MUCH AND DAYDREAMS."
SOME THINGS NEVER CHANGE.

I WATCHED THE BEATLES ARRIVE IN AMERICA,
AND DECIDED I WANTED TO GO TO ENGLAND.
I SAW HAIR GROW OVER EARS AND DOWN OVER COLLARS
    AND ONTO
SHOULDERS AND BACKS ALL OVER THE COUNTRY.
I WALKED WITH THE FIRST PROTEST MARCH IN
    WASHINGTON
AND EVERY OTHER FOR TEN YEARS.
AND WE STILL HAVE CROOKS RUNNING THE COUNTRY.

I SAT IN STREETS, CAFES, CORNER BARS AND COFFEE HOUSES
AND LISTENED TO THE BEAT OF A NEW GENERATION BEING
    BORN.
I WENT THROUGH PUBERTY WITH JANIS AND JIMI
AND TOOK LSD WHEN IT WASN'T CUT WITH SPEED OR
    POISON.
I SMOKED POT IN FIFTH GRADE AND LAUGHED ALL DAY
AT A FAT SUBSTITUTE TEACHER NAMED "MRS. POTTY."
I DATED BLACK BOYS AT FIFTEEN IN AN ALL-WHITE KLAN
    NEIGHBORHOOD.
I HITCHHIKED TO NEW YORK FROM BALTIMORE WITH
    THREE QUEENS
IN HOT PANTS, CLOGS AND LONG, BLEACHED SHAGS AT
    SIXTEEN,
AND BLEW TRUCKERS ALL UP AND DOWN THE TURNPIKE.

I'VE BEEN ADDICTED TO MDA, TEQUILA, LSD, PCP, SPEED,
    DOPE, COKE,
POT, MESCALINE, QUAALUDES, NICOTINE, SEX
AND THE MYSTERIES OF THE NIGHT ALL MY LIFE UNTIL I
    HIT TWENTY-EIGHT.

SINCE THEN IT'S ONLY BEEN NIGHTLIFE AND SEX.
I'VE WALKED BAREFOOT ON TWENTY-FOUR-HUNDRED-
   DEGREE HOT COALS
AND NOT BEEN BURNT.
GRETA GARBO GRABBED ME FROM BEHIND IN TRAFFIC AND
   SAVED MY LIFE.
I'VE HAD GREEN HAIR, BLUE HAIR, BLACK HAIR, RED HAIR,
   NO HAIR, LONG HAIR
AND ALL BEFORE 1973. I'M HAPPY TO STILL HAVE HAIR.
I'VE WALKED SUNSET BLVD., POLK ST., FORTY-SECOND ST.,
   HOLLYWOOD AND VINE,
CHRISTOPHER, FIRE ISLAND, P-TOWN, KEY WEST, BOMBAY,
   MIAMI BEACH,
LONDON, PARIS, ROME, MILAN, MONTREAL, AND EVERY GAY
   GHETTO STREET
LISTED IN THE BOOK AND I'M STILL LOOKING FOR THE
   PERFECT LOVER.
I'VE LIVED AS A WOMAN FOR A SOLID YEAR AND HAD TITS
   THANK YOU.
I'VE DATED BLACK MEN, WHITE MEN, BROWN MEN, RED
   MEN, YELLOW MEN,
AND SEVERAL DELICIOUS WOMEN.
I'VE BEEN ENGAGED, MARRIED, IN LOVE, SEPARATED,
   DIVORCED AND
BROKENHEARTED.
I'VE HAD SYPHILIS, GONORRHEA, CRABS, SCABIES,
   HEMORRHOIDS, HEPATITIS,
APPENDICITIS, DERMATITIS AND THE FLU AT LEAST FIFTY
   TIMES
AND I FEEL BETTER NOW AT FORTY THAN I DID AT
   TWENTY-FIVE.
I'VE SPENT THE LAST ELEVEN YEARS MEDITATING,
   CONCENTRATING,
CONTEMPLATING, APPLICATING, EDUCATING, INVESTIGAT-
   ING AND INSTIGATING
A HIGHER IDEAL.
I'VE BEEN A BORN-AGAIN CHRISTIAN, A CRYSTAL-HOLDING
   NEW AGE
VISUALIZATIONIST, A BUDDHIST, A HINDU, A CHRISTIAN
   SCIENTIST,

A UNIVERSALIST, A BULLSHIT ARTIST, A SEEKER OF TRUTH, A
  CHARLATAN,
A HOLY ROLLER, A SHAMANISTIC DANCER, A GURU, A
  DISCIPLE,
AND AN ENIGMA TO MY FRIENDS.
I'M A TRIPLE-GEMINI NATURAL BLONDE WHO LOVES GOD
  AND TAKES
TIME OUT TO SMELL THE ROSES.
I'VE BEEN AROUND THE BLOCK AT LEAST TEN TIMES AND I'M
  READY
TO GO AGAIN UNTIL THESE FEET WON'T CARRY ME
  ANYMORE.
I HAVE ALWAYS BELIEVED IN THE POWER OF LOVE AND THAT
THE GROOVE LIES SOMEWHERE BETWEEN THE HEART AND
  THE GENITALS.
I HAVE NEVER BEEN DELIBERATELY CRUEL AND I'VE NEVER
  HIT ANYONE
WITH MY FIST. I HOPE I NEVER HAVE TO.
I'VE BEEN A WHORE, A SAINT, A SINNER, A HEALER, A
  HEATHEN,
AN ACTOR, A POET, A DRAG QUEEN, A STRAIGHT MAN, A
  TEENAGE ZOMBIE,
A PUNKROCKER, A GREASER, A CLONE, A FAGGOT, A STREET-
  WALKER,
A SKYWRITER, A VEGETARIAN, A TEACHER, A STUDENT, A
  WANDERER, A
CARETAKER, A WILD THING, A FATHER, A SON, A YOGI AND A
  FIERCE HAIRDRESSER.
I'VE BEEN LOST, FOUND, CONFUSED, ABSOLVED, PUNISHED
  AND REWARDED.
I'VE STARED DEATH IN THE FACE AND WONDERED WHY NOT
  ME. YET.

I'VE TALKED AND LISTENED AND HEARD AND SEEN AND
  BEEN SHOWN THE WAY.
I'VE PLAYED FOLLOW THE LEADER, PIN THE TAIL ON THE
  DONKEY,
FIVE CARD STUD, AND RUSSIAN ROULETTE WITH A SILVER-
  HANDLED .38.

I'VE LOST EIGHT THOUSAND IN CASH GAMBLING AND WON
   FIVE HUNDRED
ON A BET IN LESS THAN A MINUTE.
I'VE SEEN THE EYE OF GOD AND BEEN TOUCHED BY HER
   HAND.
I'VE SEEN MIRACLES HAPPEN AND BEEN DISAPPOINTED
   DOZENS OF TIMES.
I'VE BEEN ALMOST EVERYWHERE, MET ALMOST EVERYONE,
   SEEN ALMOST
EVERYTHING, DONE ALMOST ALL OF IT, AND I'M STILL WAIT-
   ING TO BE DISCOVERED.
THE NIGHT HAS A THOUSAND EYES AND I'M A GYPSY
   DANCER
WHO'S STILL HUNGRY FOR MORE.

david mills   # G-MEN IN THE PINES

There were G-men in the pines
As he waited—stiff
Glove, white uniform, 32 oz.
Aluminum bat—for her,
Waited for the opportunity
To nick the fence, bruise the bases
Move the crowd. Somebody's
7 P.M. She always drove him
In the station wagon, to the diamond
To the bragging, to the masquerading
Of his outfit. It was a strong day:
Pompous sun scolding the sky;
Mrs. Ackerman chatting on a bench;
Fists fighting his dreams
And the truth of standing
In front of the building, waiting;
Seven evergreens cornering him,

A suburban trim in a silhouette
Of skyscrapers. Absent-eyed
She said, "There are G-men
In the pines, that's why I'm late."
"But Mom, I don't see anything!"
"Forget about the game.
Your life is dangling!"

eileen myles   PV

Today is so full, and yet today never gets spoiled.
—*Tim Dlugos*

Some old drunk who'd been
to France recently died, left
his collection of Isherwood, John
O'Hara, tobacco-stained, grungy
with tattered invites hanging out.
I come wagging out of the train
station at 59th & nearly scream,
Just the books I need!

I take my own sense of
abundance down
into the subway, the
F, Second Ave., the
bodies strewn, the
stink of human
shit   the ungodly
lights, standing, waiting
in the heat.

The mother won't repeat
for the child. If you
didn't get it the first
time . . .

Who is that Irish novelist,
he says, the one we see
in meetings in East Hampton

The train arrives & I hop
on, that lesbian poet, the
one we always see around
3:30 in Kiev, having a very
late lunch I guess.

We whiz uptown to get help.
We whiz back down. This
is an old-fashioned phone
call, Do you have
10 bucks, All Saints Day 1989.

I slept with her last night,
first time since August, she's
moving so the smells of her
neighbor's pot won't waft
insidiously into her bedroom
anymore, Jan with his
new electric piano, Jan the
monkey-faced pot dealer who
teaches tai chi.

I went to see 17 art shows on
Saturday. 17. That's not a lot.
Saw Tim in the hospital on Sun-
day. Thin Tim. We know he'll
come out. He doesn't want to
be everyone's friend Tim who has AIDS
so we won't let him be that.
We won't.

We charged around in our
dungarees watching the century
approach. Another one, nicer
than this, young again, full

of conviction, naïveté, covered
with hair and sunlight, brim-
ming with time, a wave of
invention . . .

I take my sense of abundance
into the subway & what do
I see? People bending reading
swaying, torn posters
waving in a song of
sickening movement. Why don't
they think we know about
rice, racing, . . . handsome woman
fiddling with her bag. We're
the same people who met in
a disaster, but nothing hap-
pened here. You can't call
it joy this somnolence, licking
our lips with our earphones
on. The poet got off
in the yellowing light,
the rising tile, then
Lexington Ave. Have you
gone here, did you
go there   everyone wants
to know. & there's the
EXIT. Absolutely now
I'm going & the buildings
are growing before my
eyes.

ADVENTURES OF PLASTIC MAN

HERE I LIE ON MY HOT BED
IN THE AGE OF THE JIM HAT
FORCED TO SETTLE DOWN
WITH ONE BROTHER
AS MY FINGER TIPS
ROLL DOWN THE SARAN RAP
SO HIS SAP DOESN'T SEEP

USED TO BE TOO SHY TO PEEP THE MEAT!
GREETS ME NOW
GREETS ME LATER

2 DAYS, 2 HOURS, 2 YEARS GONE BY

NOT YET TRUSTING
NOT YET BLESSED
ENOUGH TO SAVOR THE FLAVOR
OF A CLEAN FUCK

FORCED TO DUCK BEHIND
WAR-TORN TROJANS
WITH A LUBRICATED SHIELD

NOT GONNA LIE DEAD
REFUSED TO GET PLAYED OUT
LIKE A SUCKER!

LIKE THOSE
I AIN'T WEARIN NO CONDOM
MOTHERFUCKERS!

JOINTS JOIN MY DESPERATE HAND
AN' GUIDE THE BROTHER'S
RUBBER GLAND FROM THE BEACH
TO THE SAND

orion # DIRE MANIFESTO

Too many anti–World War 3 pacifists are obnoxiously making
me nauseous. I have to purge them out of my proximity. I don't
want to inhale their polluted breath. Their hypocrisy stinks
from too many civil rights marches, anti-war demonstrations,
and plucking feathers off pink flamingos. Fuck them, since they
refuse to vanquish and evaporate on their own I must kick their
butt so they'll keep their distance. I won't be astonished if
they'll perish in the perilous ire of my ransacking berserk
raid on the shit they toss on my lacquered veneer. World War 3
is a major prerogative. 46 years of braggadocio by America and
Russia which of the 2 is the strongest invites it. If these
infantile chickens remain near me, I'll polish them off with
bullets, hand grenades, and molotov cocktails. All they do is
rattle vacuous rumbles about how peace and love is exciting
and beautiful, and how war destroys what they relish and cherish.
I have no use for their antiquated treasures and my rejection
of their wares causes them to be abject and dejected. Tough
shit. They're ripe to be targeted by the fusillade of my
sprinkling ambuscade. If you're anti–World War 3 align your-
self to the aim of my pistol. It's obviously the chickens who
don't want the inception of World War 3. They hide their vanity
behind a humanitarian guise, and stage good samaritan deeds
and exhibitions in order not to be involved, because they're
scared shit. But such a manifestation must materialize. We
can't be deprived and denuded from such a spectacle forever.
It's the hope for it that gives us the motivation, the impetus,
and the incentive to continue to exist. Our progenitors and
ancestors had access to such luxurious epics, why shouldn't we.
World War 3 should be invigorating, vivifying, and vitalizing,

and no doubt about it, electrifyingly energizing. The chickens
who protest against it should be the first ones to be dispatched
and parcelled to the trenches. Their skin deserves to be at
hazard for being such cowards. And if they stay alive following
a transaction of marauding and plundering, they're to be
executed by a firing squad made of evangelistic ecclesiastical
monks. World War 3 is the most nutritional appetizer to
tickle the gullet as it glides and slides in the tunnel that
leads to the aqueduct of the conduits that obtrude out
of my channeling projectile, the antenna and radar
periscopically focuses my cannonizing sermon to flagellate
the dissent of the chickens whose aspiration is to sweat out
the anarchistic provocation I advocate.

julie patton   **"PO TREE!"**

A black man uttered d' udder day . . .
Yea, beneath day

Bereav'd of light
Both 'peared almost night.

Po-o-tree!
He splithered and splattered like a
        daffy

Duck—a drunk
Bird dance,
        Sing!

On a brass sea sassy
C B D-DO-B D Bop Bam!

Truth trippin' on a typewriter po—o
        etic justice

Resounding branch of a cocabola
Tree splintering

       into two
            front teef

Beat yo' drumsticks and sing!

Po tree,

He be . . . mused like music
Rappers recitin' Blake,

"Dese black bodies dis sunburnt face
Tis but a cloud like a shady grove"

"Po' tree," he said

To me, reading
Leaves from

Skin'd
White pulp of

Trees

Rag
Lips drooping with

The roots of speech
Twiggs leves blosmes floures

Etrange frute

Hanging from Imperial
        is 'ems populous routes

Olde english thought stems
Smoothly articulated limbs

What trees would have done with hands
Reach, reach

For an even loftier expression
The Tarzan *cry-y-y-y-y-y-y-y*

In the dark
Jumble of un-

Tamed and tethered
Tongues

Too black for words
You 'sposed to swing from

Duh *bulging* O's loose vowels
Twist'd mouths

Consonants
O dark continents

Swingin' in a southern breeze

Hear the frute o' po'
Tongue-tied roots

You ax d' uh (unh hunh), re-place the
The wit duh . . . a

Febyll tre that falleth at the fyrst strok!

Cypresses wthoute dignitee, syck
      a more

Scent of magnolia

Dutch elm disease . . .
I beshout'd at him a treatise

On dead and dying leaves
Po' tree you can gnaw on till

The sap oozes, runs like blood
Po ol' tre, he said southern style *please* . . .

Wind gatherin from m' paper sleeves
Cruel soliloquies of this

Pastoral scene

Whence came haunting
Song—cane thrashing back

Then the sudden smell of burning flesh

Way down yonder by the po'

> Po tree where
> Weepin' widows 'neath spanish moss
> Still pines away scarred human cross
> Forced sentences
> Dark subjects
> Unable to read
> Propositions
> Ol' tomatums

Pre fix'd at breakneck speed by a
Poplar's demand

Black byrds wither round 'n' wilt
    'member'n

What hands have done with trees, the
Threatening white sheets

Singe thin, ash dun shins
O dark

Tendril'd limbs
Blotted like ink

I had the impression of running,
Running down limb skin'd tree

Blood on the leaves, blood at the root

O leaf fall of scattered fingertips
Pressed for words they'll . . .

Shoot you like a mockingbird

See what they do to thee—damn!
Po' trees must do with hands for

> **This book open wound**
> Word become flesh
> Beaten to a pulp
> Dried and pressed
> *For the rain to gather*
> *Wind to suck*
> Lorde, Lorca, Dumas
> Hak Kyung Cha!
> Heads swirlin' in
> A paper breeze
> Eyes weep fo' dese
> Death sentences read
> Poet trees mutilated
> Out of breath . . .

*"For the wind was changing notes as it went through the branches
I imagined this was music, was surprised to hear someone
calling my name. Fe . . . de . . . ri . . . co . . . it seemed to be saying.
I listened for a long while and realized that the branches of an
old poplar were rubbing sadly and monotonously in the wind."*

> See, hear! who be
> done beat this 'ere

Strange 'n' bitter crop
O what's poplar
Not popular I said
Still never lifting my
10 volume head
Read the fresh way
That tree's leaves
have of stirring the
wind makes it
sound so much like
running water—

Po' trees a babblin'
Brook I spat

Watching the maenads tear
Orpheus apart

Bulging eyes, twisted mouth

Still singing
His head washes ashore

Tarred and feathered, neck
Twisted unloose

For the sun to rot, crows to pluck

They'll make a noose of
Words

Shoot

Paper

Bullets

Strangle
Piercing tongues like

Birds mocking birds
"Potree-ee, po' tree, po' et' tree!"

Blood on the leaves, blood at the root

Poetry's
Foul play that bleeds

Skinned, headless, plucked
10 cents a breast and a wing

Beat yo' drumsticks and sing

carolyn peyser   **PLEASE**

Ever notice neon
arrows pricking your
airbag? You tell me
it's meant to be. Again
I'm led to see the blinders
they fit to my soul. Thoughts
are like waves. Their motion
hides the quiet between. Who
has time to feel the ocean or
hear the stars? I'm told kittens
open their eyes in two days.
Blindfold for a week
and they will not see.
Permanently. But we
have wider windows. Brains
are like radios calibrated
to pick up every station
though most get stuck
on three: sleeping

awake and dreaming.
(And I don't remember
my dreams.) Today I'm
reading that before the Big
Bang there was a billion
times more energy than now.
Dream. Would I have found
time to learn Spanish? Cooked
more? Or stopped frantically
signing up voters last year
to hear the first guy in nine
months to smile with his
eyes and say I was pretty?
(That's twenty-two months
if you take away the smile.)
Why is it so hard to see love?
Marlys is memorizing six corny
songs so her father and she
can see each other again. Ancient
Indian rishis said Life is built by
taking part. Breathe the energy.
Burn. There's no need for virtual
reality, friend. Change the channel.

raymond ramirez (aka bori)
PROJECT BLUES

I can't sleep
I'm trying to snooze
some motherfucker upstairs is banging on my
         radiator with a pipe
and he's giving me the project blues
he's playing the star-strangled banner in reverse
         —I hope

oh how I wish I can find a fuckin' housing man
so cold in here you can only curse and I can't
          cope
I need some dope or at worst, some tylenol with
          codeine for my legs
you see
I live on the twenty-third floor and the elevator
          has been out for
forty-three fuckin' days
seven times a second I voyage up or down those
          damn stairs
filled with piss-infested corners
owned by crack neglected occupants
the so-called stockholders of the damn projects
          holding non-
negotiable shares
but who cares?
who fuckin' cares?
I have to make it to my cell-unit alive rather
          than dead
walking down mile-long hallways reminds me of
          a first degree
security lock-up instead
so many entrances and so many exits that they
          install
producing an environment conducive to crime
I guess this fuckin' project was a successful
          experiment after all
having us stacked like animals one on top of
          another
so much frustration builds, I take it out on the
          closest person to me—
my brother
there he goes again, that fuckin' lunatic
playing that damn song, I wish he'd just quit
shit!
can't get no sleep
the wardens still haven't turned up the heat
but like a fool, I'm gonna wait even though I
          know it will never arrive

always leaving life up to fate—kind of
        philosophy that destroys your
inner drive
so fuck you socrates or plato or whoever else
        this type of thinking
brings to mind
I'm gonna join my musical brother upstairs and
        sing this song to
keep me warm and try to forget all about the
        social, political and
economic bind

noel rico   EXCERPT FROM THE
SOUTH BRONX

old woman holds pale
hand belonging to child
from a velasquez canvas
you could hear
the rosary beads in her
pocket as she walked
like marbles on a string
they used to sound
old men with brims
old hats turned up
        looked
like all the hats were smiling
playing dominoes under what
was then jesus sky and
yes the father and the holy ghost too
you could hear
        even from a block away
their laughing/
        talking/

                    cursing
                            —in spanish
            "ME CAGO EN DIOS"
dominoes flying up
into the air
                    falling
        to the
                    ground
        like so
            much
        black
        and
        white

        rain.

keith roach   ODALISQUE

i desire the vision of
the nocturnal ones
the sight of slight shifting and
motive forgotten
a consummate congress with darkness

i lurk at the threshold of a pageant
the probability of a birthing—
who would be kings and queens and beasts
stalks the recesses
where thought is regressive
where all known history hides
amusing itself as habit
i bark at shadows
some wage slaves toiling for subsistence
they fear the dark
which eats them daily

they bargain for promises
from fate
they say
what goes around never ends

a midwife wanders in light and shadow
she is blind from so many illuminations
so many initiations
she is focused on every thought
incarnate or denied
every child of fornication/imagination
unholy unborn
she waits for revelations
the death of notions borders prophets and things
and waiting
what goes around is contagion

darkness beckons and teases
where i wander
looking to murder love
before i am bound
before i gamble on insight
in my quest for lucidity
without the vision of my cats
or the awareness of convenience
here
it is dark again
what goes around
will grab you from behind
and choke the living shit
out of you

will sales THAT KIND OF BLUES

I've got the kind of blues
that leaves your mouth bone dry
like a red hot fever inside.
It's like you got the news
in a telegram
that part of you just died.

You know the kind of blues
that makes a good stiff drink
taste weak as a glass of milk,
leaves you mean and evil
as a coiled-up snake,
deadly as a razor blade
wrapped in silk,
that kind of blues.

So I lie all night alone in bed,
one-third alive and two-thirds dead,
visions of suicide dance thru my head
'cause it's that kind of blues.

It's the kind of blues
that makes a preacher cuss
and the devil break down and cry,
the kind of blues
that lays you down so low
six feet deep is high.
It's that kind of blues.

It's the kind of blues
that makes a strong, young man
feel old as his great-grandpa.
The kind of blues
that makes a boy leave home
when he catches the landlord

in bed with his ma.
That kind of blues.

So I beg and steal
and pawn all I got
to stay on my diet of cocaine and pot
and still I'm all fucked up
and tied in a knot,
'cause it's that kind of blues.

It's the kind of blues
that makes a mother wrap
her newborn baby
in a garbage sack.
The kind of blues
that makes a man become
chopped-up meat
on a railroad track.
That kind of blues.

It's the kind of blues
if you ain't never met 'em,
I hope like a motherfucker
you ain't never gonna get 'em.
It's like slipping down slowly
in a quicksand ditch.
It's like scratching outside
for an inside itch.
That kind of blues
is a son of a bitch.
That kind of blues.

raúl salinas   ## PUEBLO QUERIDO

En aquel
        AUSTIN
maldito/bendito
        Where ragged/jagged
tender bits of my body/flesh/
        ¡PEYEJO!
still adorn
        Tejas barb-wire
existence of courtroom injusticias
        down desolate doper streets.

There/where
        tomás wolfe's
fool proof-read novela
        contain no truth pa'mi.
¡SI SE PUEDE!
        volver al canton
once again.

ex-Convictos/Activistas
doing righteous gente work
        involved in sharing
homeboy   (cockroach poet)
        with the WORLD!

Doing Good
        in city
of chavalo gone BAD
Inspiring tender mentes
        de gente nueva
related to
        parentela out of the past.

Vast memorias/
        (norias of nostalgia!)
gush forth   como el

raging río Colorado/
whose banks once served
        (still might today)
as jardines primeros of grass
        despues shooting gallery/
aguáje to abate   madrugando mendicants'
        narcotic-ridden
nerviosidad.

        La universidad calls
up! jump (hopin' IT falls!)
        seís vatos locos
listos to prowl otra vez/
        vecindad of worldly
(teenage) vagabundo days
        spent
"skelly-bibbing"
        student apartamentos
to survive.

        Live
assembly hall address
        en Austin Hi,
escuela que dejé long abandonada/
        missing out en
senior prom & ring . . .
        Class of '52

¿Y tu?
        Some anti-prison lobbying
and back to being
        cantor de cantina/
hanging out en la esquina
        (del barrio)
pasándole poems a
        perrenial pachucos prendidos
(hoping somewhat to ease their pain)
        as the rain entertains us
con su

Tattooed Tecato Tap Dance

WhirlWIND quincena/
      Escena
de muchos colores/
      bastantes sabores
de multi-café.

REviviendo
      reLIVING/Re-Viving
rose-gardens that never ceased to bloom
wounds that scarcely (muy despacio) heal
      yet feeling good 'n tight
on birthday party night.
"*La fiesta se celebraba*
el mero día de san juán,
      cuando llegaron al baile . . ."
four levels of
incestuous promiscuity.

El Hurráca con su current
      Love
affair/his primo
      w/ la second ruca d'el.
Su primer esposa (having been
      primo's movida's sister-in-law)
con el vato d'ella
      He having been poetic cuñado
(making his movida-chueca/
      primo's cousin/ cuñada)
in those confusing times
      before the "raids,"
in those confusing times
      before the bust.

      Just as the evening is ending,
just as night comes to a close
      having chosen
Buena Suerte Lounge,

          just as the party is over
Palomia del pasado
attempt somewhat debil . . .
¡adios!

          "*Despedida no les doy . . .*"
on this day que ya me voy,
          because i knew we'd cry
as grown men/ women cry.
          As tender warriors cried/
shed tears (for years!)
          devoid of prison fears
while shackled/
          bound in chains—
chattel slaves—
          Prisoners-of-War,
headed for that Marion Monster
in my never—
                    to be—
                              forgotten

prison past.

ricardo sánchez   25 MAYO 92 EN
PULLMANIA, WASHINGÓN

mi muy querido hijo
sets up
his tripod
& camcorder
to record a jive moment
in the living colors
de la familia, all the while
there is much
to amplify, to create

an aesthetic
which might make sense
in some other universe,
three years from now
there will be another
familia here in this
jive space in Pullmania,
perhaps there will be
others to galavant
through CAC/English, I
do not foresee staying
here much beyond the jive
of this time-frame, nor
can I care to do so . . . I
merely want to finish up
this moment, to conjure up
new ones as I find a way
to escape earthen sensibility,
to journey forward
into new galactical byways . . .
meanwhile
mi muy querido hijo
plays with camcorder
venues as new parvenues
come and go
twixt Prufrockian valleys
and Macondian quackeries, oh,
let it all be merely what it
shall be, there is no rhyme
no reason, just a jest
from achey lesions. . . . i
have simply run
out of intelligence,
my buffoonery is showing,
the camcorder catches
my twitching unsanity,
as i struggle toward
discarding another sense
of self, of city, of being

while re-ordering
my disborderedness. . . .

gail schilke   LOS BRAVOS

I wouldn't bet on it
I mean, I could walk from here
To tomorrow and nothing
Would be any different
I spent days pitching my tent
In your front yard
Only to get invited indoors
Where the servants live

Look, I skate all over this city
I hit taxi cabs with my fist
Kiss my middle finger
Shove it up their face

Maybe I can't find my way home anymore
But it's better than sleeping
With your eyes open
Guessing what everyone has to say
Before they lay flat their mouths

Listen, I know how to make pretty
You boys are easier than you think
But I don't want it that way
I want to shove it in your face
Wake you up then get you lost
I want to part you like a river
And spread my words
Inside of you

susan scutti   **EPITHALAMIUM**

And then there's this incredibly long pan
where the camera moves from the dirty china
to the empty Heinekens
past a few slices of fluffy cake
and a single cigarette burning to ash in the tray
until the pan ends with a brief shot
of some burgundy stain spread dead center
in the white tablecloth.

There's another part, too, at the beginning of the video:
the camera zooms in on the couple
alone at the altar
and you see Maria move—
just a flicker.
She turns to take a last
look at this man she's marrying.
Even through her veil you see
fear scorch her face.

But the best part comes near the end
when the camera starts on the dance floor
then slides from table to table
and you see all of us there
and every expression on every face
looks the same.

> *we have held desire in adulterous arms*
> *we have loved selfishly and aborted desperately*
> *we have wanted what is not ours*

We are related.

Finally, the camera returns to take a departing
shot of the married couple
who stand united
against the chaos of living.

476

> having tasted the body
> having drunk the blood
> we walk free in the bondage of family

danny shot   MY BAD ANGEL

doesn't always watch over me.
She puts things in my head.
She tells me things like:
"While having coffee this morning, put your arms around
the young pretty teacher
you are friendly with
and pull her close to you . . .
kiss her passionately . . .
you know she wants you . . . look into her eyes . . .
real men take what they want."
But I know better.
My bad angel loves me deeply.
She is my angel
but I don't trust her.

My bad angel is a beautiful
twenty-five-year-old woman
wearing too much lipstick,
a primitive woman dancing naked
in the moonlit forest of the mind
beheld by amber eyes.

My bad angel buys me drinks and
then has no money to pay for them.
She always lights my cigarettes.
She serenades my daydreams with Spanish love songs
of unrequited love.
She tells me to write poems when
I should be paying bills.
Her lips taste of bitter absinth kisses

drunk in all-night underground cafes.
She suffers me with longing.

My bad angel comes to me at night and invades my dreams.
She takes the change from my pockets when I'm sleeping.
She took my leather jacket.
She wants me to shave my head.

My bad angel needled her way into angel land
self-destructing and obstructing
my emotional merry-go-round.
My bad angel tried to strangle
my wife in her sleep.
She wants me all to herself.
We have a special relationship.
She tells me things she tells nobody else:
       "Death is the truth of life.
       Life is the air that we breathe,
       the love that we keep,
       the desire we touch,
       the thoughts that we feel.
       The body is a shell
       that gives form to the living."

My bad angel tells me I'm a ladies' man
in spite of my face.
She makes me forget my anniversary.
She makes me buy presents for imaginary lovers.
She says it's okay to read my poetry to rich people
at trendy Soho restaurants because I've already paid my dues.
My bad angel always reminds me to wear my grapevine suit
to dramatic happenings on Avenue B.
My bad angel makes me undress women in my mind.
She makes me look at dirty pictures.
She touches me yet can't be touched.
She would like to babysit my children
but I won't let her.
She pushes me into the middle of fights at school.
She wants me to buy a gun.

She helped me assemble my switchblade.
She doesn't give a damn about my history.
She never listens to me.

My bad angel keeps other angels away from me.
She hardens me with desire for bodies
that are out of reach.
She has followed me from New York to Hoboken.
She is here right now.
She doesn't need wings to fly.
My bad angel plays outside of time.
My bad angel took her own life
and still blames it on me.

She shows me glimpses:
>   The body a shell
>   that gives form to the living.
>   The living interconnected
>   to all the living that ever were.
>   Time, a road built upon shadows
>   of souls of all ever alive.
>   Time measures life,
>   God measures death.
>   God the Word . . .
>   Lovers embrace the edge of eternity,
>   naked forever after . . .
Smile angel smile
your secrets are mine.

marc smith CHICAGO: SANDBURG
TO SMITH, SMITH TO SANDBURG

Once, you were the Hog Butcher for the World.
>   *Elmo, from Dakota, stuck those pigs because it was a job*

nobody wanted, and he had to take it. The blood came to his waist
and the pigs squealed. And everytime a street car turned a corner
those squeals came back to him.

> *Bloodthirsty men. Hogs to kill.*

Once, the tools were made here. Are they now?

> *Buy 'em at Sears. Buy everything at Sears. Buy the whole god-*
> *damned world and stick it into a thirty-foot lot. Renovate it. Re-*
> *juvenate it. Hire a Polish immigrant to polish the floors. A Czech*
> *to point the bricks.*
> *Make the tools with Japanese steel.*

Stacker of Wheat he called you.

> *It must move through here somewhere. Piled onto a boxcar.*
> *Piped down into a ship's hold. Stored in a concrete silo. But where?*
> *Louie Gomez quit school at sixteen to shovel grain spill off the*
> *slip docks of the Calumet Harbor. It was hard fuckin' work but he had*
> *to take it. Now, a Champaign biz-grad who builds his body with free*
> *weights and cleans his Caribbean suntan in a health club sauna, trades*
> *stacks of wheat we never see making Louie's wages at sixteen times sixteen*
> *times the years of inflation in the tick tick seconds of a market that*
> *closes at mid-afternoon when and where Louie, now forty, sweeps the floor.*

Player with railroads, eh? Handler of freight?

> *There is no more romance to handle there now. No pride.*
> *Just sleepy-eyed union stooges who walk the yards killing time,*
> *pressing a button now and then. Robots, mechanical and in the flesh.*
> *Half hour coffee at ten. The gin mill at 12:15. Timetable says:*
> *a smoke at two-thirty; punch the day's end ticket at a quarter to four;*
> *go home; eat the dinner; watch the TV; bawl at the kids; do it all again.*

Stormy, husky, brawling,
City of Big Business ventures and routine subsistence.

> *They told him you were wicked, a hooked pin. He saw painted women*
> *under the gas lamps luring the farm boys. I see hot crack tricks,*

almost naked, prowling on Dearborn, pulling North Shore football
heroes upstairs into fifty-buck rooms for thirty-buck wipes of their runny noses.
   And they said to him "You are crooked." And still crooked you
are. Crooked at the top. Crooked in the middle. Crooked at the bottom
where you should be crooked, where there's an excuse for being crooked,
where gunmen still kill and go free to kill again, for those at the
crooked top, for those at the crooked middle, too moral to pull the
triggers themselves.

Brutal? Yes, you are brutal.

   On the faces of women and children, and even on the faces of men,
I see the brutality, the acts of violence, the actors of violence.
And I say to myself what's the use in turning to the old pages of pride
and optimism. What's the use in throwing back the sneer saying:

Come and show me another city with lifted head
singing so proud to be
alive and coarse and strong and cunning.
Flinging magnetic curses amid the toil of piling
job on job.
Here is a tall bold slugger set vivid against
the little soft cities;
Fierce as a dog lapping for action,
Cunning as a savage pitted against the wilderness:
Bareheaded,
Shoveling,
Wrecking,
Planning,
Building, breaking, rebuilding,
Under the smoke, dust all over its mouth,
Laughing with white teeth,
Under the terrible burden of destiny laughing
as a young man laughs,
Laughing even as an ignorant fighter laughs
who never lost a battle,
Bragging and laughing
that under his wrist is the pulse,
and under his ribs the heart of the people,

Laughing!
Laughing the stormy, husky, brawling laughter of Youth,
half-naked, sweating, proud to be . . . proud to be . . .
proud to be . . .

What's the use in being so proud
   when the things that change shouldn't
   and the things that should stay fixed
   in the blind imbalance of Liberty
   That Hamblin and Masters and Sandburg saw so long ago?

Come show me now Hog Butcher, Tool Maker, Stacker of Wheat,
   Player with Railroads and Freight Handler to the nation.
Show me where we're going now. Show me our proud new destiny.

pamela sneed   THE FINAL SOLUTION

Last night
in your arms
touching your tongue
to mine
I forgot
lesbianism is an illness
caused by a deficiency
of good dick
which might mean
this love
lingering on my lips
is a disease
according to our parents
who chant daily
with the moral majority
on Channel 5
for our exile
from society

482

In your arms
I forgot
about the man
behind us
screaming
we were unnatural
his behavior was
unnatural
so I crossed
the street
afraid
he'd give me
some good dick
and I'd be found
in an alley
with my vagina
ripped open
and my panties
stuffed in my mouth

This morning
as I sat
dreaming of you
last night
a well-known newspaper
in the Black community
printed a letter
saying
we should be made
to wear stars
on our clothes
be forced into
ghetto camps
and if
our perversion
is still
not cured
There will be
a Final Solution.

sparrow   A TESTIMONIAL

I have lived in this city
25 years
and all that time
I have dropped things.
I've dropped
tissues,
letters from women
in Santa Fe, N.M.,
money,
the keys to my house,
books by
Jacques Prévert.
And all this time,
you,
the people of this
city, have pointed
to me, and said,
"Hey!" "Sir!" "You!
You dropped something!"
and then I've picked it up.
You have watched
over me all these
years,
and I've waited till
now to thank you.

carlton t. spiller   PANAMANIAN NIGHTS

It was one year ago today you took your leave,
  eyes wide open,
   a thin smile across your lips.

484

Your memory choking me,
  like a windless sandstorm
  covering my lungs
  in the dunes of my childhood.

I can still see me,
  gazing down from the balcony,
  piercing the Panamanian night
  with a starless longing,
  lost in the blackness.
  Black tar roadway etching its signature
  on your vanishing car.

That long walk, taken too many times,
  down the tunneled hallway,
  too thin for my wheelchair
  as it closed in on the door to my room.
The hospital walls smelling
  thick with jungle cries of my isolation,
  the howl of the jaguar buried
  in my cry for release.

I was not quite three
  when I was pried loose from
  my mother's frightened grasp
  by those long bony fingers of polio.

Placed in isolation,
  outside the children's ward,
  into the sealed corridor with locked rooms,
  into the damp cave of my repose,
  seeking that one point of fearlessness
  that a three-year-old can find
  deep inside pools of hopelessness
  where walls are built brick by brick,
  shaped by small hands,
  in the woodfired ovens of fear,
  moved only by the endless tick
  of a clock I could not read.

Too young to understand
  the unseen plague raging through my legs
  like a black bull gorging the belly of the toreador.

My mother only permitted to visit
  for two hours twice a day,
  unable to explain
  that each time she left she would be back,
  that she was not abandoning me to the desert stillness
  that burnt a scorched path
  along the endless cracks in the hospital walls.
  That cloudless wind now only a memory to push my tears.

It was then I learned
  to trust only the song of my own voice,
  chanting a veil of protectionism
  down the hardened black mahogany path of my dreams.

I can still see the desperate anger in your eyes
  each time the hospital orderly nodded for you to leave.
I can feel the grip of your white knuckles
  squeezing me in a prayer of fear
  hidden behind your smile of tears,
  as you put me screaming back into the crib.

That final look over your shoulder, each day,
  trying to tell a three-year-old of the volcanic rush
  of emotions
  erupting into lava flows that would swallow my isolation if you
  could,
  . . . if you could only
  spoonfeed me the trust
  I buried deep inside
  and encased in the cooling
  molten rock that surrounded my heart.

Thirty-four years later I hear the echo of your footsteps
  hidden deep in the moist caves
  where only the inner I of truth roams.

lamont b. steptoe   **FOR GWEN BROOKS**

Ancient Mother,
Nile Woman/Queen Mother,
Nubian Woman:
You, rule words like
Cleopatra ruled upper Egypt.
Yours, are the eyes that cap
the pyramids,
Yours, are the eyes that
are the fulcrum of the universe.
Stolen African child,
Your screams of anger
and longing for home are
poetic symphonies that build
libraries and create villages.
You, snipe from rooftops
with your sentences,
You, plow fields and chop
cotton with your exclamation
points,
You, cook cabbage with your
poetry,
You, bake fresh bread,
You, pull up greens from city
backyard gardens,
You, play numbers everyday with
your poetry,
You, fill up the house with your
chitlin' smellin' poetry,
You, fry chicken on Sunday
with your poetry,
You, rub lineament on arthritic
joints with your poems,
You, set traps with your words
breaking fat rat necks,
You, hunt down roaches in

tenement kitchens with your rhymes,
You, clean windows, scrub floors,
open doors with your poetry,
You, heal the sick, feed the hungry,
give sight to the blind with your poetry,
You, set chained souls free
and raise the dead,
simply by the things you've said.

everton sylvester   **WELL?**

I got cash in fuck-you quantities
Now what?
            that makes you uncomfortable?
Fuck you
            and the Range Rover you drove in on
Fuck your Saab convertible
And fuck your twice weekly trips to the analyst
Stoopid motherfuck.
Fuck the Hamptons, Maine,
            and fly-infested south of France.
I am paid,
                        Asshole
Got more cash than god can count
So why don't you just . . . die?.
Choke to death on your damn designer
bagel from Balducci's
low cholesterol, naturally.

Fuck your big old Sunday NY Times
Fuck the Wall Street Journal and Newsweek and the lot
including Nation, Village Voice, Guardian
and the rest.
Stupid set o' privileged motherfuckers
think it's fashionable to have
"an alternative view."

And Fuck, if you can
your pencil thin
Evian drinking
calorie counting
caffeine limiting
sodium sparing
Nutrasweet sweetening
rear-view mirror preening
carrot nibbling, bunny.

Go drown in a lake of Diet Coke, Fucker.

I got cash
What else matters?
Slave!
Fuck your fencing, screw your squash
Yo,
Piss on your polo and your Pavarotti.
Fuck all that shit you call music and pretend to enjoy
I got cash,
megacash.
Unhappy with that?
Oh, go sit on your ski rack.
Money talks, you little pussy
And let your politically correct pals know
that I think you're a dick also.
Neutered asshole!

And your idea of multiculturalism . . .
Japanese restaurant on Monday
Indian on Tuesday
And on Wednesday, Caribbean.
"Not too spicy please."
Well,

I got stash on stash.
And it ain't nouveau cash.
Money's in ma family for generations
Ma great great great grandfather made the bag

selling European slaves
in Africa.
I got cash motherfucker.
And you can't tell whether or not I'm joking
Can you?
Dumb fuck!

nate tate   PARANOIA AT ITS FINEST

Today I read a story in the *West Side Spirit*
'bout a four-year-old
Wears a bullet-proof vest made of kevlar.
Can withstand a full blast from an uzi.

Few daze ago r-rested three-year-old
Carryin' .45 automatic to nursery school.
Jus' heard they'll be givin' out condoms
To kindergarten kids.

Child of eight got caught
With 800 vials of crack.
He was holding it for his brother.
Making 800 dollars a day.

Newborn baby born wit' AIDS.
Today some still call it
"The Gay Plague."

Bess friend went to Kuwait last year.
I might be goin' next year
Spite of all that . . .

Still can't wait
To see the uncensored version
Of Madonna's new video.

vipin LANGUER/LANGUOR

Fatigue

My hands are powerless
they lie in my lap, loaded with gravity
not even wriggling their feeble fingers.
The musk of her presence
lies heavy in my lungs
my eyes sting and burn and smart
my ears are crazy with bees,
my sweat glands are working overtime
they irrigate my helpless skin
with tepid honey.
I glance at her
my insides seize up with
wretched departure, my tongue is dry
and it rolls around in my mouth
seeking a bit of moisture
my throat shudders in a paroxysm
of unsaid words.
I watch the flushed face of the day
recede from my sight with a tremor
for tomorrow may never come
with her lucent laughter
and cooling fingers.
She's here
but she's ever on the point
of packing her bags.

michael warr BREAKING TILES

In movements more
Expressive than words

We break ceramic tiles
Behind the shower curtain
With the centrifugal force
Of our bodies.
Nurtured tension verges
On bending burglar bars
Across the bathroom window.
The streams cascading down
Your back leave your taste
Inside my mouth:
A spice that always has been
More than supplemental.
In our secluded chamber
Of lashing water,
Momentarily oblivious
To the outer world,
We breathe in impulsive
Synchronization.
Under taut strain of
Our unrestrained intimidation
Even hard walls crack
In awed acknowledgement.

jack wiler
MEDITATIONS ON NATURAL MAN

The street outside is littered with begging drunks and begging addicts.
Their faces are scarred or bandaged.
Every last one of them limps.
Guys curled up against a wall with
piss running out onto the sidewalk.
Women limping and screaming all at once to no one in particular.
Standing in line to get my cheap Chinese food,
five of them, in this case, black guys,

all with their little dixie begging cups
arguing over what they wanted to eat
start to pull and tug and tumble out onto Ninth Ave.
I left the restaurant and I wasn't hungry anymore.
35 Street is filled with trucks and cars all going nowhere.
More drunks are arguing outside my office.
One drunk is weaving on the top step of a stoop.
Two drunks, a man and a woman, are showing their kid to
two other drunks.
All the heels on all their shoes are crushed.
They all do a little stutter step,
limp and shuffle,
limp and shuffle.

This is a nature poem.

I feel like tossing my lunch in the trash.
I sit in my office and read and the first thing
I pick up is a poem by Carolyn Forché
describing in detail the tortures and degradations of the El Salvador
    military and police.
Balls are crushed.
Mice are inserted in vaginas.
Razors and lime and barbed wire loop through the poem.
Men and women are thrown in open graves,
have their hands cut off,
their heads staked and posted as a warning and
outside over the din of all this ugliness in the book
I can hear the stupid loud drunken arguments,
the truck drivers cursing,
the bleating of horns.
An iron slab is dropped over an open hole with a huge clang.
Someone in the office is fighting with someone else
but it's hard to hear for all the other noise.
And finally Willie interrupts my lunch to ask me
what kind of glueboard we're using now to trap rats,
Catchmaster
or Victor Holdfast?
And now *I'm* pissed,

now I yell at him,
What fucking difference does it make!

I add my little bit of grace to this natural scene.
I step back now.
Add up all the natural wonders.
Place myself in the world and bring you this little epiphany.
We use Catchmaster Rat Glueboards
Because they're cheap and they work.

jeff wright   COURT APPEARANCE
for Bob Rosenthal

Do you speak English?
You are charged with stripping
an abandoned vehicle.
That is a misdemeanor.
It is a crime.
The vultures will have your liver.
If you plead guilty
I'll charge you with a violation.
That is not a crime.
Do you understand?

NOTES ON THE POETS

Elena Alexander is a performer and poet, creator of the Biblio reading series in New York, and dear spirit. She appears in the Penguin anthology *Brought to Book*. "I'm most happy when I'm in a room full of writers." Ergo: Cafe denizen!

Miguel Algarín wrote his first poem on April 27, 1967, to cure a terrible headache.

"Things needing to be said, and said tersely" brought **David Allen** back to poetry. Born in Kingston, Jamaica, in 1968, he is a student at Brooklyn College.

"I came to the Cafe after a Poets Theater Festival and stayed because of the wall-to-wall energies." **Sheila Alson** taught for many years in New York City's public schools, and is a poet, gadfly, and activist on the Lower East Side.

Alurista is a poet, a professor, and a mythical figure in Latino letters. His book *Spik in Glyph* (Arte Publico) is un classico.

Sri Lankan native **Indran Amirthanayagam** follows his father in being both a poet and in the foreign service—"it's a family impulse." Author of the extraordinary *The Elephants of Reckoning* (Hanging Loose, 1993), he says, "You must love the land when you leave to build your house on the sea. That's poetry."

Godfather of Chicano fiction, **Rudolfo Anaya** is the author of *Bless Me, Ultima* and *Alburquerque*, and has been acclaimed as la ultima palabra among the writers of the Southwest.

Cynthia Andrews has published two books with the New Press: *Saving Summer* and *Homeless*.

"Poetry literally means my name," says **Zoe Anglesey**, tireless poetry worker/translator/teacher, who hails from Forest Grove, Oregon. She has published many anthologies in Central America, and most recently edited and brought to the Cafe the young poets of *Word Up: Hope for Youth Poetry* from El Centro de la Raza in Seattle.

Yo, Pauly! **Pauly Arroyo**, autentico nuyorriqueño, nineteen years on the scene, Low Ball Slam Champ, icon. Black belt karate; black belt poetry.

Richard August is a cofounder of the Nuyorican Poets Cafe and has had a lifelong commitment to the survival of poetry in the United States.

The leading master of Chicano poetry in the nineties, **Jimmy Santiago Baca** wrote the screenplay for the acclaimed motion picture *Bound by Honor*. Author of *Black Mesa* (New Directions) and other books of poetry, he is at work on a novel. He lives in New Mexico.

Asha Bandele, born in New York City in 1966, appears in the anthology *In the Tradition* (Harlem River Press). "Asha is a Black poet, not a poet who happens to be Black."

Born in Puerto Rico, **Carmen Bardeguez-Brown** came to the United States in 1985. Her poetry is sound and sense in a dense mix of bilinguality: "I have to go to the Cafe! That's where the poem is spoken, where I can exist."

The T. S. Eliot of the Cafe, first Cafe Grand Slam Champ, author of *Big Bank Take Little Bank* (Nuyorican Poets Cafe Press) and *Joker Joker Deuce* (Penguin), **Paul Beatty** is the hinge between hip hop and poetry on the page. He was born in L.A. in 1962.

Poet Laureate of Harlem **Denise Bell** has seen her one-act plays *Again* and *One* produced at the Nuyorican. "My poetry is urban grit."

"Poetry is what happens when I can't say what I want to someone I love."—**Nicole Blackman** (New York City, 1968).

Jennifer Blowdryer: "Born in 1961, Northfield, Minnesota. Faculty brat. Started writing because nobody would talk to me and I liked *Harriet the Spy*." Author of five books, most recently *Don't Call Before Noon* (Apathy Press) and *The Laziest Secretary in the World* (Piranha Press).

"Welcome to Heaven! The Party's on me!"—**Shorty Bón Bón**

"The first artist is yourself. The second is the larger catharsis, the meeting of work and society/audience. If the two are in sync, the work endures." **Alaan Bowe** was born in Brooklyn in 1966.

Catherine Bowman was born November 26, 1957, in El Paso. Peregrine-Smith published her first book, *1-800-HOT-RIBS*, in 1993. She is a Cafe regular whose humor and bite have changed bricks to brains with a single simile.

El Coco Que Habla, the Talking Coconut, ayee! He is the repository of God's Tongue, the veteran street poet, muttering to himself the poems that everyone else will write. El maestro, **Jorge Brandon**, father of Nuyorican Poetry. The Grand Orator and Prime Mover, born in Puerto Rico in 1905.

Nicole Breedlove: "June Jordan said once, 'The purpose of poetry is to make the revolution irresistible.' I hope to be a vehicle for that change." Currently a student at Barnard, she appeared in the PBS program "Words in Your Face." She was born on November 14, 1968, in New York City.

Sleeping bag on his back, **Jim Brodey** (1942–1993) was literally the first poet-in-residence when the Cafe reopened in 1989. We miss him and his nasty humor and cutting insights. His Open Room poem "Little Light," inspired by Eric Dolphy's "Little Light," in turn inspired *Little Light,* the literary magazine edited by Susan Cataldo.

Props to **Kymberly Brown-Valenzuela**, who helped put this anthology together! Born in Montclair, New Jersey, in 1968, she studied with Miguel Algarín at Rutgers. Her recipe: "A poem bridges the loneliness of the soul and the imperfect world, pulls out the bits of glory, and destroys false sentimentality."

Warner Brothers recording artist/poet **Dana Bryant** is one of the first poets to cross over to that side of the CD. An extraordinary performer, she was born in Brooklyn and is a former Grand Slam Champion of the Cafe.

Anishinabe most recently from Wisconsin, **Diane Burns** has been a poetic force in Loisaida for over a decade. Her book *Riding the One-Eyed Ford* (Contact II Publications, shouts to Maurice Kenny and Josh Gosciak, editors) is in its third printing.

Lisa Buscani (aka Regina Divina) is the author of *Jangle* (Tia Chucha Press) and has reigned as Individual Slam Champion of the United States of Poetry. She resides in Chicago.

"The Cafe baptized me in Pure Art," swears **Regie Cabico**, a Grand Slam Champ and performer in theater as well as poetry. Filipino-American, born May 18, 1970, he checks "Other." Always.

Professor **Steve Cannon** has a reserved seat at the bar every Friday night for his free-lance exhortations. Born April 10, 1935, in New Orleans, he has inspired generations of Loisaida writers, from the Umbra poets of the sixties to the current Cafe. He is the publisher and editor of the arts journal *A Gathering of the Tribes*, publisher of Fly by Night Press, and proprietor of Tribes Gallery in New York City. He is professor emeritus at Medgar Evers College. "Read the goddamn poem!"

Nick Carbo was born October 10, 1964, in Lagazapi, Albay, the Philippines. He is the author of *Amok* (Monday's Mango Press), and is currently poet-in-residence at American University. "Once I had to slam against Denise Duhamel, my wife-to-be! But it was OK. We both lost."

Member of the performance ensemble Thought Music, **Laurie Carlos** was in the original cast of *for colored girls who have considered suicide/when the rainbow is enuf*. An arena poet with an eternal voice.

Born in Cabo Rojo the day after Valentine's Day, 1951, **Américo Casiano, Jr.,** holds down the Bronx chair of Nuyorican International.

"I know her poetry seems like the opposite of mine, but it was seeing Dana Bryant that made me think, 'Maybe I can do that!'" says poet and experimental prose writer **Elizabeth Castagna**. She was born in the Bronx in 1961.

A Chicano from Moses Lake, Washington (born November 13, 1970), **Xavier Cavazos** says that "Richard Hugo once said that Theodore Roethke showed him you can take the most absurd stance in poetry and still be legitimate in the academic world." And if that's not the oral tradition, what is? Winner of First Poetry Ball Ever dual trophies and the 1993 Fresh Poetry Prize, Cavazos currently slacks in Seattle.

Creator and belle of the First Poetry Ball Ever, **Marcel Christian** would like you all to know that "poetry is a ball."

The man of One Hundred Fires is still lighting up the skies of Loisaida. **Lucky CienFuegos**, in residence at the Eternal Poetry Workshop.

"Mr. America" is an excerpt from *Signs* by **Gabrielle N. Lane Clarke**. Rome Neal, resident director of the Nuyorican Theater Festival, has made the piece an integral part of Cafe lore by laying the language inside a whirling jump rope.

Born 10:25 A.M., September 20, 1971, **Samantha Coerbell** is a Green Card poet of Trinidadian parentage. Her poems sear the eyes open.

Lead singer for Cafe house band Drunken Boat is our own Rimbaud, poet **Todd Colby**.

High Priestess of Word **Wanda Coleman** is the essence of Los Angeles poetics. Her most recent book, *Hand Dance*, joins her six others from Black Sparrow. "Today there is a two-level assault on the creative spirit in America. One, the jealous critic who seeks to control or destroy the creative entity. Two, the cultural power-brokers who force the creative entity into a posture of mediocrity or self-censorship to make money."

Born April 4, 1969, **Matt Cook** left the Milwaukee Slam Team (Sean McNally and Tim Cook, known collectively as "The Cook Boys") and moved to New York City in the fall of 1993. "I write like I talk, and fortunately I talk cool."

Ah! The books of the poet **Victor Hernandez Cruz**, from *Snaps* in 1968 to *Red Beans* in 1991, have turned on generations to the Nuyorican voice. A winner of the World Heavyweight Poetry Bout at the Taos Poetry Circus, he currently lives in San Diego, Puerto Rico, Califas, and La Tierra.

At the glorious wake for Audre Lorde at St. John the Divine, it was clear that the transcending voice of **Malkia Amala Cyril** was speaking the Future of Poetry, the tradition ongoing. Born May 2, 1974, in Brooklyn, Malkia was fifteen when she won her first Slam at the Cafe. She is currently a student at Sarah Lawrence College.

Thulani Davis, born in Hampton, Virginia, in 1949, is the author of four books, most recently the novel *1959* (HarperCollins) and *Malcolm X: The Great Photographs*. "Words to build, not vent."

Cristina Desrosiers, born in Quito, Ecuador, on May 6, 1971, says, "Words scratch the surface. The poem digs in." She is a member of the poetry and performance collective the Pussy Poets.

A painter as well as a poet, **Carol Diehl** is a contributor to *Art News*. "Art and poetry are the same thing. Where else besides the Cafe can you write a poem in the morning and get your feedback that night?"

"I miss the Cafe terribly! There's nothing like it anywhere else," bemoans **Denise Duhamel**, poet-in-residence with her husband, Nick Carbo, at American University. She has a book out, *Smile!* (Warm Spring Press), which was preceded by three chapbooks. We miss you too!

Slammer, MTV poet, and Pussy Poet, Ms. **Kathy Ebel** takes the work seriously: "I love words, and poetry allows me to play with them, intensely."

Evert Eden was born in South Africa in 1950. His play *The Interrogation* was performed at the O'Neill Playwrights Conference. He is the dedicated host of the Wednesday Slam Opens at the Cafe, where whoever walks through the door, slams.

"My first poem was inspired by a few dreams. I learned poetry from dreams." **Anne Elliott** started slamming, met the other Pussy Poets, and found a new home for her work outside the performance-art world, where she had earned an M.F.A. at the University of California, San Diego. You must read her book, *Stories Inside a Crawling Skin*.

Alvin Eng was born in Queens in 1962. He made it to the Cafe from the Poets Theater Workshop that Bob Holman led at St. Marks and La Mama. A recent grad of the NYU Musical Theater Program, Eng blends rock, poetry, and solo performance into what he says "Poetry is! and that is all."

A jet of energy or **Janice Erlbaum**? A Pussy Poet born in New York City in 1969, she is currently studying writing at NYU. "At fifteen, I left home. That's when I became a poet. Poetry helps me to cope. The Cafe inspires me to keep at it!"

Martín Espada's four books include *Rebellion Is the Circle of a Lover's Hands* (Curbstone) and *Trumpets from the Islands of Their Eviction* (Bilingual Press). He is a lawyer, a legend, and currently a professor at UMass in Amherst.

MTV Poet Laureate **Maggie Estep** is not a normal girl. "I sort of wrote my first poem so that I could use the word *cheese* a lot."

"I've witnessed the deaths of (too) many of our distinguished Nuyorican poets, as well as Padrino Miguel Algarín's giving birth to the Poets Cafe. It is a center within the universe where we become family, where elders empower children, where our souls find a watering hole and, no matter where we came from, our hearts cultivate the space our minds call home."—**Sandra Maria Esteves**, author of three books of poems, including *Bluestown Mockingbird Mambo* (Arte Publico).

With the 1993 publication of *It's Not About Time* (Fly by Night Press), Loisaida legend **John Farris** will at last be known to a larger audience. "My approach to poetry is to sit down and make poems and hope you know what you're doing." With John, it's always clear he does.

Born in Mayaguez, Puerto Rico, November 28, 1946, **Jose-Angel Figueroa** is the author of three books, most recently *La Patria/The Homeland*. "Poetry is the heartbeat of great literature."

Poet, teacher, lecturer, and Grand Slam Champ **Reg E. Gaines** has appeared on MTV's "Spoken Word Unplugged" with poems you'll find in his books *24-7-365* and *Headrhyme Lines* (both from Iota Press/Poet Tree). *Please Don't Take My Air Jordans* is a first rap-poetry crossover for Mercury Records.

"I had readingphobia until I stood up at the Cafe and won an Erotica Slam," confesses **Eliza Galaher**.

Gary Mex Glazner is a sometime cowboy poet from Oklahoma who is Slam Meister Emeritus of San Francisco, his current adobe abode. "Heard my first Slam at Chicago Blues Fest. Turned me green with excitement and red with embarrassment."

Gloria was a sculptor till she walked in on an Open Room at the Cafe. Now she's a Pussy Poet and a slammer, with music holding together the bittersweet syllables.

Hattie Gossett, aka Sister No-Blues, says: "Did you ever see her with a *man?*"

It would not be the Cafe without **Lois Griffith** standing at the front of the bar. Lois says, "Get to the writing every day," and she does (having just finished a novel) while doing the daily at the Cafe and also professoring at Manhattan Community College. Truly, "the Spirit of the Cafe." *Con amor, a Lois!*

Dog Eaters, a real and surreal tale of Filipino life under the Marcos regime, broke poet **Jessica Hagedorn** from the world of letters to the world at large. She recently edited *Charlie Chan Is Dead: An Anthology of Contemporary Asian-American Fiction* for Penguin, which also brought out her *Danger and Beauty* collection.

Kimiko Hahn: "The work of Bob and Miguel inspires me to continue putting poetry back in the street where it belongs!" She was born July 5, 1955, in Mt. Kisco, N.Y., and has published four books, including *Air Pocket* and *Earshot* from Hanging Loose Press.

Mia Hansford digs her poems out of air. "Too many *l*'s in this one," she has been known to ponder. A member of the Poets' Chorus, she was born in 1964, in Somerset, Kentucky.

Christian Haye has seen his writing in the *Village Voice* and *Vibe*. He has directed the plays of Steve Cannon and produced the work of Pamela Sneed and is a contributing editor at *Tribes*. He was born in New York City in 1969.

David Henderson is *De Mayor of Harlem* (Dutton), Mr. Henderson's birth-place. Author of the "greatest rock biography ever written" (*'Scuse Me While I Kiss the Sky: The Biography of Jimi Hendrix*, Bantam), David has published three books of poetry and is at work on many illustrious and mysterious projects, including books on reggae and rap.

A native puertorriqueña, **Diana Hernandez-Correa** was one of the new Cafe's first bartenders. Now she is known for her art (her show graced the Cafe walls in 1991) and her singing (she's a jazz-salsa chanteuse) as well as her poetry. She designed the logo and T-shirts for the Cafe.

Bob Holman would like to thank Elizabeth, Sophie, and Daisy for putting up with his hopeless addiction to poetry.

Susan Hornik has published two chapbooks: *Dedicated to the One I Drink* (The Poet Tree Press) and *It's a Mistake to Think You're Special* (Wild Strawberry Press). One of the hardest working forces in po-biz, she hosts the Poets' Erotica readings at the Cafe, where she also has helped with press and other organizing. Cheers, Susan!

Founder of the Left-Handed Poets (you know who you are!), our man **Indigo** is the charming scorekeeper of our Slams. Current Champ of the

Hecklers' Slam, Mr. Indigo, out of Ohio, keeps the room honest and relaxed. "I use my work to try to preserve those aspects of the gay subculture that are rapidly disappearing due to the spread of AIDS."

Arkansas traveler **Patricia Spears Jones** is the author of *Mythologizing Always* and *Seven Sonnets*. "Poetry is the second-oldest art form! It deserves greater respect!"

R. Cephas Jones, known as one of the great jazz poets around the Cafe, played Lee Morgan in the Cafe production of *Don't Explain*. Born in Jersey City in 1957, he is a member of the performing group the Poets 4.

Eliot Katz is a poet and political activist who currently works full-time as a housing advocate for Central Jersey homeless families. His first book, *Space and Other Poems for Love, Laughs, and Social Transformation* (Northern Lights), was published in 1990.

Author of *American Cruiser* (Zeitgeist Press) and *Before I Wake* (Cyborg Productions), **Alan Kaufman** currently lives in San Francisco, where he organized poetry juggernauts to Germany and Austria. "Poetry is the last uncorrupted art form. The Cafe was the first uncorrupted art place I ever encountered."

Rick Kearns is a Nuyorican who sings love poems from Pennsylvania direct to Loisaida.

Mike Ladd was born in Boston in 1970. "My struggle is to keep not just my words but the words of all poets unadulterated and pure as possible. That struggle is very painful and frustrating and confusing but it also makes me strong."

Born in Queens in 1951, **Patricia Landrum** came to the Cafe through the Open Room. "Words," she says, "are Music for Soul." She has two chapbooks in print: *Sweet* and *For Our Times*.

Following in the footsteps of Master Orator Jorge Brandon, **Tato Laviera** is a Loisaida prophet living between interplanetary mambo steps. He has published four books with Arte Publico, including *Mainstream Ethics*.

Shirley LeFlore is a Grand Slammer and jazz poet from East St. Louis and a charter member of the Eugene B. Redmond Workshop and Fan Club. Shouts out to Eugene!

Award-winning documentary filmmaker (*Azul: Poetry in Nicaragua*) **Roland Legiardi-Laura** is a codirector of the Cafe. "Poetry is like a toothbrush, a kiss, or a hammer. Use it or lose it."

Gary Lenhart used to hang at the Cafe in the seventies when he was also spending many hours at the St. Mark's Poetry Project. With Greg Masters and Michael Scholnick he edited the seminal little mag *Mag City*; he later edited *Transfer*. A stalwart at Teachers and Writers Collaborative, he has published two books, *One at a Time* (United Artists Books) and *Light Heart* (Hanging Loose Press).

"The rock that drinks the water from la Pampa of Life," is la poesia to **Tito Lespier**, autentico nuyorriqueño de Loisaida. He played the Mambo King at the reopening celebration for the Cafe, Halloween 1989.

Robbie McCauley remembers Bimbo Rivas daily; was identified as "the race doctor" by Jessica Hagedorn, Laurie Carlos, and Nicky Paraiso in 1990-something; is an innovator in the Content as Aesthetic School of Performance Theater; has written, done workshops, and performed throughout the United States using theater to confront people's bad habits about race, class, gender, and style; received a 1992 Obie for her *Sally's Rape;* and has been in and out of the Cafe since it was on Sixth Street.

For thirteen years, Binghamton, New York, has had the glory of the Big Horror Reading Series due to the heroic efforts of poet-maniac **Richard Martin**, author of *White Man Appears on Beach*.

Greg Masters appeared in the original Cafe production of Lucky CienFuegos's *Flamingo, Flomongo*. "We rehearsed daily for a year and a half, the greatest year and a half of my life." Two books: *In the Air* (Remember I Did This for You/Power Mad Press) and *My Women and Men, Part II* (Crony Books). It was during his revolutionary stint as editor of *The Poetry Project Newsletter* that the switch from mimeo to offset was made.

"I come from a revolutionary tradition of vanguard literature," says **Tony Medina**. "The Black Arts Movement of the sixties, the Harlem Renaissance, Third World resistance literature . . ." Born in the South Bronx in 1966, author of *Emerge & See* (Whirlwind Press), you'll find him on street corners reading to people listening always with delight to his insight.

Nancy Mercado, born in Atlantic City in 1959, is a director of and writes for the Roberto Clemente Center in Elizabeth and has been on the Cafe scene since 1980. Her poem "Milla" was mentioned honorably for the Allen Ginsberg Poetry Award. She is an editor of *Longshot* magazine.

Wild man, wise man **Bobby Miller** was born in 1952 in our nation's capital, changing the course of everything, *especially* life as we knew it, forever. His self-published masterpiece, *Benestrific Blonde,* being the opposite of *catastrophic*, is seen on all the city's finer bookshelves. He runs his own reading series at Flamingo East and is, in his own words, "a fierce hairdresser."

David Mills was born in Brooklyn on October 10, 1965. He appears in the anthology *In the Tradition* and has been known to write essays and journalism, but "it's all poetry."

We proudly present the General of the Royal Chicano Air Force, Sr. **Jose Montoya**.

Ed Morales read the original Nuyorican poets when in college, then headed Downtown. He knows that "the Cafe is the intersection of Bohemia and the neighboring P.R. community," and he's been a member of both for twelve years. A journalist for the *Village Voice*, he knows poetry as "the truth and ways to disguise it."

"I wrote my first poem as a personal response to a social predicament," remembers Grand Slam Champ **Tracie Morris**, "and after that—thanks to Steve Cannon and the Stoop!" She is the author of *Chap-T-Her One* and often performs with her band Words-N-Music. Her decidedly improvisational performance style roots jazz, hip hop, and blues, for starters. And on top of all that, she still has time to be the 1993 National Haiku Slam Champion.

Who once was a reporter for *People* and now is a student at the Harvard Divinity School? **Gavin Moses**, founder of the Poets 4. He represented the Cafe in the 1991 National Slam in Chicago.

Not Me (Semiotext[e]) and *Bread and Water* (Hanuman) are the most recent books by **Eileen Myles**; Black Sparrow Press will be releasing *Chelsea Girls* (stories) shortly. Ted Berrigan dubbed her "the last of the New York School"; in 1980, she coordinated a collaborative series between the Cafe and the Poetry Project. "Poetry is a private universe that came out in public thought."

Ninety 9 is a slammer and hip hop artist who has been seen on MTV and other finer orbits about the planet.

"Let's put it this way: there are innumerable poets who could be seen as decorous stylists, very few who could be categorized as offensive and provocative. I see myself in the role of troubleshooter." **Orion** is a street poet, a citizen of Tompkins Square Park who was born in Switzerland (1945) and lived in Israel for the first twelve years of his life. He does a mean Elvis.

"The beautiful and the ugly is the uncomforting truth of poetry." **Dael Orlandersmith**, poet and actor, reads it like a riot act of the heart. Born in 1959, raised in Harlem and the South Bronx, she was the winner of the Fresh Poetry Prize, 1993.

"Twisting sound into speech. And verse vise" is the art of painter and jazz poet **Julie Patton**. She was born in Cleveland on March 17, 1956, and is also a well-known arts educator.

Where a Nickel Costs a Dime is **Willie Perdomo**'s first book. A Grand Slam Champ, he was born and raised on the border between Harlem and El Barrio.

Carolyn Peyser wandered into the Cafe one evening and kicked a Quincy Troupe poem for the room, amazing all. Even more amazing, she proceeded to give up her day job, move downtown, and now finds herself in the center of the Cafe whirlwind: she is in charge of documentation of Slams, helps coordinate *The Fuse,* and is associate producer of the *Nuyorican Symphony* CD. She is also director of public relations at Poets House. Gracias, Carolyn!

A native New Yorker from Ponce, Puerto Rico, the Rev. **Pedro Pietri** carries his Condom Cross everywhere but is not making available his "Rent-a-Coffin" (how long do you need one?). Already a New York City icon, he can be found on postcards and T-shirts in Village souvenir stands. The Cafe has proudly presented many of his masterpieces of theater, including *Happy Birthday, M.F.* A two-time champ of the Hecklers' Slam (by dint of his infamous "silent heckles"), Pedro became a poet because of the Latin Insomniac Motorcycle Club (Without Motorcycles). When he does not come into work today, you will find him at the Cafe, boycotting death.

Miguel Piñero (1947–1988) was the cofounder of the Nuyorican Poets Cafe. Miky's masterpiece *Short Eyes* turned American theater out. He is the author of twelve full-length plays, sixteen one-act plays, and many episodes of "Miami Vice." A great actor, poet, and playwright, he is the Philosopher of the Criminal Mind.

Editor, with Ras Baraka, of the influential anthology *In the Tradition* (Harlem River Press), **Kevin Powell** is a staff writer at *Vibe* magazine. He was the poet on MTV's "The Real World," and says that in the *real* real world, "Let's take poetry back to where it belongs—to the people!"

Originally from San Francisco, performer and poet **Kathy Price** now spends her time at el Cafe, mixing and matching Life and Art, crossing over multi- and pop cultures. With her, language becomes a weapon. Or a kiss.

Raymond Ramirez drives out verses from the South Bronx Stairwell Poetic.

Noel Rico is currently on a round-the-world diplomatic poetry tour.

Bimbo Rivas (1939–1992) was the inventor of Loisaida. He laid down the laws of Nuyorican aesthetics for Theater and Poetry. He's another one of Master Jorge Brandon's disciples and is currently handing down the Tablets for the New Poetics.

Hardworking activist **Louis Reyes Rivera** is the publisher of Shamal Books and also a scholar and performer of extraordinary spirit. He is a living bridge between Latino and African-American poetics.

Keith Roach, the Ceremonial Master of the Open Room, was born in 1954. "For all of those thoughts that seem inappropriate, for all those words that have nowhere to go—hey, it's poetry time. Time for the Open Room."

Luis J. Rodriguez oralizes the simple belief of the new poet—"Poetry is an innate ability in all people"—and then goes out and activates it through publishing (as editor of Tia Chucha Press) and working with diverse communities, from the homeless to the incarcerated to street gangs, to get the word out. A hero in our midst, he is the author of two books of poetry and the astonishing memoir *Always Running: La Vida Loca—Gang Life in L.A.* (Curbstone Press).

Fine playwright, director, and poet **Carl Hancock Rux** is now the lush baritone voice heard emceeing "Live from the Nuyorican Poets Cafe" over WBAI New York, 99.5 FM.

Independent candidate for New York City Council, housing activist, and ur-rapper **Will Sales** was a participant in the oral tradition before there was a name for it. Originally from Cincinnati, he is a fixture of the Low East and a member of the Poets 4.

Raúl Salinas lives and works in Austin, Texas. He is a pioneer of the Great Chicano Literary Bashes of the 70s, 80s, 90s and into the 00s.

Ricardo Sánchez, the ultimate archivist of SW culture, has recently moved his files to the research stacks of Stanford University, so all may come to learn the history of Chicano literature.

Sapphire, born in Fort Ord, California, in 1950, is a survivor; her poetry speaks to that. "Writing takes me out of the shamebound constrictions of isolation and self-hate and connects me. Lost pieces of myself return when I tell my story. I re-member myself." She lives and teaches in Harlem.

Originator of the Knitting Factory Poetry Series, **Gail Schilke** remembers, "When the Cafe reopened, there was no heat, no bathrooms, so we shivered in our sweaters, under the layers of coats—nothing could stop the poetry!" She has two books, *From the Margin* and *Stilltrauma*, and is a visual artist as well as a poet. She was born in Hartford, Connecticut, in 1950.

Michael Scholnick (1953–1990) studied with Miguel Algarín at Rutgers and was a regular at the Cafe and St. Mark's in the seventies. He set a world's record in synapse leaps; his poems blossom ever. Books: *Perfume* (Crony Books) and the collected poems, *Heroism* (Yellow Press).

Schooled in classical poetry, **Susan Scutti** says the Cafe helped her to find a way to the contemporary in her own work; "Epithalamium" was the first poem she wrote for oral presentation.

Ntozake Shange is the only poet to have her poetry (*for colored girls who have considered suicide/when the rainbow is enuf*) translate successfully to Broadway. (*Short Eyes* doesn't count because it's not a poem. Please do not mention *Cats*.) She is the inventor of the choreopoem and is the world-class Energizer of the Word.

Editor of the effervescent *Longshot* magazine, **Danny Shot** studied with Miguel Algarín at Rutgers and states, "The Cafe is the only place in New York that's always been there for me." Danny was Bronx-born in 1957.

How many poets in their lifetime have an anthology devoted to imitations of their work? The *Hal Sirowitz Anthology* is the only one we can think of. Winner of the Toyota Funny Poem Slam (no joke!) and a member of the

1993 Cafe National Slam Team, Hal has five books out, most recently *Fishnet Stockings*. "I'm not sure why people like me. I write a lot about my mother and we all have mothers, so it's possibly that." He was born (and still lives) in Queens.

Composer of *Nuyorican Symphony* (Knitting Factory CD), **Paul Skiff** runs the Knitting Factory readings with Gina Bonati. He's from the Midwest.

Originator of the Slam and dedicated to poetry for the people with the audience in control, **Marc Smith** still hosts Slams every Sunday at the fabled Green Mill Tavern in Chicago. A construction worker before becoming a poet, he's been known to slide into New York on the rare moment and visit the Cafe. "Thanks to Pedro Pietri for putting me up at the Men's Shelter."

Slam Champion of the Multiverse, **Patricia Smith** recently moved from her native Chicago to Boston, where she is a reporter for the *Globe*. Author of three books of poetry, most recently *CTD (Close to Death)* (Zoland Books), she says, "If I could visit everyone to read [my poems] personally, I would."

Pamela Sneed is a poet and performer, theater worker, and cultural activist. She works at the Hedrick Martin Institute; her one-woman show *A Contemporary Tale of Harriet Tubman* was a sensation at the Cafe.

Sparrow ran for President in 1992 and is founder of the One Size Fits All Movement. Author of *Sparrow's Coloring Book* and *Esprit de Questionism* and editor of *The 11th St. Ruse,* he says of poetry: "It's always dark inside an egg."

Carlton T. Spiller is a leading legal beaver who moves from law to poetry just to keep it on the sane side.

Peter (Pete) Spiro has published five books of poems, including the classic *Work*. His play *Howya Doin' Franky Banana*, produced at the Cafe, pushed multi-culti into the outer reaches of Bensonhurst. He is a Grand Slam Champ whose commentary on the gung-ho bare-knuckles National Slam became the classic "They're doggin' me."

Lamont B. Steptoe is the author of six books, including *Uncle's South China Sea Blue Nightmare*. A Vietnam vet and father, he is also a poetry activist. He was born in Pittsburgh and now lives in Philly and works at the Painted Bride and the Walt Whitman Cultural Center in Camden, New Jersey.

The quiet formal lyric utterance of **Adrienne Su** has shushed the most formidable of hecklers. Born August 10, 1967, she is currently writing at the Provincetown Fine Arts Center. She represented the Cafe in the National Slam in Chicago, 1991. "Poetry was meant to be spoken."

Poet and performer, pioneer at Black Rock Coalition and Nu Yo Records, leader of the band dadahdoodadah, poet in residence at the New School, and creator of *The Circle Unbroken Is a Hard Bop* at the Cafe? Must be **Sekou Sundiata**, mentor to the new jacks at home at el Cafe.

Jamaican **Everton Sylvester** is a New York City cabdriver who teaches English at Westinghouse High School in Brooklyn. A Green Card Poet and '93 Grand Slam Finalist, he says, "I have given no thought to why I write poetry."

Born in the South Bronx on June 21, 1959, **Nate Tate** is the author of *Get Black to Where You Once Belonged* (Mulberry Press) and *Soul Brother #10029* (Iota Press). He urges the following question upon our readers: "Who's worse, the Devil or his Demons?" At the Cafe he once insisted that a love poem for his girlfriend, Leslie, could only be read if she would join him on stage, becoming his single audience. Leslie complied—the first time a Muse physically worked the Open Room.

Home is Trinidad for **Cheryl Boyce Taylor**, and she sets many of her poems there. Books include *Birthsounds, Rhythms, and Other Contractions* and *The Caramel Pecan Collection*. "Poetry is my religion, and there will I do worship!"

Piri Thomas: his classic *Down These Mean Streets* (Vintage Books) is what we call home. Punto.

Edwin Torres says *"I Hear Things People Haven't Really Said,"* or at least that's the title of his book. We'd best believe him, for to hear him is to hear things no one else has ever heard, so rare and bold are his unique NuYoFuTuRismIc Riddimings. Thus the utterance "The History of Why I Am Who I Am. I grew up hearing two languages thinking they were one language so concluded that there was one language which you just made up yourself." Born in 1958, he was awarded the first Cafe Fresh Poetry Prize, in 1991.

Every time he reads, we give thanks that a poet from the Future has been dropped in our midst. **Mike Tyler** got to the Cafe by subway. Born on some other planet, some time ahead, he is the author of *From Alabama to California* (The Art Cannot Be Damaged Press), a "Share Book: if you want to keep it, send the money; if not, leave the book somewhere." Mike's dictum: "Poetry is sexy moral language."

Born in Trivandrum, India, **Vipin** is the author of *The Vulgate Heart*, an all-new version of the Upanishads. His poetry has inspired generations of dust-into-spirit-via-word.

Winner of the Gwendolyn Brooks Award in 1989 for his book *We Are All the Black Boy*, **Michael Warr** is a poet and national poetry activist based in Chicago. There he edits for Tia Chucha Press, with Luis Rodriguez, and is director of the Guild Complex and the Windy City branch of the National Writer's Voice Series.

It was at the Cafe that **Jack Wiler**, poet and exterminator, first read aloud. He was born in Darby, Pennsylvania, in 1951.

Jeff Wright, editor of NYC's hip arts monthly *Cover*, is a West Virginia poet whose Hard Press postcard series defined the late seventies.

Emily XYZ's definitions for poetry: "1. Sonic effect. 2. Transcendence." Her poetic duets with Meyers Bartlett always definitize the air: "Jimmy Page, Frank Sinatra," come to you live in the stere-ereo of her performance. She got born in 1958, in Herkimer, New York.

ACKNOWLEDGMENTS

"At Ease" by Paul Beatty appeared in *The Portable Lower East Side*; "Darryl Strawberry" appeared in *In the Tradition* (Harlem River Press) and *Big Bank Take Little Bank* (Nuyorican Poets Cafe Press). "Sex Goddess of the Western Hemisphere" by Maggie Estep appeared in "Bomb." "Thomas the Burnt English Muffin" and "Please Don't Take My Air Jordans" by Reg E. Gaines appeared in "Bomb"; all of his poems are taken from his books *Headrhyme Lines* (Iota Press/Poet Tree) or *24-7-365* (Iota/Poet Tree). "Sendin' Out A P.B." by Christian Haye appeared in *Longshot*. "New York City Rundown (European on Me)" by Tony Medina appeared in *Emerge & See* (Whirlwind Press). "Rebirth of New Rican" by Ed Morales appeared in *Performance Journal*. All of Tracie Morris's poems can be found in *Chap-T-Her One*; "Project Princess" appeared in *The Source*; "Morenita" appeared in *Longshot* and "The Fuse." "Mother Love" and "She's Come Undone" by Dael Orlandersmith appeared in *Raw Girls*; "Poem II for Anne Sexton" appeared in "Bomb." "Nigger-Reecan Blues" by Willie Perdomo appeared in *Words in Your Face* (PBS), *City Sun*, and *In the Tradition* (Harlem River Press); "Reflections on the Metro North" appeared in "Bomb." "celibacy" by Kathy Price appeared in *Longshot*. "Deformed Finger" by Hal Sirowitz appeared in "Hanging Loose"; "Sons" appeared in "Lips." "We All Need" by Pete Spiro appeared in "Bomb"; "Work" appeared in *Labor in the Post-Industrial Age* (Pig Iron Press); "Cause and Effect" appeared in "Aim." "Address" by Adrienne Su appeared in the "Harvard Independent." "Dig on the Decade" by Edwin Torres appeared in "Movement Research Performance Journal." "Dust-Bowl Memory," "Bells," "Choices," and "Black Mesa" by Jimmy Santiago Baca are from *Black Mesa Poems*. Copyright 1986, 1987, 1988, 1989 by Jimmy Santiago Baca. Reprinted by permission of New Directions Publishing Corp. "1-800-Hot-Ribs," "Mr. X," and "Deathwatch Beetle" by Catherine Bowman appeared in *1-800-Hot-Ribs* (Peregrine-Smith). "American Sonnet" copyright © 1993 Wanda Coleman. Reprinted from *Hand Dance* with the permission of Black Sparrow Press. "Rebellion Is the Circle of a Lover's Hands," "Two Mexicanos," and "Latin Night at the Pawnshop" from *Rebellion Is the Circle of a Lover's Hands/Rebelion es el giro de manos del amante* by Martín Espada. Curbstone Press. Copyright © 1991 by Martín Espada. Distributed by

InBook. Used with permission of Curbstone Press. "Latin Music" and "Skull Food #2" appeared in *Dangerous Beauty* (Penguin) by Jessica Hagedorn. "The Heat" by Kimiko Hahn appeared in *Earshot* (Hanging Loose Press). "Evergreen" by David Henderson appears as the video performance "Eternity." "1990" by Bob Holman appeared on the CD "Live at The Knitting Factory: vol. 4" as well as in "Scarlet" and the "South Dakota Review"; "ROCK'N'ROLL MYTHOLOGY" appeared in *Panic DJ!* (University Arts Resources); "Love Poems" appeared in "Cocodrillo"; "Modern Lovers" was a bookmark from the Alternative Press. "Sly and the Family Stone Under the Big Tit, Atlanta, 1973" by Patricia Spears Jones appeared in "The Kenyon Review." "God, Mingus and Myself" by R. Cephas Jones appeared in the "Tel Aviv Review." The poems by Eliot Katz appeared in *Space and Other Poems for Love, Laughs and Social Transformation* (Northern Lights). "In My Father's House" by Sapphire appeared in "Outweek," "Caprice," "Downtown," "Eyeball," and "Central Park"; "Wild Thing" appeared in "Portable Lower East Side," "Eyeball," and *Critical Condition* (City Lights). All three poems by Michael Scholnick are found in *Heroism* (Yellow Press); "For Irwin Heilner" appeared in "Mag City," and "Good Graces" appears in *Out of This World* (Crown). "Skinhead" by Patricia Smith appeared in *Big Town, Big Talk* (Zoland Books) and "Agni"; "Sweet Daddy" also appeared in *Big Town, Big Talk* as well as *Life According to Motown* (Tia Chucha) and *CTD* (Zoland). "Sunday, August 11, 1974" by Miguel Algarín appeared in *Nuyorican Poetry* (Morrow); "HIV" and "Sheets" appeared in *Longshot.* "Poem to a Wood Sculpture" by Lucky CienFuegos appeared in "Dodeca"; "In the Pocket and Spend It Right" and "Piss Side Streets" appeared in *Tick Tock Mental Clock* (Taino Press). "An Essay on William Carlos Williams" by Victor Hernandez Cruz appeared in *Red Beans* (Coffee House Press); "Three Songs from the 50s" appeared in *Tropicalization* (Reed, Cannon); "Art—This" and "Haikukoos" appeared in *By Lingual Wholes* (Momo's Press). "Bacalaitos and Fireworks" by Lois Griffith appeared in *Women's Writing* (Canada Anthology) and was a "Poetry Spot" on WNYC-TV. "Soledad," and "my graduation speech" by Tato Laviera are reprinted with permission from the publisher of *La Carretta Made a U-Turn* (Houston: Arte Publico Press–University of Houston, 1981); "sky people" and "tito madera smith" by Tato Laviera are reprinted with permission from the publisher of *Enclave* (Houston: Arte Publico Press–University of Houston, 1985). "You Jump First," © 1973 by Pedro Pietri, appeared in *Puerto Rican Obituary*. Reprinted by permission of Monthly Review Foundation. "Prologue for Ode to Road Runner" appeared in *Text Sound-Texts* (Morrow). "La Bodega Sold Dreams," "A